TONIGHT. . . .IN THIS VERY RING!

TONIGHT. . .IN THIS VERY RING!

A FAN'S HISTORY OF PROFESSIONAL WRESTLING

Scott Keith

CITADEL PRESS
Kensington Publishing Corp.
www.kensingtonbooks.com

CITADEL PRESS BOOKS are published by

Kensington Publishing Corp.
850 Third Avenue
New York, NY 10022

Copyright © 2003 Scott Keith

All Kensington titles, imprints, and distributed lines are available at special quantity discounts for bulk purchases for sales promotions, premiums, fund-raising, educational, or institutional use. Special book excerpts or customized printings can also be created to fit specific needs. For details, write or phone the office of the Kensington special sales manager: Kensington Publishing Corp., 850 Third Avenue, New York, NY 10022, attn: Special Sales Department, phone 1-800-221-2647.

CITADEL PRESS and the Citadel logo are Reg. U.S. Pat. & TM Off.

Photos by Darren Smith, courtesy of Lincoln University.

Designed by Leonard Telesca

First printing: January 2003

10 9 8 7 6 5 4 3 2 1

Printed in the United States of America

Library of Congress Control Number: 2002104526

ISBN 0-8065-2437-5

Contents

Acknowledgments   vii

Introduction: Everything in This Book Is a Lie   ix

Glossary   xiii

Rating the Matches   xvi

Tonight . . . In This Very Ring! . . . *Starring:*   **1**

Prelude: Thirty Years, One Chapter (1963–1993)   **5**

Act One: King Lear (1993–1996)   **15**
Scene One: The Lex Express   16
Scene Two: Don't Cry for Me, Yokozuna   18
Scene Three: Too Many Undertakers   21
Scene Four: That's MISTER Bob Backlund to You   23
Interlude   24
Scene Five: Diesel (Non-Drawing) Power!   26
Scene Six: Billionaire Ted   28
Scene Seven: The Problem   29
Scene Eight: The Solution   31
Scene Nine: The Resurrection   32

Act Two: Lazarus (1997)   **35**
Scene One: Titan Strikes Back!   35
Scene Two: Lost—One Smile. If Found, Contact S. Michaels   37
Scene Three: Hero of the Day   39
Scene Four: Reunited and It Feels So Good   41
Scene Five: Canadian Stampede   43
Scene Six: Austin Finds Himself   45
Scene Seven: Things Fall Apart   47
Scene Eight: Suck It!   49
Interlude   50
Scene Nine: That's Gotta Be Kane!   50
Scene Ten: Dogg-Ass   54
Scene Eleven: What Happened Before Montreal   55
Scene Twelve: What Happened in Montreal   58
Scene Thirteen: What Happened After Montreal   60

Act Three: Austin v. McMahon (1998)   **63**
Scene One: Shawn Michaels Gets His   63
Scene Two: Dumpsters and Boxers   65
Scene Three: Eric Bischoff Does Something Stupid(er)   66
Scene Four: Four Point Six   69
Scene Five: Look Out Below!   71

Contents

Scene Six: The Gang Warz Begin   73
Scene Seven: The Brawl for All   76
Scene Eight: Changes Come Around   77
Scene Nine: The Sock Puppet Heard
    'Round the World   79
Scene Ten: The Deadly Game   80
Scene Eleven: This Book Must Weigh 300
    Pounds, Then   82

Act Four: The Russofiction (1999)   **85**
Scene One: The Royal Rumble   86
Scene Two: HHH's Larger, Twin Brother
    Returns   90
Scene Three: Russo Screws Up Wrestlemania   92
Scene Four: UP YOURS, Corporate Ministry!   94
Scene Five: Over the Edge   96
Scene Six: The Lamer Power   98
Scene Seven: The Magic Briefcase   100
Scene Eight: True Love (Even Badly Acted)
    Conquers All   102
Scene Nine: This Is Your Life, Rocky!   103
Scene Ten: And Don't Let the Doorknob
    Hit You on the Ass on the Way Out   105
Scene Eleven: The Ladder Match Returns   107
Scene Twelve: Can the Belt Actually Fit Him?   109
Scene Thirteen: Stephanie Sets Rape
    Victim Rights Back Twenty Years   110

**Act Five: The McMahon-
Helmsley Era (2000)**   **113**
Scene One: The Rock Wrestling Federation   113
Scene Two: Goodbye, Mick. See You in Six
    Weeks   115
Scene Three: The Dudley Boyz Get the
    Tables . . . and the Titles   117
Scene Four: The Good Guys Finally Win   120
Scene Five: Dance, Fatass, Dance   123
Scene Six: Morality Sucks   124
Scene Seven: This Is Elevation?   127
Scene Eight: Idiots of All Sorts   130

Scene Nine: Kurt Strikes Out   133
Scene Ten: Kurt Makes His Comeback   134
Scene Eleven: HHH No-Sells Death   136
Scene Twelve: Some Other Stuff Happens   137

**Act Six: There Goes the Neighborhood
(2001)**   **139**
Scene One: Monopoly Isn't Just a Game
    Anymore   139
Scene Two: The Glass Ceiling   142
Scene Three: Monday Nitraw   144
Scene Four: The "X" Is for "Excellent"   146
Scene Five: The "X" Is for "Excrutiating"   148
Scene Six: Did I Mention the Glass Ceiling?   151
Scene Seven: No, Seriously, Glass Ceiling,
    Ever Heard of It?   153
Scene Eight: The WCW Invasion Begins!   156
Scene Nine: Did We Say WCW? We
    Meant WCW/ECW   158
Scene Ten: Did We Say WCW/ECW? We
    Meant Shane & Stephanie   160
Scene Eleven: What?   162
Scene Twelve: However You Spell It,
    They Suck   164
Scene Thirteen: Jericho Shatters the Glass
    Ceiling! Just Kidding   166

Afterword (One Last Thing . . .)   **169**

Appendixes   **173**

Pay-Per-View Revenue History   173
Composite TV Ratings, 1997–1999   177
Composite TV Ratings, 2000   178
WWF Tag-Team Title History   179
WWF World Title History   183

Index   **187**

Acknowledgments

Much props to my various homies, yo:

Thanks to Jeremy Botter for webmastering and offering to mention me in his band's liner notes, even if the record deal didn't happen. Thanks to Don Becker for putting up with the nonsense involved in the transition from Rantsylvania.com to TheSmarks.com.

Thanks to Mike, Mattie, Taryn, and Linz for offering early feedback on the book.

Thanks to John, Huy, Tyler, Zen, Rahim, and Karim for being Canadian and keeping it somewhat real.

Thanks to Dave Meltzer for putting out the best damn newsletter I've ever paid an arm and a leg for (after exchange) and will continue to do so.

Thanks to John Petrie for inspiring the format of my reviews many, many years ago.

Thanks to David Bixenspan for being my anal-retentive fact checker.

Thanks to Darren Smith for generously donating the pictures you see within these pages.

Thanks to Undertaker and his various opponents for providing me with years of great jokes at his expense. Ditto Hulk Hogan. Ditto Ultimate Warrior.

Thanks to all the various people who have written for the various forms of my Web site over the years. Except the Scotsman.

Acknowledgments

Thanks to Paul Orndorff for turning on Hogan in 1986 and thus reaffirming my faith in mankind and hooking me on wrestling for good.

Thanks to Ed, for at least trying to get me the Smackdown tickets on time.

Thanks to Frank, editor/agent/cool guy, even if he does love Hogan.

And most of all, thanks to the endless stream of wrestling promoters backed by money marks who never fail to fail, and thus give me years of material on how not to run a wrestling promotion. Truly, your stupidity has not gone unnoticed by me.

Introduction
Everything in This Book Is a Lie

They say life imitates art and vice versa. If that's the case, I don't know what wrestling is imitating because it certainly bears no resemblance to any life I've ever lived. In wrestling, people regularly get hit on the head with chairs and develop split-personalities. Referees fall like bricks from the sky after being nudged even slightly, and have the uncanny inability to see more than six inches in front of their faces. A fifteen-minute-long beating can be shrugged off by merely shaking one's head and getting the fans to clap loud enough, if only you are on the side of good and not evil. A straight punch to the face does virtually no damage, but put a roll of quarters in your fist and the poor recipient is out like a light.

Stop to think about this stuff for more than five minutes and you'll go crazy wondering why you even watch it. I went through that phase briefly, around 1987, then simply formulated the same answer I always use now whenever I'm asked why I watch wrestling: "Because I like it."

Others look more deeply into things, wondering about the moral questions involved in heavy steroid use (and abuse), painkiller overdosing, frequent injuries with no health-care plans, and, most heinously, attempted acting done by non-

union actors. Personally, these things no longer bother me on a moral level because I came to the conclusion long ago that if I had to stop and worry about every morality question that came with my viewing habits, I'd have had to give up baseball and Arnold Schwarzenegger movies years ago.

As for wrestling, I personally quit defending it in 1999 when my favorite wrestler ever, Owen Hart, plunged from the rafters during a botched entrance stunt and broke his neck after dropping fifty feet and hitting the top turnbuckle on the way down. That's not to say I don't look at some of the bigger problems facing the sport with a concerned eye, but at the same time I've come to grips with the realities of what I choose to watch. So when people ask me, I just tell them up front that it's a scummy business and you have to be stupid to get involved in it given the inherent risks of being a wrestler and the minuscule chance of breaking into the only major promotion left.

But as a fan, I still watch because I've learned to separate the rationally thinking part of my brain, the part that knows that what's going on is wrong on many levels, from the more visceral part of my brain, which just enjoys two guys beating the crap out of each other, using nothing but pure athleticism and the occasional piece of furniture. More often than not these days it's the rational side that controls my feelings on the sport, but as long as the visceral side is still there, I'll keep watching.

See, *Tonight . . . in This Very Ring* isn't really what you'd call a straightforward history of the WWF. The thing with wrestling is that "history" for promoters is made up of half-truths and imaginary situations, and you can't just go up to a WWF PR guy and ask for attendance figures and gate receipts (like a normal journalist would). Why? Because all the information is filtered carefully through the whims of Vince McMahon, according to what he wants the public to believe on a given day. So you're forced to seek outside sources like newsletters or "insiders" or whatever meager scraps of information you can squeeze out of wrestlers in hopes that they're not lying today—because generally they are.

Hell, early in 2001, Vince McMahon did an interview with Bob Costas on the subject of the then-floundering-but-not-dead XFL, and once Costas strayed from Vince's comfort zone of what he considered the "truth," it nearly turned into a fistfight. That's their life—lying. Normal actors play a part on stage, then go home to be themselves. Not wrestlers—when HHH goes home, for instance, he's still Hunter to his friends, not Paul Levesque (his real name). Most wrestlers live their gimmicks 24/7, and that's why it's so frustrating to try to get any kind of useful information out of any of them, or anyone else associated with the sport for that matter. Basically, we only know as much as they want us to know. For a sport that's been so gung ho about reveling in its own fakeness for the past few years, it's sure hard to get a straight answer out of a wrestling promoter.

Take, for instance, the topic of "sports enter-

tainment." I hate that phrase with a passion. "Sports entertainment" has no defined meaning; it's simply a convenient way for the WWF to weasel out of accepting responsibility for their programming. Actor's union? "No, we're sports." On-site medical personnel? "No, we're entertainment." It's two great tastes that taste great together!

Vince McMahon seems to have the notion that if only the general public would stop thinking about his product as "wrestling," then suddenly all the negative stigmas and stereotypes would go away—as though "sports entertainment" was somehow a clean and unfettered term without the inherent biases of the press to sully its name. Meanwhile, guys still cut one another with razor-blade fragments and suffer career-ending injuries on botched powerbombs. But I'm sure if that "wrestling" term got shitcanned, it'd all go away. Right.

So in a sense, everything in this book is a lie. Just like wrestling isn't actually wrestling, it's "sports entertainment." Well, I'm a rebel, so you won't see that phrase repeated anymore in this book except in an extremely sarcastic sense. But that is to say, everything here all happened to the best of my or anyone else's knowledge. But you never know when Vince is going to change his mind and suddenly decide that it *didn't* happen, ya know? Trust me—if the WWF were running the White House, Vietnam would have been wiped from the record books and replaced with the plot of *The Green Berets* because there's more money to be made that way.

On the other hand, with wrestling, you don't want to know the whole truth of everything, because then that sucks the fun out of it and you end up a cynical jerk like me. So they lie, we as fans accept those lies in order to maintain our sanity and move on with our lives. So rather than a dreary history of what happened according to the WWF (which would take about ten pages, since history is rewritten from the ground up for political purposes every four years or so), this is more of a personal recollection of what being a fan of the WWF was all about during its biggest years, down periods, and embarrassments. And since I'm a fan of the wrestling part of the product first and foremost, it's also an overview and detailed history of the defining matches of those years.

Please note: No wrestling promoters were harmed during the making of this book. Well, at least not by me.

Glossary

Before we begin, let's make sure everyone is on the same page by going over some of the more scary words that I tend to use when discussing wrestling on a level deeper than "Whoa, dude, he really nailed him with that chair!" I'm going to assume that you know *something* about the "insider" terms in wrestling, or else why would you be reading this book?

Angle No, not Kurt Angle. An angle is the short name for the story line—the reason why a match is happening. In a broader sense, it's a catchall phrase for anything within wrestling that's not what it appears to be on the surface. As in "Is he hurt?" "No, it's just an angle." Angles don't necessarily lead to matches, but that's the intention.

Gig/Blade/Juice All words used to describe the act of slicing open your own forehead with a razor blade to draw blood. I tend to use them interchangably as verbs, with "blade" being my personal favorite. My own personal pet peeve is wrestlers who allow themselves to be seen doing it on camera, which I tend to gripe about a few times during the course of this book.

Stiff or "working stiff" When I refer to a match being "stiff," it means that they're either hitting each other *really* hard in reality, or just making it look like they are. The desired goal is to put forth as much illusion of real pain as possible while doing the least amount of actual damage. Either way, the end outcome is the same as far as the viewer is concerned.

Shoot Something that's real. This word has since become something of a running gag in wrestling now that seemingly everyone on the Internet knows in theory what a shoot is. Many wrestlers, like Tazz, now slip it in to lend an air of authenticity to their promos. In wrestling, it is very rare that *anything* is a shoot anymore, though. In fact, the word has become so trite and overused that I don't think we're really going to be able to tell when something really is a shoot because even when they're lying, wrestlers call things "shoots" now. Blame Vince Russo.

Workrate This is the essential word that separates the casual fans from the "smart marks" who tend to be cynical and analyzing. The idea is that because wrestling is worked (that is, fake), wrestlers can thus control the pace of their own matches and how quickly they hit their spots (i.e., moves and countermoves) during that match. The goal is to work hard and provide a fast-paced, but believable, match, and when that happens, it is said that a wrestler has good "workrate." Workrate is not the most important part of the overall package by any means, but it is generally the one thing that casual fans don't really think about until they start learning about what's going on behind the curtain, so to speak. Many people, myself included, count themselves as fans of the in-ring action first and foremost, and thus we are said to be fans of workrate.

I think by now that all the other "inside" terms you might encounter have been beaten to death enough on TV in recent years that you don't need me to define them for you (like "babyface," "heel," "pop," "heat," and even previously taboo phrases like "hot tag," which is when a babyface makes the big tag to his partner after a long beating). I have a few of my own personal catchphrases that you may encounter and wonder about, so here's some of them defined:

Blind Charge refers to someone taking a mad dash at someone else in the corner and missing by a mile, usually because they weren't paying attention and didn't see their target move out of the way. This happens a lot because it's an effective and time-honored transition move that allows one person to act stunned while the other sets up the next big move.

Canadian Violence is when someone of Canadian heritage delivers an open-hand slap (or chop) to the chest of their opponent. The joke is that people in Canada do it best because there's nothing else to do up here.

Double KO is another shorthand term, this one for when the two opponents need a break

and "knock each other out" via a collision in the middle of the ring so they can rest. This is followed by the referee making a count, which in theory goes to ten before a double countout is declared (but has never made it there to my knowledge), and generally sees both guys getting up for one last big sequence once the count reaches eight or nine. This is a very clichéd and tired part of a match, but since the crowd tends to enjoy counting along with the referee, it happens a lot.

Heel beatdown is my shorthand for two or more heels running in at the end of a match and beating the crap out of a hapless babyface. Usually a friend of the face will then run in to even the odds, and "make the save." If the babyface is a particularly big loser, the referees will have to save him.

KICK WHAM STUNNER is my pet name for Steve Austin's Stone Cold Stunner finisher, so called because the kick to the gut that precedes it is so devastating that the poor victim is paralyzed for another two seconds afterward, and thus falls prey to the Stunner portion of the move. In his heyday, Austin did the move all in one fluid motion, but time and injuries have slowed him down to the point where that's no longer possible. I have also added the sarcastic "KICK WHAM" prefix to HHH's Pedigree ever since he started posing in-between the "kick" and the "Pedigree" portions of the move.

Playing Ricky Morton refers to Ricky Morton of the '80s teen-scream sensations The Rock 'N' Roll Express. Morton was a blond, pretty-boy stereotype who had the unique ability to take a superhuman pounding for wholly unreasonable lengths of time (usually 10–30 minutes nonstop) while somehow enticing all the women in the audience to want to jump into the ring to defend him from the big, bad heels. This was truly an amazing talent and the amount of sympathy heat Ricky could draw from the crowd while getting his ass kicked by people one hundred pounds heavier than him was truly an awe-inspiring sight. Unfortunately, drugs and partying outside of the ring took a toll on him far worse than any heel could, and his reign at the top of the *Tiger Beat* scene only lasted until he suddenly started looking his age in 1990. But in tribute to Ricky's pioneering of the "face in peril" formula for tag-team matches, I generally refer to any poor babyface getting clobbered for the bulk of a tag match as "playing Ricky Morton."

Plunder is a Dusty Rhodes term that refers to the various weapons, garbage cans, and ladders that magically appear underneath the ring just in time for a hardcore match. When someone starts pulling something out and throwing it into the ring, they are "loading up the plunder."

Potato refers to a stiff punch to the face (accidental or otherwise) that draws unintentional blood from the nose or eye. I don't know why it's called a "potato punch," it just is.

Stomping a mudhole is a Jim Ross favorite from way back that got turned into a regular term with the rise of Steve Austin, and it refers to someone basically putting the boots to a fallen opponent who is cowering in the corner for protection. Generally, the babyface stomps any mudholes that need stomping because the crowd likes it better that way. For extra points, pausing to soak in the cheers before suddenly turning around and kicking the heel in the head one last time is referred to as "walking it dry." It's an Oklahoma thing, don't ask.

Stuntman Bump refers to a particularly sick fall (usually taken by Shane McMahon) that has no meaning within the context of the match and doesn't directly affect the outcome one way or another. It's just like a set piece in a movie—something so that they can show off how far they can fall.

"...OF DOOM" Finally, when I'm in a particularly sarcastic mood (which is pretty much 24/7), I will refer to certain completely ridiculous and insulting moves as "...OF DOOM," as in Hulk Hogan's "LEGDROP OF DOOM" or Undertaker's "ROPEWALK OF DOOM," because in reality there's no way these things could possibly do any kind of damage to the victim, but the poor guy has to act like they're scared before the move and dead after the move. But then, if we wanted to shoot for realism in wrestling, the phrase would be out the door the first time someone bounces off the ropes, so consider it a mere poke at the wrestlers in good fun and we'll leave it at that.

Rating the Matches

At some points in this book, you'll come across star ratings for certain matches. The star ratings system is the smart mark's best friend, because it's a (supposedly) universal way for wrestling fans to compare the quality of the matches, although it rarely works out that way. The basic premise is that a match is "rated" from DUD (0 Stars) to ***** (5 stars), using scary words like workrate, psychology, transitions, heat and other intangibles to define just how good it was. It was invented by manager Jim Cornette and Norm Dooley and has since been taken by the Internet community and modified for their needs. Here's how it works:

*****	Match of the Year Candidate
****½	Almost perfect
****	Excellent
***½	Extremely good, but with some important flaws
***	Good, but lacking in many ways
**½	Above average, but nothing special
**	An average match—most of the wrestling matches on TV will top out here due to time constraints
*½	Below average, but watchable
*	Bad match, but enough action to make it worthwhile
½*	Terrible match
DUD	No value whatsoever
Negative numbers	Completely offensive to the viewer in every way

Tonight . . . In This Very Ring!
Starring:

Vince McMahon as "Vince McMahon"

A wrestling promoter, multimillionaire, and mild-mannered announcer for WWF TV programs with a penchant for miscalling three-counts. He also may or may not be a steroid distributor, depending on the outcome of a federal trial.

Terry Bollea as "Hulk Hogan"

A tanned, muscular wrestler and former four-time WWF world champion who is craving one more shot at the title, whether or not it comes at the expense of everyone else around him. Due to sudden restrictions on steroids, he is dramatically smaller than usual at this time, although still a weird color of orange.

Bret Hart as "Bret Hart"

A Canadian hero, given the WWF title in 1992 as an experiment due to his growing fanbase and in 1993 awaiting Hulk Hogan's putting him over once and for all to be established as the wrestler of the '90s. Called "The Excellence of Execution" for his solid technical skills, although he is almost as well known for having the greasiest hair known to man.

Michael Hickenbottom as "Shawn Michaels"

A former tag-team specialist turned pretty-boy, blond primadonna heel after ditching drug-addicted partner Marty Jannetty, his power increased exponentially as he made friends with bigger and bigger people and took more dramatic bumps, until he was primed to be WWF champion and the star of the next millennium by the end of 1996. After a so-so run with the WWF title in 1996, Shawn began solidifying his power, changing his entire attitude and style to fit with the upcoming swing to upstart writer Vince Russo and the "Attitude" era. If that meant faking a knee injury here and there, so be it.

Kevin Nash as "Diesel"

A former middling basketball player turned WCW reject, before a friendship with Shawn Michaels earned him a job in the WWF as Shawn's bodyguard, at which point his "awesome" talents (holding his fist in the air, rubbing his gloved hand, and glaring menacingly at fans) propelled him to the WWF championship faster than should have been possible for someone as awesomely untalented as he is. Best known for being close to seven feet tall and playing a character based on the Wizard of Oz while in WCW.

Larry Pfohl as "Lex Luger"

A legendary choker while in WCW, Luger's Hogan-like physique and steel-plated forearm seemed to guarantee a top-card spot for as long as wanted it, despite his horrid work and seemingly total lack of care for the business. Amazingly, his penchant for being booked to look like a chump followed him to a new promotion with new bookers.

Mark Callaway as "The Undertaker"

Yet another WCW refugee who, like Nash, also had the benefit of being extremely tall and a natural badass, plus the additional benefit of not being a total slug in the ring. However, he was given the ultimate cartoon gimmick: an undead zombie controlled by the spirits of his dead parents, contained in an urn carried by a guy named "Paul Bearer." So to keep in character he had to move really slowly all the time and thus negate his natural speed.

Steve Williams as "Steve Austin"

One of the lucky survivors of the Hulk Renaissance in WCW, he managed to make it out under the electric fence merely by having a gruesome triceps tear that nearly ended his career. WCW President Eric Bischoff's secretary fired Austin over the phone for not providing proper medical documentation of the injury—and because a wrestler who just wore plain black boots and trunks would apparently never sell merchandise—then he was into the WWF after a cup of coffee in badboy promotion ECW. After a false start as the lame-o Ringmaster, he settled into his badass rebel image as "Stone Cold" Steve Austin and was primed to set the world on fire as 1997 began.

Mick Foley as himself

Playing the psychotic Mankind upon his entrance into the WWF, he was on the fast track to upper-card heel status before getting derailed when washed-up Terry Gordy's run as his crony—The Executioner—killed his momentum and sent him back to square one personalitywise. Replacing Gordy with bigger and badder monster heel Vader was a good first step, but a babyface turn proved to be the magic formula . . .

Paul Levesque as "Hunter Hearst Helmsley"

As Shawn Michaels's real-life best friend, and sole Clique member not to defect to WCW in 1996, Hunter was always going to be around TV whether he was successful or not. His hair alone guaranteed that. But in the beginning of 1997, they finally found the secret to his success, and as an added bonus he was already sleeping with it. Three years and as many character makeovers later, a star was born.

Glen Jacobs as "Kane"

A six-foot-odd monster with almost no talent when he started, Glen Jacobs floated through a variety of gimmicks ranging from Jerry Lawler's evil dentist, Isaac Yankem, to a reprise of the Diesel character during the WWF's attempt to fool fans into thinking that Kevin Nash was back with the WWF late in 1996. Jacobs developed into a passable worker, however, and when they needed someone to play an especially goofy gimmick late in 1997, he stepped up to bat again and hit a home run . . .

Dwayne Johnson as "The Rock"

Son of '80s star Rocky Johnson, The Rock was originally an annoying "rookie sensation" who was turned into an actual heel sensation after a well-timed knee injury and sudden injection of personality created the superstar for the next century. His knack for catchphrases and unique connection with the fans catapulted him to the top faster than the WWF could keep up with him.

And also starring (in alphabetical order . . .)

Kurt Angle as "Kurt Angle"

After winning Olympic gold for the U.S. in 1996 as a wrestler, Angle was heavily pursued by the WWF for a professional career, finally debuting on TV in 1999 and shooting to the stratosphere from there.

Chris Benoit as "Chris Benoit"

After idolizing the Dynamite Kid as a teenager, Benoit started in Calgary in 1987 and worked his way up to the big time, despite his lack of size and personality, by being an intense mo-fo who could rock the ring with the best of them.

Adam Copeland as "Edge"

Known for his gigantic teeth and rock-star looks, Edge debuted in 1998 as a young sensation and has floundered at the mid-card level ever since, although a teaming with partner and story line–brother Christian resulted in a tag-team title run that totally reeked of awesomeness.

Solofa Fatu as "Rikishi"

Starting early on as a member of the Samoan Swat Team with partner Samu in the late '80s, Fatu spent a few years in the WWF in the early '90s before bouncing through a series of lame gimmicks, including The Headshrinker Fatu, Makin' a Difference Fatu, and The Sultan, before putting on another fifty pounds and becoming an evil sumo wrestler with a heart of gold.

Matt and Jeff Hardy as "The Hardy Boyz"

Wrestling fans from a young age, the Hardyz honed their craft in the Carolinas with lame gimmicks and highspots so crazy that most thought they'd be lucky to live to see twenty-five, let alone break into the big time. But they survived and became the WWF's newest pretty-boy team phenomenon in 1999, upsetting the Acolytes to win the tag titles and becoming two of the bigger stars of recent memory.

Booker Huffman as "Booker T"

A black man from Texas, he discovered his nonexistent Harlem roots in WCW in the early '90s along with brother Stevie Ray when they formed Harlem Heat. Booker was given a singles run in 1997 as a result of Rick Martel forgetting his trunks for a title match, and he soon became one of the most popular stars WCW had. He became only the second black WCW champion in history in 2000 when he beat Jeff Jarrett to win that title, then signed with the WWF in 2001 after the death of WCW, bringing that belt with him after regaining it from Scott Steiner on the last Nitro. He is best known for the "Spinaroonie," a breakdance move to taunt his opponent. It usually backfires.

Chris Irvine as "Chris Jericho"

Son of hockey legend Ted Irvine, Jericho learned most of his craft in Japan while maintaining a rock-star alter ego in the form of "Moongoose McQueen," lead singer of Fozzy. With his long blond hair and short stature, WCW used him as a pretty-boy babyface from 1996–98 before trying him at a heel turn, transforming Jericho into a whining, prissy, conspiracy-obsessed lunatic in the process . . . and a very big star. However, politics prevented Jericho from even getting a glimpse of life above the glass ceiling, and his frustration led him right into the arms of the WWF in 1999.

Andrew Martin as "Test"

A former bodyguard for Motley Crue, Test debuted in 1999 as a lackey for HHH and because he was so darn tall and had long blond hair, was given chance after chance to establish

3

himself in the mid-card and higher, failing each time.

Shane McMahon as "Shane McMahon"

Originally brought into WWF story lines as a coconspirator with father Vince McMahon, Shane was bitten by the wrestling bug and soon became known for his insane bumping and willingness to do just about anything to make the crowd pop. In real life, Shane runs the media division of the WWF machine.

Stephanie McMahon as "Stephanie McMahon-Helmsley"

Introduced in 1999 as Undertaker's kidnapping target, Stephanie developed her own on-screen personality after a heel turn and soon became a fixture on the TV shows—because she was writing them all.

Jay Reso as "Christian"

Longtime partner of Edge, Christian entered the WWF in 1998 as his estranged brother under the spell of vampire Gangrel. Once reunited with Edge, first as heels, then faces, then heels again, Edge and Christian discovered that offbeat shenanigans were the key to success.

Al Sarven as "Al Snow"

The very definition of "journeyman," Snow spent years on the indy circuit before getting a break with the WWF in 1996 as Leif Cassidy, a spoof of Shawn Michaels's rocker persona. After getting fired and sent to the ECW in 1997, he changed his act to "psychotic mannequin lover" and earned his ticket back to the WWF as a result.

Ken Wayne Shamrock as "Ken Shamrock"

A tough-guy wrestler in the '80s, Shamrock switched to his real love, fighting, when the Ultimate Fighting Championships debuted in the early '90s. He made a name for himself, albeit not a very successful one, before returning to the wrestling rings for the WWF in 1997 using an ultimate-fighter gimmick, and thus helped to revolutionize submission wrestling as a result.

Ray Traylor as "Big Bossman"

A former prison guard who started wrestling in 1986 to earn some money on the side, Traylor was discovered by Jim Cornette and turned into a bodyguard named "Big Bubba Rogers." His amazing speed, for a man over 300 pounds, earned him a push, and then a contract with the WWF in the late '80s. After making big money on a run against Hulk Hogan, he became one of the most successful babyfaces of the early '90s, first with the WWF and then WCW before age and injuries turned him into a shell of his former self. He returned to the WWF in 1998 and has been trampling on his own legacy ever since.

And Chaz Warrington as "the Beaver."
(don't ask)

Prelude

Thirty Years, One Chapter (1963–1993)

"From nothing we have risen, And from nothing we still rise."
—Author Unknown.

[Fade In]

One of the main problems of the printed medium, unlike the Internet, is that you only have so much space to devote to stuff. For instance, where originally I had in mind a broader historical scope for the book, in practice I found myself with about 80,000 words to play with and a lot of years to cover. So what we're going to do now is catch you up on everything that happened in the WWF from day one until the beginning of 1993, because when it comes right down to it, we'd all like to forget the '80s anyway.

I do feel a little guilty about shafting poor Bruno Sammartino yet again, as it seems like every modern history of the WWF completely omits him and his era, so rest assured that Bruno *did* exist and he was champion for a very long time and drew lots of money.

Back in 1963, a bunch of promoters banded together under the name NWA—National Wrestling Alliance. Two of these promoters were Vince McMahon, Sr., in the northeast portion of the U.S., and his crony, Toots Mondt. Toots's big draw was "Nature Boy" Buddy Rogers, a notorious heel who won the NWA's world title from Lou Thesz (himself no slouch in the wrestling and money-drawing departments). After a certain point, however, the NWA wanted Rogers to lose the title back to Thesz, but Mondt and McMahon had a better idea—keep the title for themselves and tell the NWA where they could get off. See, McMahon virtually owned Madison Square Garden, and if you controlled MSG, you controlled the wrestling world. So Vince had some very solid ground to stand on when he made his decision to break away from the NWA.

The NWA, in keeping with the traditions of wrestling, has a fictitious history dating back to the turn of the twentieth century, but in fact they were only created in 1949. In order to lend a more credible air to their world title, it was decided that all programs and literature dealing with the history of the organization would reference a world title first seen in 1904, a little white lie that has endured even until today.

Rogers did eventually lose the title back to Thesz, but the result was disputed, which gave McMahon the excuse he needed to split away from the NWA and form his own major promotion—the World Wide Wrestling Federation. It sounds kind of weird to have that extra *W* in WWWF, but it was there for the first fifteen years of the company's existence, so get used to it for a bit. Rogers "won" the title in Rio de Janeiro, which is one of the all-time classic inside jokes in wrestling—anytime you see someone "winning" a title in a South American country, it means that they were just given the belt. Now, this would have been great for all concerned, except for one problem—Rogers had a pretty serious heart condition and couldn't perform to the best of his ability, so they needed a new champion.

The infamous "Rio de Janeiro title change" reared its ugly head again in 1979 when Pat Patterson "won" the first intercontinental title in a sixteen-man tournament that only happened in Vince McMahon's imagination.

Enter Bruno Sammartino.

Now, unfortunately, history has erased Bruno from the annals of WWF greats because it's the WWF and, well, that's what they do once you leave the promotion and can't help the company make money anymore. But Bruno, who was an untested Italian bodybuilder, swept into the WWWF and was immediately put over the ailing Rogers, in much the same way that Hulk Hogan would take the WWF by storm twenty years later. Rogers had in fact suffered a heart attack earlier that week, so the match was cut dramatically—down to under a minute, in fact, as Bruno polished him off with a backbreaker to win the title.

Sammartino held that title for an astonishingly long eight years, and while I'd love to reminisce longer about all the great things he did for the WWWF (and there's a lot of them, including selling out Madison Square Garden more times than anyone thought was humanly possible for one person), I've got to move past him for the moment. Besides, his first title reign ended years before almost anyone reading this book was born. Sammartino finally lost the title in 1971 to the most generic of all generic "Evil Russians," Ivan Koloff, so that the title could be moved on to the hot new thing of that time, Pedro Morales. Here's my review of the match:

Ivan Koloff v. Pedro Morales

Koloff defeated Bruno in 1971 to become the third WWWF champion, ending Bruno's insane eight-year run as champion. He would hold the title for only three weeks before meeting the next big thing: Pedro Morales.

Both men were not so good.

Big, long headlock to start. Koloff was actually pretty ripped for the time. Koloff does his headlock. Morales monkey-flips out of a knucklelock, then Koloff goes into a bearhug. Pedro comes back with a slam, and we get a collision for the double knockout. Crowd is absolutely rabid—my call of the match can't do justice to how hot the fans are for Pedro. Another slam, but Koloff falls on top for two. Koloff goes to the top for his dreaded finisher—the top-rope kneedrop—but misses and Morales hits a flying bodypress for two. Then they ruin the match by doing the stupidest ending in wrestling—Koloff hits a German suplex, and Morales lifts his shoulder at two and gets the pin. I HATE THAT FINISH. Morales wins his only WWWF title, and MSG absolutely EXPLODES. Holy shit! Match was good enough, if kind of slow and plodding. **

While Morales was no great shakes in the ring, he appealed to a wide audience and got some great reactions for his matches. Morales is more a footnote in history than anything, however, despite being a champion for two years until running into the dreaded Heart Punch of Stan "The Man" Stasiak.

Stan "The Man" Stasiak, bad as he was, can't hold a candle to his son Shawn, who debuted for the WWF in 1999 as "Meat," slave boy to Terri Runnels and Jacqueline, before getting fired for secretly taping private conversations between other wrestlers. He was allegedly having an affair with Jerry Lawler's girlfriend and was trying to cover his own tracks. He returned to the WWF in 2001 after the sale of the WCW, at which point he was given the gimmick of "Planet Stasiak," a hopelessly deluded loser who lost his matches in under thirty seconds and spoke in bad poetry. Kinda makes the heart punch look highbrow by comparison.

A word on the Heart Punch, if I may: The idea behind it is that Stasiak would punch the poor guy in the chest, presumably stopping his heart long enough to pin him. Hey, it was the '70s, a few grams of coke would work just as well, but I guess he liked doing things the old-fashioned way. Now, in *good* wrestlers this kind of silliness might be easily overlooked, but Stasiak's title reign baffles people to this day, since he was horrible by any standard and there were other perfectly good killer heels floating around capable of carrying the title better than Stasiak, like Koloff, Killer Kowalski, the popcorn vendor, a little kid at ringside . . . pretty much everyone in the world. Now, if Stasiak was fighting a dead guy and needed to give him CPR in order to revive him long enough for a match . . . well, then the Heart Punch was just about the perfect move to use.

Stasiak got crushed by Sammartino, who was still so over that he got another two years with the title while the next wave of wrestlers

prepared to storm the scene. Unlike today, however, Vince McMahon, Sr. had a very firm and unshakeable view of where his promotion was headed in the next few years, and that direction was with a guy so far ahead of his time that he could come out of retirement tomorrow and still be over: superstar Billy Graham. After decades of in-ring skill being a necessary element for maintaining the integrity of the world titles in wrestling, Graham was unapologetically 'roided up and obnoxious, setting the template from which Hulk Hogan (in his later heel days), Jesse "The Body" Ventura, and "Big Poppa Pump" Scott Steiner would base their own personas. Graham was more concerned with posing than wrestling, he ran from conflict, and told anyone in the audience who would listen what a god he was. Plus, he was very over and had defeated Bruno Sammartino to capture the WWWF title by 1977.

By this time, forces elsewhere were aligning to eventually shape the WWF's rise in the '80s. Vince McMahon, Jr. was gaining power with his father, even as Vince, Sr.'s own cronies prepared to choose sides in the inevitable power struggle. A very young and green Hulk Hogan was breaking into the sport in Florida as Terry Boulder. Veteran wrestler and promoter Angelo Poffo's son Randy Savage was helping his father wage war in Tennessee against Jerry Jarrett, while building his own reputation as a badass heel and a fantastic worker. Andre the Giant was touring the world as the McMahons wondered if they should keep him closer to home as the business got bigger. The Junkyard Dog ruled the South, making more money (and scoring more drugs) than thought possible for a black wrestler at the time. A young Rodney (later Roddy) Piper was doing indy shows in Canada, L.A., and Portland and was told numerous times that he was too small to be an effective money-drawing heel.

Bob Backlund quickly won the WWWF title,

which became the WWF title midway through 1979 when the company underwent a cosmetic name change with the slow changeover in ownership from Vince, Sr.'s Capital Sports Group to Vince, Jr.'s Titan Sports. The differences in the product weren't immediately noticed, mainly because the old man still held a tight hand over his own company and Bob Backlund was definitely still the man for the top spot as far as he was concerned. The younger Vince had some drastically different ideas about what direction the company was going to be headed—namely a national one.

Unbeknownst to Vince, Sr., his main men (Gorilla Monsoon, Arnold Skaaland, and Phil Zacko) were already lining up on his son's side of things. By 1983, the WWF was becoming a muscle show with a circuslike atmosphere as Vince, Jr. gained more control over the company, until he finally forced a hostile takeover on his own father, using Monsoon/Skaaland/Zacko to leverage the old man out of his lifelong career. No one said it was a pretty business, that's for sure. Vince, Sr. died shortly after.

Vince McMahon (assumed to be the only one from here on) now had a dream of going national and obliterating all the competition, and toward that goal he had one major ally and one major problem: his own arrogance, and his own arrogance, in that order.

His arrogance helped out a lot because he clearly knew what he was after, and the other promoters were either smart enough to back off (like Stu Hart) or tried to stand up to him and went out of business shortly after (like, um, everyone else). By the end of 1983, it was really just the WWF, the AWA, and whoever was lucky enough to be a member of the NWA.

McMahon's arrogance hurt him a lot, however, in late 1983 when it dealt him a nearly crippling blow to the ego in the form of the Georgia Championship Wrestling fiasco. It might shock newer fans that in fact, 2001 was

There's a whole other story behind Vince's purchase of Stu Hart's Stampede Wrestling promotion in 1984, but the short version is that Stu proved to be the smartest of the smaller promoters—he sold out to Vince in exchange for deferred payments, and when Vince conveniently started ignoring those payments after only a year, Stu claimed breach of contract and took his promotion back, having used the buyout to secure son Bret a permanent place in the WWF.

not the first time that Vince McMahon had bought out the WCW—sort of.

In 1983, Ted Turner's Superstation WTCG (later WTBS) was rapidly expanding to homes all across America, and McMahon, being the true believer in the American dream, saw an already overcrowded market and said "Me, too!" Unfortunately, this came with a heavy price as Ted Turner (according to McMahon legend) wanted a piece of the WWF. Quite desperately, apparently.

McMahon wanted the plum timeslot on Saturday afternoons occupied by Ole Anderson's Georgia Championship Wrestling (although the show was called "World Championship Wrestling" to keep it from sounding too "Southern"). So failing Turner buying the WWF, McMahon convinced the Brisco brothers (who were backing GCW) to betray boss Ole Anderson and sell their stock to Vince McMahon and the WWF.

Admittedly, Ole Anderson wasn't the brightest lightbulb in the package to begin with and likely would have run the company into the ground anyway, but we'll never know for sure since Vince's scummy end run around the front office made it a moot point anyway.

McMahon has a different story, but as with lawyers and politicians, assume he's lying 99 percent of the time and you'll be better off. And thus,

World Championship Wrestling was sold to Vince for about the price of a bowl of soup. Vince ended up with the Saturday timeslot on WTBS just as his national promotion was expanding, and Turner had an "in" with the new badboy on the wrestling block to provide cheap programming and great ratings for his station.

One problem that you won't hear the WWF tell: the ratings *sucked*. From the first day that Georgia Championship Wrestling fans tuned in, expecting to hear Gordon Solie but getting Hulk Hogan instead, the response was overwhelmingly negative and it turned into a huge PR nightmare for everyone involved. Cards and letters poured in by the hundreds begging for Gordon Solie to return, so Turner quickly relented and gave Ole Anderson a new timeslot on Saturday morning, creatively called "Championship Wrestling from Georgia."

McMahon's side of things (from an interview in his own *WWF Magazine* in 1996) was that Turner kept making overtures about buying the WWF out until Vince finally yelled "No, you brute!" like a girl getting felt up on a first date. Turner twirled his evil moustache and swore revenge on the virtuous, independent, free spirit, forcing him off the station on a technicality and necessitating a sale of GCW to Jim Crockett—then the owner of Mid-Atlantic Championship Wrestling—who then merged his two companies into what was until 2001 known as WCW.

Most of this is all bullshit—ratings were a disaster from day one, and continued to plunge until Turner simply decided to cancel McMahon's programming from his station in record time (less than two months) and return to the proven track record of Jim Crockett. Turner was no angel to be sure, and there's another really nasty political story involving Mid-South owner Bill Watts and *his* involvement in all this and how he got screwed over worse than anyone thanks to Turner's backstabbing, but that's not relevant for the moment. The whole thing showed that

McMahon's "national" dreams probably wouldn't be able to penetrate the redneck populace without some help (ironic, considering the extremely lowbrow nature of McMahon's product as compared to the more mature and athletic product offered by Jim Crockett at the time), and it was his first embarrassing setback on a large scale. It wouldn't be the last.

> **J**im Crockett was himself no great shakes as a promoter in the long run. Although he won the battle against Vince by winning the timeslot on WTBS, his horrendously bad decision-making resulted in booker Dusty Rhodes running the promotion into the ground by 1988, necessitating the Ted Turner buyout of the entire operation. Had there not been Turner Broadcasting to bail them out, NWA world champion Ric Flair was ready to jump to the WWF and the "war" would have been over thirteen years prior to the purchase of the WCW by the WWF in 2001.

Times they were a-changing under the new guard with McMahon, as he mercilessly drove any competition out of business wherever he could, and in the cases where they had too deep a foothold in a given territory (which was almost everywhere), he simply signed all the major talent away and left the promotion for dead. You have to understand something right now—the way the WWF tells the story, in 1984 their product swept over the wrestling landscape like Moses parting the Red Sea and everyone went "ooh, ahh" when Hulk Hogan came to town.

This could not be further from the truth—the people who went "ooh, ahh" were the TV producers who saw the flashy new presentation and dumped the smaller "rasslin'" promoters from their normal timeslots in favor of the better deal from the WWF. In fact, most longtime fans *hated* the WWF's slower, clumsier freak show and wanted nothing to do with it and still don't today, but were forced to watch it because McMahon simply waged a war of attrition on anyone who opposed him. By 1985, Vince and the Traveling Hulk Hogan Ego Fest had alienated almost the entire wrestling fanbase—the audience they were now catering to was created almost out of thin air from new fans who had never seen an alternative to the WWF before: sports entertainment fans.

Marketing wrestling is like marketing smoking—hook 'em young and hook 'em good. The same thing happened with WCW in 1996 when the nWo angle was created and WCW's entire previous fanbase simply stopped watching wrestling. Fad audiences are great to have in the short term, but once the talk shows don't care about you anymore, look out below.

The king of the fad audience was undoubtedly Hulk Hogan. The prototypical muscular, tanned god who set the public image of what a pro wrestler should look like for years to come, Hogan burst onto the WWF scene in 1983 and never looked back. Hogan gets a lot of credit for saving wrestling during the national expansion, but the truth is that Hogan is one of a few guys who could have carried the load. Junkyard Dog was actually more widely known on a national scale at the time, and could have helped the WWF break into the South thanks to his previous experience there as the biggest hero since Davy Crockett. However, JYD was hindered by deteriorating ring work thanks to the insane amount of cocaine that he was doing and a penchant for Twinkies that kept him pleasantly plump, whereas once he was ripped and chiseled.

The other contender for superstardom was Jimmy "Superfly" Snuka, and in fact he was pretty close to Hogan's level without the same push. However, Snuka was another well-known abuser of all sorts of substances, and by 1985 he self-destructed in spectacular fashion, culminating in a night during which his girlfriend was murdered and he was the prime suspect. Hindsight, however, is 20/20, and it would have been just as easy for McMahon to go with Snuka at the time and still make millions. But luckily for us, it was Hogan, the Orange Goblin, who got the call to glory, and he crushed Iron Sheik to win the WWF title and start things down the road to riches for Vince McMahon.

McMahon actually wasn't that rich to start—when he forced his own father out of the business and then stared down all the other promoters, he was mostly bluffing. His investments were all based on potential earnings, and even Vince admits that had any of the "good old boys" in the older territories found out, he would have been run out of the business before he'd even got started. By 1985, he had talked NBC into taking a huge risk on promoting WWF programming in *Saturday Night Live*'s timeslot as *Saturday Night's Main Event*, a risk that paid off huge for everyone.

Vince then created *Wrestlemania* and avoided bankruptcy by a hair when the show got a huge, last-minute walk-up for the closed-circuit airings, then he made millions off the videotape revenues. Hulk Hogan only worked a couple of dates a month, but whatever arena he main-evented sold out instantly and made tons of money for everyone on the show. MTV took another risk in melding their music videos with the WWF product, and the result was a definitive '80s fad: "Rock 'N' Wrestling"—as if Cyndi Lauper has ever rocked in her entire career. But the exposure on MTV made huge stars out of not only Hogan, but also his archrival, Roddy Piper, who then went to Hollywood and continued spreading the buzz of the WWF by actually being a decent actor.

Selected Hulk Hogan Filmography: *Rocky III, No Holds Barred, Suburban Commando, Mr. Nanny,* and *Santa with Muscles.* And they say wrestling is embarrassing.

In 1987, the WWF peaked for the '80s with *Wrestlemania III* from the Silverdome, a legendary show that saw Hulk Hogan pin Andre the Giant to retain the title in one of the worst matches in wrestling history. Here's my review:

Main Event, WWF Title:
Hulk Hogan v. Andre the Giant

The very definition of a money match and a dream match, as wrestling fans debated this one for months previous and talked about it for years after. You've heard pretty much everything about this one on all the documentaries that have sprung up recently, so there's not really much more I can add to the hype for it. Andre, undefeated for twenty years and a hero for more, against Hogan, reigning world champion and unbeatable superman.

The story: Hulk and Andre are friends for years, through everything. Jack Tunney presents Andre with a trophy for his accomplishments one week, and then presents Hogan with a bigger trophy the next week, which annoys Andre. So much so, in fact, that Andre comes out the next week and challenges Hogan to a match for his title, then rips off Hogan's shirt and cross. Andre takes on former rival Bobby Heenan as his manager, and the rest is history. Bob Uecker is guest ring announcer and Mary Hart is guest timekeeper. Andre nearly gets booed out of the damn building. Now THAT'S heel heat. When Jesse Ventura says that it's the biggest match in the history of professional wrestling, it's NOT hyperbole.

They do the big staredown and then Hulk tries a bodyslam, but Andre falls on him for two. The crowd is pelting Andre with garbage at various times. Andre destroys Hogan with knees and two bodyslams. He does everything slow and deliberate, mainly because he was having trouble moving by this time in his life. Comeback number one for Hogan goes nowhere as Andre won't go down. Bearhug from Andre, which lasts about five minutes, literally. Comeback number two from Hogan goes nowhere again as Andre boots him out of the ring. They fight outside, and Andre headbutts the post by accident. Hulk pulls up the mats and tries to piledrive Andre on the floor, but he gets backdropped. Wow, a bump. Sort of.

Back in the ring, and Hogan finally knocks Andre down with a clothesline. He hulks up as Andre gets to his feet, and then in the most famous moment in wrestling history, he slams Andre and pins him with the legdrop. Match was atrociously bad, but for sheer history there's none greater. ¼*

While not the absolute worst match ever, it can be conclusively stated the Hulk v. Andre is one of the only ones to utilize a bodyslam as a finishing move. Andre was in severe pain due to his physical condition and nearly unable to move as a result, but in later tellings Hogan has revised the story to where he was worried about Andre "shooting" on him (not cooperating) and it was his lucky break that Andre agreed to do the job that night. Of course, this discounts Andre saying "Slam me, boss" before the big move and then doing all the work therein himself, but that's the kind of stuff you have to deal with where Hogan is involved.

Professional wrestling had reached an incredible height, and every night was a party filled with women, drugs, and money, and every day they counted the money from the night before. But just like all the other two-bit promoters that McMahon thought he was above, he made the same mistake they all had: he assumed that his fad audience was his core audience, and that they'd be around forever. They weren't. By 1988,

Hulk Hogan was losing steam with his standard "Hogan v. Big Fat Heel" and "Hogan v. Big Fat Foreigner" formulas, and when it came time for a rematch with Andre the Giant on prime time TV, Vince decided that it was time for a change. Here's my review:

WWF World Title:
Hulk Hogan v. Andre the Giant

This was quite possibly the most important single moment in the modern era, just because of all the historical significance, the precedent it set, and all the things that followed from it. This was the debut of the new WWF title belt that had been promised prior to Wrestlemania III, but had never showed up for whatever reason. It was of course the familiar design that was just retired in 1998 when Steve Austin won the thing.

Hogan does his posing before the match starts. Hogan cleans house on the seconds, then starts punching Andre. This goes on FOREVER, and Andre just keeps absorbing blows from Hogan and won't go down. Hogan tries going to the top finally, but gets slammed off and suddenly starts selling a back injury like he was just in a career-ending car accident. Andre chokes a lot. He works a bodyslam in, then does a Hogan big boot and falls over in the process. Only quick camera work prevents him from looking like a total idiot. More choking. Still more. Choking, you say? Have some more. Hogan comes back and goes aerial, hitting a clothesline from the second rope and the STINKY WART-INFESTED NASTY GIANT-KILLING LEGDROP OF DEATH, but Virgil is distracting our referee.

Hogan stops to argue the point, but Andre lumbers up and grabs him from behind, hitting a half-assed suplex/hiptoss thing and getting a one-count . . . which is extended into three because the ref keeps counting despite Hogan's lifting his shoulder. The crowd is in SHOCK as Hogan's four-year title reign has come to an end under suspicious circumstances. HULK SCREWED HULK!

Mean Gene pops into the ring for a word with Andre, who barely has the celebratory speech out of his mouth before he hands the title over to Ted Dibiase, becoming the shortest reigning champion in the WWF to date. The weirdness continues, as a SECOND Hebner comes out of the dressing room to argue with the first one. One of course was Dave Hebner, senior WWF referee, and the other was his twin brother, Earl, current senior WWF referee. Earl eventually punks out Dave, which is good enough proof of Evil Intentions for Hogan, so he tosses Earl like a shotput into the arms of Dibiase (sending him about fifteen feet into the aisle in the process) and that's that. ½*

This show scored the most ungodly high rating ever for a wrestling match—a 15.2 rating on prime-time network TV—and was preceded by levels of paranoia unmatched by the CIA circulating through Titan Towers in the weeks leading up to the show. Vince, in desperation to keep the finish from being leaked to any sort of media, kept it entirely to himself and only told the people involved a few hours before the show. This included concocting an elaborate story for the pre-taped syndicated television shows to explain why nothing was being said about the incredibly controversial finish even two weeks afterward. In fact, they COULDN'T say anything about it because those shows were taped BEFORE the big match and Vince hadn't clued them in to what the controversial finish was going to be at the time they were taped!

By this time, Andre the Giant was having dire health problems as his body just couldn't support his own weight anymore, and he was having trouble walking normally. It was kind of a metaphor for the whole WWF because it had started to collapse under the weight of its own excesses.

Randy Savage ended up with the title, and was doing just fine as champion before the WWF panicked and turned him heel again, putting the belt back on Hogan for another kick at the can. But the magic was gone and you could tell—Hogan wanted out of the business by 1989 and got into movies like *No Holds Barred*, leaving Vince floundering for a main-event draw to replace the Hulkster. He tried Ultimate Warrior, but the audience was leaving for good and wanted no part of him. Warrior's unstable personality and bizarre interviews weren't much help, either. Rick Rude was looking like a good draw on top, but McMahon screwed him over while he was injured and ran him right into the arms of WCW as a result.

In 1991, the WWF was handed the biggest story line in its history on a silver platter, and they blew it. Ric Flair left WCW during a contract dispute and showed up on WWF TV—carrying the other promotion's world title with him! An immediate feud with Hulk Hogan (who was having try number three at being champion) seemed a natural, but we never saw that particular match on PPV—just on largely unknown house shows—and Flair (considered by most to be the single greatest wrestler of the modern era) was made to "pay his dues" before getting a serious push in the WWF. This was mind-boggling to everyone involved, even though Flair got the WWF title in early 1992.

The NWA actually got the last laugh on the Ric Flair situation, as he showed up on WWF TV carrying the NWA world title and claiming to the "Real World's Champion." The NWA promptly sued and Vince quietly gave in to them and dropped that aspect of the Flair character. You'll never hear Vince tell it that way, of course.

But the one thing that nearly killed the WWF for good was not the dumb mistakes made on the way down, but the one made on the way up. Namely, steroids. And lots of 'em. And when the federal government started investigating the WWF for distribution, suddenly all those muscle-bound circus freaks were out of a job all at once and business went into the toilet with Ric Flair and a skinnier-than-usual Randy Savage battling for the top spot.

And then it got even worse. . . .

Act One

King Lear (1993–1996)

"Drugs are bad, m'kay?"
     —Mr. Mackey, *South Park*

O nce upon a time . . .

The dark ages of wrestling (for the WWF) came from about 1989 (the downside of Hulk Hogan's drawing power) until Ric Flair left at the end of 1992, at which point things got *really* awful. It was almost a Shakespearean tragedy in terms of the scope of bad things that started happening to the WWF on a regular basis. In fact, McMahon, who was making increasingly bad choices in booking and whom to trust, started to resemble the main figure in the Shakespearean tragedy *King Lear*.

For those who haven't read *King Lear*, here's a very rough summary of what happens:

King Lear is a once-wise, aging ruler of a large kingdom who is in need of an heir. He summons his three daughters to him and decides that whichever one loves him most will be given his kingdom. Regan and Goneril lie and profess their love with various hyperbole, while Cordelia simply states her loyalty to him and no more. Lear loses control and punishes Cordelia for her answer, denying her the kingdom and giving it to his other, more "loving" daughters instead.

As Lear moves away from his ruling duties, he is shuttled back and forth between his two daughters, both of whom are using him for their own gains. Soon Lear's only true friend is the Fool, who ironically is the only one who speaks the truth. Cordelia is courted by the king of France, who soon invades the weakened Lear's domain, nearly costing Lear his entire kingdom. The invasion is barely held back by Lear's army, and as his other daughters desert the kingdom, Lear reconciles with Cordelia and finally realizes who his true allies are—only to discover that it's too late. Cordelia has been mortally wounded in the battle, and Lear has gone so mad that he is unable to see that, and, thinking that she is still alive and able to rule his kingdom, he gives up and dies.

Rather gloomy little play, isn't it? So what does that have to do with the WWF? Well, let's rewrite it, substituting some names. . . .

15

Vince McMahon is a once-wise, aging promoter of a large wrestling company who is in need of a new long-term draw. He summons his three biggest names to him and decides that whichever one kisses the most ass will be given a run as champion. Diesel and Shawn Michaels lie and profess their respect for Vince with various hyperbole, while Bret Hart simply states his loyalty to him and no more. Vince loses control and punishes Bret for his answer, jobbing him to Bob Backlund and giving the WWF title to Diesel instead. As Vince moves away from his creative duties, he is manipulated back and forth by his two champions, both of whom are using him for their own gains. Soon Vince's only true ally is Jim Ross, who ironically is the only one who speaks the truth.

Bret Hart, in the meantime, is being courted by Eric Bischoff, who soon invades the weakened Vince's domain, nearly costing him the WWF. The invasion is barely held back by Vince's loyalist workers, and, as the Clique deserts the WWF, Vince reconciles with Bret Hart and signs him to a twenty-year deal—only to discover that it's too late. Bret has been morally scarred by the changing face of wrestling, and Vince has gone so mad that he is unable to see that, and, thinking that Bret is still a viable draw and able to carry the WWF title whenever the need should arise, he gives up and instead allows Shawn Michaels an extended reign as champion, thus effectively conceding defeat in the Monday Night Wars.

Heavy, no?

So this, then, is why the WWF died, and how they got there.

SCENE ONE
The Lex Express

1993 didn't start too well, as Yokozuna was pushed as the primary heel in the WWF, the main factor in his favor being the enormous amount of fat he carried around. He would be dead six years later as a result of his eating habits. Hulk Hogan came back (off the juice and looking the part) in January, hungry for one final run at the top. The idea was for him to win the WWF title back later in the year, and then put Bret Hart over at *Summerslam* to establish Bret as the next big star of the WWF. Hogan was completely in agreement with whatever Vince said at that point. Hogan had leverage because they were trying out a new format for their flagship show, *Prime Time Wrestling*, as it became the newer and edgier *Monday Night RAW*. They wanted big ratings to impress the network, and Hogan certainly could deliver that.

By *Wrestlemania*, things were changing. Bret lost the title to Yokozuna to cap off the god-awful ninth edition of the show, and Hogan immediately came down to ringside to challenge the new champion (before he ate the belt, presumably) to a title match even before Bret Hart had left the ring. This was the wrestling equivalent of jumping into bed with your best friend's wife before the ink on the divorce is even dry. Hogan won the title in ten seconds with the legdrop, and then suddenly told Vince that he wouldn't do any jobs for Bret Hart and would instead be taking three months off to make another box-office blockbuster. By June, Hogan was no longer welcome in the WWF and his last main event featured him getting manhandled by Yokozuna and pinned with his own legdrop to lose the title because, even in leaving the promotion, he wouldn't put Bret over.

So suddenly lacking his number-one guy from the last ten years and sulking about it, Vince did what all jilted exes do—he tried to re-create the magic with someone else. In this case, Lex Luger, who was fresh off headlining the Hindenburg of PPV—*WBF Body Stars*—and wanted back into wrestling full-time again for the money. Vince's big plan was to create another

The WBF—World Bodybuilding Federation—was Vince's attempt to market bodybuilding as a competitive sport by airing a weekly TV show and a PPV, which was an amazingly hypocritical move for someone who had just fired Davey Boy Smith and Ultimate Warrior for steroid use a few months before. Vince was saved from having to explain this sort of discrepancy when the bodybuilding craze failed to sweep the nation in much the same way as the XFL also failed to sweep the nation eight years later and died a quick death.

American hero, so on July 4, Luger emerged from a helicopter to win a bodyslam challenge issued by Yokozuna, and suddenly even his shit was red, white, and blue. Vince spent millions marketing his new sensation in preparation for a big title match against Yokozuna, with the Lex Express bus and tour, Lex Luger ice-cream bars, Lex Luger T-shirts, and Lex Express–brand home pregnancy tests. Okay, I made that last one up. But it was still the biggest push in history, and to everyone's surprise (although deep down no one was really surprised), he blew the big match and only won by countout at *Summerslam*. Here's my review:

WWF Title Match:
Yokozuna v. Lex Luger

Luger slammed Yokozuna onto the deck of the USS Intrepid to set this up, thus throwing away a great Narcissist gimmick in hopes of creating another Hulk Hogan. The Lex Express toured America in hopes of getting Luger over, and it didn't really work. But nevertheless, we got this main event anyway. This was also Luger's one and only title shot. All conventional common sense and logic pointed to Luger wiping the mat with the evil Yoko and winning the title, but that never had stopped Luger from choking before.

He actually hits the HORIZONTAL ELBOWDROP OF DOOM (the move he hits once every five years) early on. Lots of "USA" chants in case any tourists forgot which stop on the itinerary this was. Yoko fights back with devastating chokes (in honor of Luger) and attempted cheating from Fuji. Luger tries the slam, but Yoko blocks and hits sweet thirty-four chins music. Luger is stunned outside the ring! Can our hero recover? More choking by Yoko and an avalanche against the post.

Back in the ring and Luger goes aerial with a double axehandle. Nice to see him vary the offense. Yoko won't go down even after two of them. FLYING STEEL FOREARM OF DEATH, but only gets two. So how come a running, loaded forearm is more devastating than a top-rope one? Oh, right, the elbow pad.

Malfunction at the junction and both guys are out. Yoko nails him with the salt bucket, but only gets two. Belly-to-bellies suplex and more choking. Have I mentioned how grotesquely fat Yokozuna is?

Bellies-to-back suplex for two. And a nerve pinch, oh great. Whose bright idea was it to book Yokozuna in a twenty-minute match? Bodyslam attempt number two, but Yoko falls on him for two. Hulkbuster for two. Banzai drop misses and the superman comeback begins. Luger slams him, nails Fuji, and pulls off the armpad for the LOADED FOREARM OF DEATH! Yoko falls out of the ring and . . . gets counted out??? Uhhh . . . that's not supposed to be how a match like this ends. . . .

They kind of gloss over the fact that titles don't change hands on a countout as the faces storm the ring to celebrate and balloons drop. Still, not a bad effort from both guys, all things considered. **½

Bret Hart, who was supposed to be beating Hulk Hogan here to become the star of the next century, had to settle for winning the inaugural *King of the Ring* PPV and feuding with commentator Jerry Lawler.

In November, the shit hit the fan for Vince McMahon.

SCENE TWO
Don't Cry for Me, Yokozuna

The first player in our little tragedy is a guy you've probably never heard of, but who nonetheless single-handedly changed the WWF. Dr. George Zahorian. See, from the mid-'80s until the early '90s, steroids were legal for use in the U.S. as long as they were prescribed by a doctor. So Vince McMahon simply hired himself a doctor, under the pretext of having him there on behalf of the state athletic commission, and away he went distributing the juice to any WWF wrestler who had the cash. And even if they didn't have the cash, no problem, he'd just advance them some money on their next paycheck.

Problem: In 1991, Dr. George Zahorian is sent up the river by the government, and arrested on several charges of distributing steroids. Suddenly, the WWF is *very* nervous, and rightly so. Just as they had feared, upon his arrest Zahorian squeals to the feds that Vince McMahon has been using and distributing steroids himself for years, and now the government has a solid and tangible way to nail McMahon on felony charges, something they'd been wanting to do. Amazingly, getting rid of all the steroids in the promotion until Randy Savage was down to something like 150 pounds and firing all the steroid freaks didn't suddenly convince the government that no funny business was going on. It sure drove away the fans, however, because they'd been conditioned to think that bigger = better, and Vince's World Bodybuilding Federation sure didn't do much to change that perception.

Vince actually brought in ex-WCW choker Lex Luger (fresh off a motorcycle accident that essentially had ended his usefulness as a wrestler, but which didn't stop him from wrestling another eight years afterward) to be his pri-mary star, booked TV time on the USA network for his *Body Stars* program, scheduled a PPV for the big bodybuilding contest, and even started his own line of "nutritional supplements" called ICOPro to help budding bodybuilders look like his guys. Of course, the only nutritional supplements that most of the WWF was using at the time sure wasn't wheat germ, so most people didn't buy into ICOPro's claims.

And so, on Friday, November 19, 1993, the Brooklyn, N.Y. office of the U.S. Department of Justice handed down an indictment against Vince McMahon and Titan Sports Inc. The indictment contained charges of conspiracy, possession, and possession with intent to distribute. Vince was, in a word, screwed.

If Vince's trial had gone the wrong way for him, legendary Memphis promoter Jerry Jarrett was the guy tapped to take over the reins of the WWF while Vince was in jail. Thankfully it didn't to come to that, or else we might be talking about "eighteen-time WWF champion Jeff Jarrett" today.

The effect on the WWF was immediately noticeable. Pat Patterson took over most of the major creative endeavors in Vince's absence, and the result was *Royal Rumble '94*. The *Rumble* was built not around the match itself that year (although there's an interesting story there, too), but around the main event: Undertaker v. Yokozuna for the WWF title, which was set up when they got into a brawl at *Survivor Series* in November '93 and were both eliminated from their matches. A casket match was signed for the *Rumble* to settle the issue, and the result scarred many people for years to come. Here's my review:

WWF Title Casket Match:
Yokozuna v. The Undertaker

And yes, this was THAT match. And if you're reading this and wondering "What does he mean by 'THAT match'?", well, obviously you've led a very sheltered life and have never heard of this match before, and are thus much more mentally stable than the rest of us poor bastards who had to watch it in 1994. I'd just like to point out, for the record, that all the free tapes from the WCW, exposure from Web sites, money from the same, and ass-kissing from fans STILL isn't enough to justify the mental anguish that this match has caused millions of people and the suffering I have to go through in order to review it for you, the reader.

But I guess a man's gotta do what a man's gotta do. So please, before we begin, bear in mind that I am making NONE of this up, and everything I am about to describe actually happened, live on PPV. This was not, just to clarify, an LSD hallucination gone wrong, or a dream sequence that ended with Pat Patterson waking up in the shower the next morning. And please, for the love of God, put the kids to bed before you read this match review, or skip to the Royal Rumble match. I wouldn't want any of them to read it and later become a booker with these kinds of ideas lodged in their heads. God knows there are enough bad influences on TV these days without the added mental problems caused by watching Undertaker matches from 1994.

Presenting the all-time champion of overbooking and general stupidity . . . Undertaker v. Yokozuna, part one. On to the match . . .

Undertaker gets a quick start, chasing Yoko to the floor. They brawl a bit. Then a bit more. Yoko gains the upper hand with the CEREMONIAL SALT OF DOOM and some weak chairshots. First casketing attempt goes to Yoko, but UT blocks and comes back. Belly-to-bellies ends that, but Taker does the zombie situp. Chokeslam follows and a HUGE swinging DDT. Undertaker tries to finish, and you might want to skip ahead now because it REALLY starts to suck.

Crush blocks UT's win attempt, and Taker fights him off. Now the Great Kabuki (as an agent of Mr. Fuji) tries his luck, along with Genichiro Tenryu. Taker fights them all off. Now Bam Bam comes down and it's four-on-one. Yoko awakens from his nap in the casket, so now it's five-on-one. Is the point hammered home yet? Of course not, so here's Adam Bomb to make it six-on-one. Throw in Jeff Jarrett for seven-on-one, then the Headshrinkers make it NINE-on-one, which is getting excessive even by ECW standards. Diesel joins us last (lazy bastard) for an even ten-on-one, and they STILL, ten guys mind you, can't get Taker into the damn coffin. So what would YOU do? Steal the urn, of course, and dump the ashes out.

Then, just when you thought it couldn't get sillier, it does: Green smoke pours out of the urn and everyone acts all shocked. LET'S KICK IT UP A NOTCH.

On the subject of the urn, it was supposed to contain the ashes of Undertaker's dead parents, which is why the green smoke coming out of it was doubly irritating: It was not only stupid and cheesy, but contradicted its own internal story line logic. By *Summerslam '94*, the urn had morphed into a giant, self-contained spotlight system, this leading me to believe that Undertaker's dead parents would be proud to know that they were being carried around in a truly state-of-the-art piece of equipment.

Vince deadpans as the entire match (and indeed his promotion) falls apart in the ring: "It appears that the power of the urn is escaping, and with it the Undertaker's powers." I swear to God he actually said that without a trace of irony. That's why I couldn't be a wrestling announcer—I'd get fired for ripping stuff apart as soon as I saw how dumb an idea it was. Finally, after all that, they put the Undertaker down for good and shut the lid to give Yokozuna the win at 14:19, although the actual one-on-one match lasted all of five minutes. The crowd is left completely numbed and in shock by the ending.—★★★★

Suck it in, because we're not done yet. The heels then lock the casket and wheel it to the dressing room, but it starts to smoke on the way down the aisle. A video of UT appears on the video wall (which the announcers naturally assume is a live feed of Undertaker inside his casket, thus indicating that Ockham's Razor is a foreign concept to Vince McMahon, Jr.).

Undertaker, who is now "dying," stops his decomposition long enough to give a speech. I was so touched that I transcribed it, because you all deserve to share my pain. I was gonna split it into individual haikus to really be a smart-ass, but it's late, so here's the Undertaker's last words:

"Be not proud, because the spirit of the Undertaker lives within the souls of mankind, the eternal flame of life which cannot be extinguished, the origin of which cannot be explained. The answer lies in the everlasting spirit. Soon, all mankind will witness the rebirth of the Undertaker. I will not rest in peace."

Is that fucking deep or what? I feel like humming "Personal Jesus" right now. I wonder if Sid was watching this show and taking interviewing notes or something? By the way, Mark Callaway wanted time off to spend with his wife, so Vince thought up this whole wonderful "sports entertainment" moment to explain his absence. Whatever happened to "he hurt his leg" or "he's in jail" like in the good old days?

Oh, wait, sorry, I bet you thought this segment couldn't get any more stupid and offensive . . . FOOLISH MORTAL! I'll break your spirit yet! The video wall image of the Undertaker goes to a reverse-color scheme, then starts to "rise" out of the video wall, to be replaced by Marty Jannetty dressed in an Undertaker costume, "levitating" to the ceiling (with wires clearly visible) while Vince earnestly sells the whole thing as a deep and meaningful spiritual experience.

Dear Federal Investigators:

Obviously whoever conducted the investigation of Mr. Vincent K. McMahon on suspicion of drug distrib-

ution in 1994 and failed to get a conviction was either retarded or coked out of their mind because if the above thirty minutes doesn't conclusively prove that the entire booking team was on mind-altering substances of some form then the American legal system might as well pack it in now, because justice is not only blind, it's stupid.

Yours Truly,
Scott Keith

P.S. If you do indeed fire your lead investigator, consider forwarding his resume to WCW, because even though retarded and on mind-altering substances, he's still one up on Russo & Ferrera at this point.

It was widely considered one of the stupidest things ever seen in wrestling, to say the least. Ridiculous gimmick wrestlers like Doink the Clown and Men on a Mission were pushed down the fans' throats, and the overall quality of Monday Night RAW declined at an alarming pace.

Doink the Clown actually was a pretty cool character in his early stages—based on Pennywise the Clown from Stephen King's novel It, he was portrayed by Matt Bourne and slanted toward the nightmarish archetypes of the evil clowns that many children seem to fear. Sadly, this proved to be too highbrow for the WWF marketing department, who had replaced Bourne with bland jobber Ray Lichacelli by 1994 and changed Doink into a lovable misfit with a midget sidekick whose most notorious acts became throwing cream pies at Jerry Lawler. My personal theory at the time was that the creative decline of any great villainous character can be traced directly to the addition of a midget sidekick, but then Austin Powers 2 went and made $350 million and shot that line of thinking all to hell.

SCENE THREE
Too Many Undertakers

One of the bright spots of the early 1994 period, however, was the feud between the Hart brothers—Bret and Owen, which resulted in Bret being more over than ever. When a tied result of the *Rumble* was booked, and with Bret and Lex Luger both hitting the floor at the same time (although sharp-eyed fans pointed out that Lex clearly hit first), the crowd so decisively voiced their approval for Bret that the WWF had no choice but to drastically alter plans. Bret was given the WWF title in the main event of *Wrestlemania X* after defeating his brother in a classic match that people still talk about today. Here's my review:

Bret Hart v. Owen Hart

This was not only a great match, and one of three matches generally considered the greatest openers of all time (alongside Pillman/Liger and Mysterio/Psicosis), but it was also the match that turned Owen Hart from mid-card joke to main-event threat. It also marked the debut of Owen's current choice of tights. The heat for this match was unreal as the fans are firmly behind Bret Hart's side of the story. Owen gave Bret the big stink-eye, which made Bret distinctly uncomfortable.

And now, the match:

They lockup, and Owen pushes Bret off, then celebrates. Cheap heat, but hey, you take what you can get. Owen gets the best of a wrestling sequence and celebrates. Bret retaliates by sending Owen to the floor, which pisses him off and he slaps Bret upon returning to the ring. Bret takes control, working on the arm. Bret gets two off a cradle, then goes back to the arm. After another terrific wrestling sequence, Owen ends up getting tossed to the floor again, and now Bret celebrates. Crowd is much more appreciative of this.

Owen has another fit and a shoving match results, off which Bret gets a rollup for two. Bret back to work on the arm. Bret gets a crucifix for two, then back to the arm. Good psychology here. Owen takes control with his SWANK leg lariat and sends Bret to the floor. He rams Bret's back into the ringpost, establishing the back injury for Bret. Owen gives Bret a cross-corner whip (first time I've seen Bret sell it back-first, actually) and hits a backbreaker. FIVE MOVES OF . . . oh, wait, wrong brother. Owen slaps on a camel clutch while trash-talking his brother. Bret escapes, but gets caught with a belly-to-belly suplex for two. Sweet sassy molassy, I love that belly-to-belly. Another cross-corner whip, reversed by Bret, and Owen comes off the ropes with a bodypress, which is reversed by Bret for a two-count. Owen goes back to the back. Rest hold from Owen, thus dropping it from *****.

Owen tries to slam Bret, but Bret falls back for a two-count. Owen's kickout sends Bret to the floor. Beautiful sequence as Owen suplexes Bret from the apron, and Bret reverses to a waistlock, which Owen reverses again for a German suplex for two. Just gorgeous wrestling. Legdrop from Owen for two. He goes for a suplex, but Bret cradles for two. He goes for a backbreaker, but Owen flips through and tombstones Bret. Nasty one, too. Flying headbutt misses. Inverted atomic drop and clothesline from Bret for two. Wait for it . . . wait for it . . . FIVE MOVES OF DOOM!

Owen hits an enzuigiri to break it up, then goes for the Sharpshooter. Bret counters. He goes for his own, and Owen counters. Owen cradles for two, but gets kicked out of the ring. Pescado from Bret, but he fucks up his knee. Owen circles in like a vulture, working on the knee and mocking his brother. What a jerk. Dragon-screw legwhip (called "Look at that!" by the ever-astute Mr. McMahon) and a submission move of some sort follows. Another dragon screw, then a figure four, which gets a two-count. Bret reverses to break the hold. Owen goes back to work on the knee. Another dragon-screw legwhip attempt, but Bret counters with an enzuigiri. Cross-corner whip and legdrop gets two. Bulldog for two. Piledriver for two. Superplex, and both men are out.

Bret revives long enough to get a two-count. Both get up and Bret hits a sleeper. Owen breaks with a Flair uppercut (Where? Down there . . .) and Bret drops like a rock. Sharpshooter! Bret powers out and applies his own, but Owen makes the ropes. Bret with a cross-corner whip, Owen reverses. Owen eats foot coming into the corner, and Bret goes for a victory roll, but Owen reverses the momentum and lies down on top for the pin! The crowd is in SHOCK. ****¾ . . . Oh, hell, who am I kidding? This is the one of the best matches I've ever seen. ***** just because Bret continued selling the leg injury to the end of the show.

After that show, Luger was buried. Owen was subsequently pushed into the main event as a foil for Bret. It was the first real sign that the WWF was willing to change with the times. That proved to be a premature hope.

On July 22, 1994, after deliberating for sixteen hours, the jury found McMahon and Titan Sports not guilty of the charges. Despite testimony from Zahorian and Hulk Hogan, there proved to be too many flaws in the evidence, holes in the stories, and reluctance from wrestlers to testify and thus be branded a traitor in the locker room, and Vince was a free man. Specifically, the testimony of Kevin "Nailz" Wacholz for the prosecution was so unbelievable that despite roasting Pat Patterson alive on the stand, they just couldn't nail Vince down with anything. While indeed everyone in the WWF came out of the proceedings looking like the sleazeball offspring of Satan and Jerry Springer, there was no actual evidence tying Vince to the crimes charged, and that was that. And with the Dark Period looking to be over, Vince triumphantly returned as the creative force behind the WWF.

The first major story line to emerge after this was the "Fake Undertaker." Ted Dibiase had "found" the Undertaker (after he "died" at the *Rumble*, remember?), only it was SMW mainstay Brian Lee with his hair dyed red. Lee was a fel-

The testimony against Vince was largely a joke and proved to be one of the biggest mistakes the prosection would make. Kevin "Nailz" Wacholz was immediately shown to be testifying out of spite due to Vince's firing him in 1992 over a money dispute. This dispute led to Wacholz attacking Vince in his office, and then later suing for sexual harassment, claiming that he was merely fending off Vince from making a pass at him. Hulk Hogan got onto the stand and turned the thing into a sympathy ploy for himself, contradicting dozens of earlier statements he had made to the press in the process, most notably an appearance on Arsenio Hall where he had denied ever taking steroids. By the time all the witnesses were called, the government's case was so full of holes that Vince himself didn't even bother taking the stand.

low redneck biker in his spare time, and Undertaker had been wanting to work an angle with him for a while. It has been said that when watching the Underfaker, you were 99 percent sure it was the wrong guy, but it was that 1 percent margin of error that made the angle work in the form it did. However, just as fast as the faker was introduced, the build to *Summerslam* was rushed with a match between the two Undertakers, which was announced before the original was even back on TV again!

The "real" Undertaker returned soon afterward (in reality he wasn't dead, he was just on vacation with his wife), and they began hyping the *Summerslam* match with little buildup or interest from the fans. The main focus of the hype was put on weird skits with Leslie Nielson and George Kennedy doing lame detective work and ordering Dominos Pizza. No, seriously. Have I mentioned that this was a really bad period for the WWF? Here's my review:

Undertaker vs. Underfaker

Brian Lee does a pretty decent job of pretending to be the Undertaker, right down to no-selling every single move. UT chases UF outside the ring, then suplexes him back in. Crowd has no idea who to cheer for. The faker gains control and tries the ropewalk, but gets slammed off. And sits up. Taker comes back with his own, and the crowd seems to be catching on to the fact that the purple one is the good guy. More no-selling happens. Crowd is just dead. Pardon the pun.

They "brawl" outside, and it's like listening to a forty-five record at thirty-three and a third. For those under twenty, that's, uh, like watching something really slow. Yeah. Anyway, Faker gets a chokeslam and Taker doesn't sit up, so he takes that as a good sign and tombstones him. UT sits up, so Faker tries again, but Taker reverses to his own. Then picks him up and gives him two more, just for good luck. And this time, there's no sitting up. Undertaker gets the pin at 9:20 and puts everyone out of their misery, and the words "fake Undertaker" are never, EVER spoken on WWF TV again.—****

So the real Undertaker won the match, Brian Lee disappeared, and Undertaker went back to his usual act again, a state in which he'd remain until 1996.

SCENE FOUR
That's MISTER Bob Backlund to You

Meanwhile, another interesting thing occurred: WWF veteran Bob Backlund was given a title match against Bret Hart on WWF TV, and lost. At the end of the match, Backlund snapped and attacked Hart, then stared at his hands in awe. The original idea was "possession" by the returning Papa Shango, but to everyone's surprise, Backlund managed to get himself over as a monster heel using only the "crazy old man" gimmick and his largely untested heel interview skills. The fans were hugely into the character,

so he was pushed into the main event with Bret Hart at *Survivor Series '94* . . . and won the title. Here's my review:

WWF World Title:
Bret Hart v. Mr. Bob Backlund

This was submission rules, with the winner being decided when their second threw in the towel. Bob had Owen Hart, Bret had the Bulldog. Stu and Helen Hart were also at ringside, which became important later. Backlund was drawing BIG heel heat here, by the way. The story was that he was still bitter at his manager's throwing in the towel and costing him the title eleven years prior, and he'd snapped and taken out Bret Hart a few months prior to this, along with nearly everyone else in the promotion.

Bret quickly dominates Bob on the mat, something you don't see too often. Bob suddenly tries the Crossface-Chickenwing out of nowhere, but Bret wiggles free. Again, and Bret reverses to a belly-to-belly. Bret tries building to the Sharpshooter, but misses an elbow and Bob works the arm. Shots of Bret's then-wife, Julie, are shown, and she looks way less horrible and shrewish than she did on Wrestling with Shadows. Bob does a great job of holding an armbar despite all of Bret's attempts to break the hold. Surprisingly, the crowd remains into the match during all the matwork, which is a testament to how over Bret was.

Bret finally manages a figure four, which has Backlund screaming at Owen to throw in the towel, but he refuses. So Backlund sucks it up and reverses. Bret breaks and works the knee. Bob comes back with a piledriver and tries the Chickenwing, but Bret makes the ropes. Backlund tries a sleeper, which is pretty pointless for this match. Double-KO, but Bret is fresher and recovers first with a piledriver and the FIVE MOVES OF DOOM. Sharpshooter in the center of the ring, but now Owen and Bulldog get into a footrace, allowing Owen to sneak in and break the hold. Bulldog lunges and misses, slamming his own head into the stairs. Great bump there. Bulldog is out cold, and now Backlund takes advantage and hooks the CFCW.

Bulldog can't throw in the towel, so Bret fights the move, doing an awesome selling job. There's nowhere to go, however. So Owen, in true weasel fashion, heads over to his parents and starts pleading with his mother to throw in the towel on Bret's behalf. Not with Stu, of course, because the old man obviously sees right through the act. He's literally in tears as the announcers speculate on a possible face turn. Owen continues hounding his mother, pulling her out of the audience, but Stu keeps pulling her back. Finally, she gives in and throws in the towel at 35:12, giving Mr. Backlund his third WWF title. The crowd is REALLY displeased with that one. Owen breaks into maniacal laughter and sprints back to the dressing room. Backlund's celebration is priceless. Great old-school match—Steve Corino would be proud. ****

Mr. Bob Backlund proved to be the voice of a new generation, rallying against the youth of America "eating marijuana" and the distribution of "condominiums" in schools. To everyone's shock, he actually tried running for public office in Connecticut years later. To no one's shock, he lost.

Backlund was the most interesting heel champion they'd had in years and was incredibly over. Best of all, he was still a great wrestler at forty-one despite a definite lack of drawing power, an age that seems downright young compared to the people on top of WCW at the same time. So what happened?

The Clique happened. And nothing would ever be the same again. But let's backtrack a bit.

INTERLUDE

In 1993, Shawn Michaels hit his stride as a singles wrestler, winning the intercontinental title for a second time from ex-partner Marty Jannetty. In order to give the character the last ingredient lacking, the WWF decided to give him a bodyguard. So, as a favor to WWF star Razor Ramon, WCW jobber (and good friend of Ramon's) Vinnie Vegas was hired and repackaged as the monster Diesel. The three men became friends and started working together on a regular basis.

Around the same time, independent wrestler The Lightning Kid was brought in and repackaged as hard-luck underdog The 1-2-3 Kid, getting his first win by going over . . . you guessed it . . . Razor Ramon. He soon joined their little group. A contract dispute with the WWF left Shawn Michaels out of action in late '93 and Diesel out of luck, but by the end of the year Shawn was back and Diesel was tossing out eight straight wrestlers in *Royal Rumble '94* to win over the crowd. Ramon was intercontinental champion, and set up an issue with Shawn Michaels over who was the "real" champ, which led to the show-stealing ladder match at *Wrestlemania X*.

Now they were using each other to get more over, and the push escalated. Diesel and Shawn were given the tag titles shortly before *Summerslam*, while Ramon and the Kid were positioned as buddies. The four men had a terrific tag-team match with one another on an early episode of *WWF Action Zone* (a recap show that underwent several facelifts over the years before settling in today as *Excess*) that only served to demonstrate how good they could be together and how lazy they tended to get otherwise. Here's my review:

WWF Tag Title Match:
Shawn Michaels and Diesel v. Razor Ramon and 1-2-3 Kid

Saaaaaay, what did all four guys have in common? This match was actually very famous in net.lore, and with good reason. It was broadcast on the second or third edition of Action Zone, the morning show that eventually morphed into LiveWire once it became another D-level recap show. The original idea behind Action Zone was to let the guys go out and do fifteen-minute wrestling matches, whereas RAW would be all story line intensive and stuff. And they picked a DOOZY of a match to illustrate that point.

Big brawl to start, heels collide and the faces clean house. Razor's Edge for Shawn gets two, Diesel saves. Razor tosses Shawn at Kid, who rolls him up for two. Backdrop and bodypress get two for the Kid. Victory roll gets two. A Rana is blocked with a vicious powerbomb, and Diesel comes in to pound the Kid. That was all just the FIRST MINUTE as they worked at a breathtaking pace and moved faster than I thought any of them could possibly go.

Kid tries a sunset flip, but Diesel casually grabs him and just chokeslams him out of his boots. Kid gets a dropkick, and Razor comes in. Slugfest is won by Da Bad Guy, and he pounds Shawn off the apron for good measure. Slam on Diesel for two, but he gets clubbed down. Clipped to Diesel hitting a sideslam for two. Shawn comes in with a flying elbow for two, and he takes a break. Razor backslides out of the chinlock for two, but Shawn dropkicks him for two. Diesel hits Snake Eyes for two. Big elbow to the back, and when Razor rolls over, Diesel drops another one on the chest for two. Razor escapes a neck crank, but gets shoulderblocked for two. Clipped to a double-KO. False tag to the Kid, but Shawn superkicks Diesel by mistake, and he plays dead in the corner.

Hot tag Kid, and he just UNLOADS on Shawn with spinkicks. Shawn bails, but Kid comes barreling over the top with a plancha and the crowd explodes. He rolls back in and Kid follows with a missile dropkick for two. Shawn walks into a fallaway slam from Razor for two. Backdrop superplex gets two. Kid goes up and they hit a Rocket Launcher on Shawn for two. Shawn desperately tries to revive Diesel to save him, but Razor casually slugs him for two. Shawn grabs a sleeper as Diesel rolls to the floor. Kid breaks it up as

Diesel slowly crawls to the apron. Ramon catapults Shawn to the corner and knocks him cold, and tags the Kid back in. He gets a top-rope legdrop for two, but Diesel finally gets to his feet, sticks his leg in the air, and takes Kid's head off for the pin at 13:52 to retain.

Fifteen minutes! This was aired on a Saturday-morning TV show, in its entirety, remember. Funny how everyone sold like nuts for everyone else there, and a freakin' awesome match resulted, one which I'd give ★★★★¼ without hesitation.

The booking was starting to center almost exclusively on those four, and as a result they were the only ones getting enough airtime to be significantly over. And so, at *Survivor Series '94*, Diesel and Shawn finally split up in order to begin the parallel singles pushes of both men. And mere days later, with almost no warning, Bob Backlund made his first title defense against Diesel after beating Bret Hart in a grueling forty-minute marathon. Diesel won the match against Backlund in six seconds with a kick to the gut and a powerbomb, taking the title and kicking off the wretched "New WWF Generation" era.

One of the most unintentionally ironic spots for the "New WWF Generation" featured Diesel going out of his way to sign an autograph for a young fan. This is very heartwarming until you stop and realize that the WWF generally charged upward of $10–$20 for an autograph at a meet-and-greet with one of its wrestlers. And that's if they were generous enough to send anyone more important than the Brooklyn Brawler or announcer Todd Pettingill. Certainly not Kevin "Diesel" Nash, who once left a message on his Web site telling the fans that they'd have to "drive a stake through his heart" to get rid of him. Feel the love.

SCENE FIVE
Diesel (Non-Drawing) Power!

Suddenly, the entire direction of the promotion shifted to Shawn Michaels v. Diesel. Shawn was put over several bigger men in order to build him as a viable contender. He won the '95 Royal Rumble and faced Diesel for the title at Wrestlemania XI . . . and that was the first sign of a major problem for Vince McMahon, and the first sign that he was unwilling to change with the times. For you see, the WWF had now done the impossible and made Shawn Michaels more over than Diesel. It was undeniable. For the first time in his experience since the Hulk Hogan era, the fans were actively demanding that a smaller man be given the world title push at the top of the promotion, and Vince didn't know how to deal with it.

The main event of that *Wrestlemania* was actually not the world title match, but Bam Bam Bigelow facing football player Lawrence Taylor in a novelty match. Two of the people at ringside for that match—fellow NFLers Kevin Greene and Steve MacMichael—went on to moderately successful wrestling careers in rival WCW shortly after. MacMichael's wife, Debra Marshall, divorced him in 1998 and jumped to the WWF by herself, and then proceeded to marry Steve Austin in 2000 and become a bigger star than any of the football players. Stop and think about this stuff too much and you'll go nuts, trust me.

He jobbed Shawn to Diesel at *Wrestlemania*, which only served to make him more over than he was before—because both men were so selfish that neither wanted to play enough of a heel to actually keep the fans from cheering them. So Vince gave Shawn a new bodyguard—Sid Vicious—and then had him turn on Shawn, hoping the babyface push would steer the fans toward a Sid-Diesel showdown instead. It didn't work—the fans clearly wanted Shawn v. Diesel again, and the WWF was unwilling to provide that for whatever reason.

Instead, they provided Diesel v. Sid, Diesel v. Mabel, Diesel v. Yokozuna, trying everything in their power to build Diesel as a Hogan-like babyface to recapture lightning in a bottle. Diesel soon became known as the lowest-drawing champion in WWF history, and the WWF paid him in line with that, to which he didn't take too well. In fact, none of the Clique did, and they started throwing backstage temper tantrums and pulling increasingly mean and sick gags on other workers.

One notable incident saw Scott Hall shitting in Sunny's food as a "joke," but the bigger message was for boyfriend Chris Candido: This is *our* locker room and you're not welcome here. Later in 1995, they staged a "strike" because of their feelings about the direction of

Tamara "Sunny" Sytch, once the most-downloaded celebrity on AOL and a major ratings draw for the WWF, is currently running a softcore porno Web site with fellow skank Missy Hyatt after battling addictions to alchohol and crack as a result of her celebrity. Normally you wouldn't think you could sink lower than having someone take a dump on your food, but there you go. She originally managed boyfriend Chris Candido in his guise as fitness guru "Skip Bodydonna," but later Tom Pritchard was added as his partner Zip. Originally the name was going to be "Flip," which just goes to show that people were actually getting paid to determine whether a better name was "Flip" or "Zip," and doing so with a straight face.

the WWF and how Vince needed to change it. Vince had to personally fly out to the house show, which started hours later as a result, and placate the whiny children that his top superstars had become.

The ultimate example of Diesel's nondrawing power and actively horrible work is *King of the Ring '95*, one of the most depressingly bad cards ever put together by either promotion. The point of it was to make the fans fear Mabel as a legitimate title threat, but what the arena was screaming for was Shawn, and by the time Mabel defeated Savio Vega in the finals the crowd was so deflated that none of them could possibly have gone home happy. Meanwhile, the Diesel v. Sid program dragged on, playing to houses of 1,000 people or less much of the time. And when the focus shifted to Diesel v. King Mabel and set up as the main event for *Summerslam*, the groans of pain from the fanbase were almost audible.

Mabel, an obese black dude, won the *King of the Ring* tournament in 1995 and thus started dressing in rather large amounts of purple ring outfits. This led to those backstage gathering around him and comparing him to Barney the Dinosaur while singing the "I Love You" song. And yes, Vince actually tried to push this guy as a serious main eventer.

Speaking of groaning in pain, Shawn Michaels got his first of many tastes of comeuppance in September of 1995 in what has come to be known as the Syracuse Incident. Although the story changes by the day depending on who's telling it, the basic idea is the same: Shawn, Davey Boy Smith, and 1-2-3 Kid are in a bar in Syracuse (I know, it sounds like the opening line of a bad joke . . .) and after getting suitably drunk they start picking a fight with some off-duty marines, the number of which varies between two and fifteen, increasing as the years go by. Shawn immediately realizes that he's started a fight he can't finish, and the three wrestlers bolt for the car, with only Smith and Kid making it in time. Left to the wolves, Shawn is quite savagely beaten to a bloody pulp by the marines and ends up spending a night in the hospital with a fairly serious concussion and some pretty dramatic facial bruises. Vince McMahon, saint above all, decides to make it into a story line. In this case, to build sympathy for Shawn as a babyface, he "comes back too soon" from the injuries, wrestles a match against Owen Hart on *RAW* the night after *Survivor Series*, and takes a kick to the head that I dubbed the ENZUIGIRI OF DOOM in subsequent references because Shawn immediately collapsed in what was the "middle" of the match and had to be rushed to the hospital. They even fooled the local hospital into thinking it was legit because he was checked in that night for observation before being released the next morning. This was quite important, being the first appearance of the "worked shoot" on *RAW*, signifying a dramatic change (and not necessarily for the better—the angle didn't draw a dime) away from wrestling's traditional kayfabe (the unwritten code of secrecy between wrestlers).

But still, matches like Michaels v. Ramon in a ladder rematch and Kid v. Hakushi were blowing the roof off the arena, while fans snored through Diesel v. Mabel or Undertaker v. whoever. The old formula of building up a big fat heel to lose to the virtuous champion was dying fast, but that didn't stop the WWF from beating it into the ground for all of 1995 and 1996 once Shawn got his run at the top. In Shawn's case, he got fed to Vader and a heel-turned Diesel. Vince's fascination with big men had killed the house-show circuit so much and left *Monday Night RAW* such a pathetic shell of its former self that the WWF was now almost begging for a challenge to its throne.

It came.

In a word, *Nitro*.

SCENE SIX
Billionaire Ted

"He beats the big guy with three superkicks."
—Eric Bischoff, referring to a Shawn Michaels
v. Sid match, running opposite *Nitro* on
RAW that night

With those eight words, the Monday Night Wars were officially launched, and WCW had the lead. In the early days of *Nitro*, Eric Bischoff counter-programmed everything that the WWF did almost to the minute, putting matches at the commercial breaks during the WWF's big matches.

Lex Luger double-crossed Vince when he jumped to WCW for their debut episode of *Nitro* in September 1995 without giving notice, as did reigning women's champion Debbie Micelli, aka Alundra Blayze (aka Medusa). And most notably, the first example of Bischoff's thinking "outside the box" was to simply give away the results of the very stale, taped *RAW*s during the *Nitro* broadcast since *RAW* was taped four shows at a time once a month.

Debbie **Micelli, aka Medusa, set a new highpoint for classy behavior when she jumped ship to the WCW without giving notice and dropped the WWF women's title into a garbage can on live TV. This led to the WCW themselves getting incredibly paranoid about their own title belts, to the point where they would not permit any champions' taking the belt home with them on the off-chance that Vince might try the same tactics. Vince finally got the last laugh in 2001 when he threw the entire promotion in the trash.**

Did it work? That's debatable at best. But people *did* talk about *Nitro* now, whether it was good or bad, and that translated into enough viewers to cause the WWF to take notice.

So what did the WWF do? Refine their approach? Push new stars? Adjust their way of thinking about the wrestling business as a whole?

No, even better . . . they mocked Ted Turner.

Yes, in early 1996, an increasingly desperate WWF began an infamous series of sketches called "Billionaire Ted's Rasslin' Warroom," using very slightly changed versions of Ted Turner, Hulk Hogan, Randy Savage, and Mean Gene to illustrate how much hipper and with it the WWF was. However, the sketches had two fatal flaws:

1) The WWF was doing the same repetitive nonsense that they were mocking WCW for doing. For example, WCW "rasslers" like Hogan and Savage were portrayed as old and slow and never leaving their feet, and to contrast this the WWF showed clips of Razor Ramon, Diesel, and Ahmed Johnson all doing their finishers. Ramon's finisher is the Razor's Edge, a powerbomb. Diesel's finisher is a powerbomb. Ahmed's finisher is a powerbomb. That's some impressive difference, no? Also, Ramon and Diesel, at the time of these sketches, were not much younger than Hogan and Savage, either.

2) The sketches ended up becoming so bizarre and mean-spirited that Ted Turner's lawyers got a judge to issue a cease-and-desist order against the WWF, something that much of the WWF fanbase agreed with. In fact, one of the last sketches had "Ted" calling a press conference and talking about how he was doing all his "evil" deeds in order to get back at his father, who had been dead for years.

This was just weird and uncomfortable for the fans to see.

The Warroom skits came to a screeching halt at *Wrestlemania XII*, when main characters Nacho Man and Huckster "fought" in a *Mystery Science Theater 3000*–styled parody match that probably set the sport back twenty years. Six years later, Vince re-signed the real Hulk Hogan and put the world title on him almost immediately.

And now, with the failure of the Billionaire Ted sketches, things were falling apart more rapidly than Vince could keep up with. Diesel's contract was up and he made it known that he would rather ply his trade in WCW for more money. Razor Ramon was suffering from a severe drug habit and was no longer welcome in the WWF. The 1-2-3 Kid's attitude was becoming so disruptive that he was also asked to leave. And so, in the ultimate slap in the face to the WWF, the departing Clique members lost their final matches one night in Madison Square Garden, and then engaged in a group hug to close the evening before departing for WCW the next day.

Now desperate for anything to gain the edge back, Vince started doing the completely wrong things—he re-signed the Ultimate Warrior and gave him free rein, he allowed Vader to be buried by Shawn Michaels's political games, and began pushing has-been Jake "The Snake" Roberts on a nostalgia trip. Goldust's quasi-gay character was stretched to the absolute bounds of good taste, and then hastily turned face for political reasons. Untested Olympic weightlifter Mark Henry was signed to a ten-year deal and immediately pushed. None of it worked. Nothing.

The only bright spot of the bunch was Shawn Michaels's carrying everything on two legs to

Speaking of desperation, the low point had to be Vince replacing Sunny as the Bodydonnas' manager with transvestite Cloudy. That went over about as well as you'd expect.

**** matches at every turn, and even that could only go so far because of Vince's reluctance to give a smaller wrestler like Shawn a proper run as champion.

And so, finally, on Memorial Day, 1996, Scott Hall (aka Razor Ramon) showed up on the first two-hour edition of *Nitro*, kicking off the nWo angle, and essentially shoveling the last bit of dirt onto the WWF's grave. WCW grabbed the ratings lead and didn't let go of it until 1998.

The World Wrestling Federation, 1984–1996, RIP.

SCENE SEVEN
The Problem

Now, let's cut open the body and see what the causes of death were.

If you could boil Vince's major problems (and there were lots) down to one simple one, it is this: gimmicks sell T-shirts, characters sell tickets. Vince's inability to make that distinction cost him dearly because fans became smarter and expected a different product as a result.

See, the problem was Hulk Hogan. For years before the big crash, Vince could just stick some guy out there with a dumb gimmick, put him up against Hogan, and the fans would have a reason to hate the guy right there. "He's fighting Hulk! Boooo!" Easy, right? It drew millions. The matches were horrible, but no one ever got injured, and the fans went home happy. The other people on the card got a huge payday. What could be better?

Well, now Hogan was gone and fans needed another reason to care. Want an example of what I mean? Take Bob Holly, for instance. When he started in the WWF, he was called "Sparky" Thurman Plugg, which is a semi-clever play on "STP" and "spark plug." Hah hah, right? But just looking at that gimmick, do you cheer him or boo him? And why?

It was that "why" that really got to the fans. Because Vince would just keep sticking guys out there with silly names and silly costumes and pretty soon no one cared anymore. Vince produced the evil martial artist Kwang, who didn't get a reaction because he didn't do anything particularly evil. So he repackaged him as the good Caribbean legend Savio Vega, and again he didn't get much of a reaction because he didn't do anything particularly good. Vince, ironically, was the last to get it.

Vintage online joke from 1994: What's the sound of 300 pounds of shit hitting the fan? KWANG!

The fans were asking "Why should we boo a plumber? Why should we cheer a garbageman? Why should we even bother to care one way or another about Jerry Lawler's evil dentist?" The WWF's answer was basically "Because we told you so" and that's where it all went bad. Because now they had to *tell* the fans what they wanted to see, when in fact the fans were already telling the WWF what they wanted, and it was Shawn bumping like a madman for Razor Ramon, or Bret Hart going thirty minutes with his brother, or Mankind and Undertaker beating on each other in a boiler room. The fans didn't care about the back story for Mankind (he was a prize-winning piano prodigy as a child, but he had failed to meet the lofty expectations of his upper-class parents, and one day his mother slammed the lid shut on his fingers and sent him to live in the sewers and

be raised by rats . . . just in case you were wondering), they cared because he was a dominant heel, and oh, my God, did he just *beat the Undertaker?*

Mankind's devastating Mandible Claw finisher (sticking his fingers into the gullet of the victim to paralyze them) used to be augmented by the victim in question biting down on an Alka-Seltzer to produce foaming at the mouth. This not only provided a more satisfying visual experience, but took care of heartburn, as well.

The people knew who they cared about all along—it was those who had characters they could relate to, or personalities they could connect with. It didn't matter what color the tights were or what profession they held (and why would someone as well-paid as a plumber bother with wrestling, anyway?) outside of wrestling. It was the wrestler that counted. That's why Sunny got over by being a hottie and her team, the Bodydonnas (evil fitness gurus who may or may not have been gay), are a footnote of history. And that's why the Goon (evil hockey player with foam skates for boots) was doomed to only doing a couple of *RAW* tapings before getting shuffled out of wrestling history. And most tellingly, that's why fans at the 1996 Slammy Awards chanted "Kill the Clown" when Vince had Doink make an unscheduled (and unwelcome) appearance during the course of the show.

But most telling and sad of all is the treatment endured by the WWF's brightest star during this whole period, and the one who could have saved them all along . . . Bret Hart.

SCENE EIGHT
The Solution

Following Bret's loss to Bob Backlund in 1994, he was almost immediately depushed into the mid-card at the request of the Clique, who didn't want their heat to be reduced by Bret. And so Bret got to face Backlund in a boring rematch at the biggest show of the year, *Wrestlemania XI*. Here's my review:

"I Quit" Match:
Mr. Bob Backlund v. Bret Hart

Roddy Piper is the special referee.

Okay, anyway, this match was set up because Backlund had made Hart submit at Survivor Series '94 to win the WWF title. And yes, I know his mother threw in the towel, but history says he submitted. So now I guess Bret wanted the job back.

Bret gets a figure four about a minute in, showing how compressed this match is. Of course, the match at Survivor Series ran about forty minutes, so anything else would be compressed.

They trade a couple more submission moves on the mat, boring the crowd. Backlund works some psychology in, working on the arm and shoulder. Yawn. Backlund was always vastly overrated. I mean, he was technically proficient and a great heel in 1994, but he never really clued into the fact that it wasn't the '70s anymore.

Bret comes back with a couple of the MOVES OF DOOM, but Backlund rolls out of the Sharpshooter attempt. Bret misses a corner charge and messes up his shoulder. This sets up the Katihaj—er, I mean the Crossface-Chickenwing. But Bret reverses the move and hooks his own for the submission. Backlund said during his big heel push that if anyone did that to him, he'd retire. Of course, Backlund never actually said "I quit" here, so I guess you could say that Bob screwed . . . oh, never mind. **

Then Bret got to put over newcomer Hakushi and Jerry Lawler. Then he got to have "Kiss My Foot" matches with Lawler. Then he got to wrestle Lawler's evil dentist Isaac Yankem in his first match on the second biggest card of the year, *Summerslam*. Then it was off to a feud with the evil pirate Jean-Pierre LaFitte. Man, can't you just *feel* the excitement Bret must have had all year with that lineup?

> The dentist was Isaac Yankem, or "I. Yankem," get it? Yes, they actually paid people to think this stuff up.

Thankfully, Vince came to his senses in late 1995 and decided that Diesel was doing his company more harm than good and jobbed him to Bret Hart at *Survivor Series '95* to end the Clique Era once and for all. Bret ended up being a transitional champion to Shawn Michaels, a situation that enraged him so much that he ended up taking six months off and nearly jumped to WCW in the process. Hindsight says that Bret probably should have left when he had the chance in 1996. The two obvious questions, "Why was he treated so badly?" and "Why did he then stay?" are harder to deal with, but both answers, whatever they may be, speak volumes about Bret's loyalty to the sport in general and to Vince McMahon specifically.

When Bret finally returned in the fall of 1996, with the WWF far behind WCW in the war, he was put into a program with upstart WWF newcomer Steve Austin, and then, finally, Vince McMahon made the decision to start listening to the fans, one that would slowly but surely swing the balance the other way and cause the WWF to rise from the grave like Lazarus and wreak vengeance on those who had put the WWF there.

Overall, the death was slow and painful—from mid-1996 until early 1998, the WWF was essentially a zombie, a walking corpse that no one had noticed was dead yet. It took a total cleansing of the heel-babyface system, the gimmick system, the locker room, and a reinvention of what weekly, episodic TV was with regard to wrestling in order for the WWF to return to its former glory. Had ECW not been around to provide a template, it's sketchy at best as to whether or not Vince would have known how to go about re-creating himself and his promotion, and it's even sketchier whether the WWF fanbase would have been receptive to those changes. In fact, given how close to total bankruptcy the WWF was at the point when Diesel lost his title to Bret Hart, it's extremely unclear whether they could have survived even another year.

But with wrestling, as with the stories crafted for it and upon which they are based, it is often darkest before the dawn for the protagonist and there is usually much soul searching and spiritual realizations to go through before redemption can be found.

SCENE NINE
The Resurrection

The first step for the WWF was to clear out all the deadwood that had accumulated in the mid- to upper-card ranks over the years, and the housecleaning became very extensive, very quickly. Diesel, Razor Ramon, Ted Dibiase, The 1-2-3 Kid, Jeff Jarrett, Mabel, Tatanka, Lex Luger . . . all gone. Some choices were better than others, but the old formula was obviously not working so the people associated with the "New Generation" were given their ticket to Turnerland or the independent circuit, as the case happened to be.

The next step was to sign a new crop of talent and start fresh. And so from late 1995 until mid-1996, a rather huge group of fresh talent was brought in to start over with: Vader, Mankind, Marc Mero, Faarooq, Brian Pillman, Goldust, Justin "Hawk" Bradshaw, Rocky Maivia, and the quaintly named Ringmaster all made their debuts in 1996. Of the bunch, Vader was the only one expected to make any kind of significant impact in the near future.

The period from *Royal Rumble '96* until *Summerslam '96* was what baseball teams call a "rebuilding phase"—the stars from the New Generation were phased out, and the next crop of stars were phased in.

Fans didn't buy into it. Buy rates tanked. *Wrestlemania XII*, featuring the long-awaited Shawn Michaels WWF title win, did a disappointing buy rate given the buildup, thanks largely to the poor handling of Bret Hart's third title reign prior to the event. Bret was made to look like a weak champion, needing interference from The Undertaker to save his title against Diesel, while Shawn was given the monster babyface push, getting clean wins over the opposition. The eventual Michaels win in the main event of *Wrestlemania* was anticlimactic at best, although an excellent match.

Vince had enough confidence to put the title on Shawn, thinking that he would make a good enough champion while he rebuilt the WWF and found the next Hulk Hogan, but no one could have foreseen the impossible outcome of WCW's "Outsiders" experiment on the other channel. For, you see, the first time in the WCW's short, nasty, and brutish history, they managed to run a successful, money-drawing angle without screwing it up.

When Hulk Hogan emerged as the mysterious third man at *Bash at the Beach '96*, the nail was pounded into the WWF's coffin, and suddenly Vince was left with a small babyface holding his number-one title and a crop of relative unknowns to build up as viable contenders for that title. In short, he didn't have a hope in hell.

> Speaking of the mysterious third man for the *Bash at the Beach* PPV, Eric Bischoff was practically chomping at the bit to sign away someone from the WWF to take that slot, most notably Bret Hart or Davey Boy Smith. Had he successfully stolen Bret, it may have been the nail in the coffin for real.

Oddly enough, fate played its hand and changed the course of the WWF in a way that no one could have foreseen.

Because in May of 1996, the Clique engaged in one last group hug in the middle of the ring in Madison Square Garden in order to thumb their collective nose at Vince McMahon and the WWF brain trust. Kevin Nash and Scott Hall left for the WCW soon after, and were thus unpunished for the heinous breach of kayfabe. Shawn Michaels was the WWF champion, and thus untouchable. That left the only available fall guy for the incident: Hunter Hearst Helmsley.

Now, HHH was scheduled to win the 1996 *King of the Ring* tournament, and would soon after get the intercontinental title and possibly a big push. But in order to make a point about wrestlers knowing their places and doing their jobs properly, HHH was removed from the pay-per-view entirely and replaced with a mid-carder of comparable stature: Stone Cold Steve Austin.

Austin had been saddled with a bad gimmick in the Ringmaster, and a manager to compensate for what the WWF felt was his lack of mike skills. Since Ted Dibiase's heat was mainly residual from the years when he could actually be an effective heel in the ring, the result was less than inspiring. In fact, Dibiase's "Corporation" gimmick generally resulted in slow and painful

death for the heat of anyone involved with it. The fact that WWF management failed to grasp that concept speaks volumes of the problems that caused their downfall in the first place. So Austin, in character and doing a partial shoot gimmick, took matters into his own hands, cutting a promo after losing a match to Savio Vega (where Dibiase had to leave the WWF because of the loss), insinuating that he intentionally lost the match in order to rid himself of Dibiase's mismanagement. And thus was Stone Cold Steve Austin born.

> And really, who WOULDN'T want to get away from Dibiase's management? His previous clients included 110-year-old Russian Nikolai Volkoff, traitorous Native American Tatanka, evil tax man Irwin R. Shyster, and Bam Bam Bigelow, who got beat by a football player.

The defining moment for the character came at *King of the Ring '96*, when Austin defeated Jake Roberts in the finals to win the tournament, then delivered his classic Austin 3:16 interview, winning over the entire arena in the process. Suddenly the WWF had a very effective heel on their hands. So they did the logical thing and had him issue a challenge to one of their top babyfaces: Bret Hart.

Austin began building a reputation as a rattlesnake, a heartless beast who would turn on anyone and had no friends. He forged an alliance with best friend Brian Pillman against Bret Hart, then turned on Pillman and shattered his ankle, using a chair, in a move that has found a place in wrestling terminology as "Pillmanizing" someone. Soon after, one of the most controversial moments in the history of the Monday Night Wars occurred when Austin made a road trip to Pillman's house, live on national TV of course, threatening bodily harm the whole way. Once Austin broke into the house, Pillman responded by pulling a loaded weapon on him, with the camera cutting out as shots were fired.

The USA network wasn't terribly impressed, especially since the show had recently been moved to an earlier, more "family friendly" time slot.

Meanwhile, Bret Hart, at home contemplating his future with the WWF and wrestling in general, wasn't around to respond to the constant threats and challenges of Steve Austin, and after weeks and months of only getting Austin's side of the story, the fans began to see things his way.

Finally, in a dramatic moment, Bret Hart returned to WWF TV in October 1996 and announced his signing with them for a long time to come, and, by the way, he would accept Steve Austin's challenge for a match at *Survivor Series '96*. That match proved to be the pivotal moment that made the career of Steve Austin and forever destroyed the career of Bret Hart. Here's my review:

Bret Hart v. Steve Austin

Austin gets all in Bret's face, and a slugfest erupts. They trade hammerlocks, and Austin gains the advantage with power moves. Bret rallies, but gets caught with a stungun. Austin works the neck, and another slugfest develops. Bret comes back with an inverted atomic drop and a rollup for two. Russian legsweep gets two. Bulldog is countered by Austin, but Bret manages a top-rope elbow for two. They fight outside, and Austin rams him into the post. Bret gets pissed and they fight into the crowd.

Austin catapults Bret onto the Spanish table and pounds him. He drops an elbow from the apron for

good measure. Back in the ring, Austin continues punishing the neck. He uses that good ol' heel standby: the rope-assisted abdominal stretch. Bret breaks and gets a stungun on Austin in a neat bit of irony. Rolling cradle gets two. To the top, but Austin gets a superplex. Bret pulls a Dynamite Kid and cradles Austin on the mat, however, for a two count. Austin manages the Stunner out of nowhere, but takes half a second too long to cover and only gets two. He keeps covering and gets two more two-counts. You NEVER see that anymore. I can understand the kickout, since Austin didn't kick him in the gut and flip him the bird first.

Austin tries a Texas Cloverleaf, and I'm thinking Vince must be going nuts trying not to jump up and yell "RING THE BELL" from ringside. Austin sends Bret crashing to the post, but Bret reverses a bow-and-arrow into the Sharpshooter. Austin makes the ropes. Bret gets a sleeper, Austin breaks and hooks the Million Dollar Dream. Bret walks the ropes and flips over for the pin at 28:34 to end an INCREDIBLE match, possibly the last, best match in North America before the Great Changeover to the Austin Era in 1997. * * * * *

The match itself was an instant classic, a superb technical exhibition that saw Bret Hart go over cleanly after reversing a sleeper more than thirty minutes into the action. It should have signaled a renaissance for Bret Hart and the end of the Steve Austin menace—but it didn't. The jaded New York fans in attendance now started cheering for the vicious heel Austin and booing the virtuous babyface Hart, and Bret Hart had no idea how to deal with that situation. Vince did, however, and the results of that would bring the WWF back from the dead like Lazarus and change pop culture as a result.

Act Two

Lazarus (1997)

"Jesus said unto her, I am the resurrection, and the life: he that believeth in me, though he were dead, yet shall he live: And whosoever liveth and believeth in me shall never die."

—John 11:25–26

"You sit there and you thump your Bible, and you say your prayers, and it didn't get you anywhere! Talk about your psalms, talk about John 3:16 . . . Austin 3:16 says I just whipped your ass! . . . Steve Austin's time has come! And when I get the shot, you're lookin' at the next WWF champion, and that's the bottom line, because Stone Cold said so!"

—Austin 3:16

Champions as the year began:

WWF Champion: Sid

Intercontinental Champion: Hunter Hearst Helmsley

Tag-Team Champions: Owen Hart and The British Bulldog

SCENE ONE
Titan Strikes Back!

Vince McMahon has long said that the WWF is like a family. If that's the case, then it could be argued that 1997 demonstrated that they were just like the Brady Bunch . . . if the Brady Bunch were all on drugs and hated one another. You had Vince McMahon, concerned father, spouting words of wisdom; Bret Hart, mature college man; Shawn Michaels, insecure middle child; and Steve Austin, baby of the family. Of course, Greg and Peter Brady didn't usually get into fistfights over whether or not one of them was doing Jan on the side, but I never said it was a perfect analogy to begin with.

Sure, some other stuff happened in 1997, but make no mistake: This year is the story of one man and how twenty years of service to the same company were thrown back in his face, and how it changed him, and wrestling, forever as a result. People kind of thought Bret was bitter over some stuff, but they had no idea just how bitter the poor guy was, and just how much Shawn Michaels was helping to egg him on backstage at the time.

Things didn't seem too bad to start the year, even though Sid Eudy was on top of the promotion, because at least the intention was in place to get the belt back on Shawn Michaels before too long. Ratings were routinely horrible for *RAW*, and *Nitro* was just having a cakewalk beating it week after humiliating week, thanks to the nWo.

Steve Austin was superhot, however, and Bret Hart seemed reenergized with the *Royal Rumble* approaching, and most people expected him to win the actual match to set up a rematch against Shawn Michaels at *Wrestlemania 13*. At the actual event, which was held in the San Antonio Alamodome and drew a respectable number of people, Shawn Michaels indeed regained the title from Sid, and Steve Austin cheated and eliminated Bret Hart to win the *Royal Rumble.* Austin actually drew an interesting response from the crowd as his pop grew larger the longer he remained in the match, a reaction that was actually kind of unexpected for someone portrayed as a heartless badass like Austin was.

However, the really notable bit about that match was Bret Hart's reaction to losing, which was to immediately begin, in the fans' eyes, whining and crying about the loss. This was actually kind of a new thing for the WWF as Vince had never been a big fan of that sort of heel in the past, and it was especially odd for a normally beloved babyface hero to begin exhibiting that sort of behavior.

The Shawn-Sid title match pretty much sucked compared to their other efforts. Shawn was suffering from the flu and wasn't up to his usual standards, leaving Sid to carry the match. Here's my review:

WWF Title Match:
Sid v. Shawn Michaels

Shawn had actually been turning heel leading up to this show, but in the weirdest thing anyone had seen in a while, he got a face pop here so enormous that the entire heel turn was scrapped and he was turned full babyface again.

And now, suddenly, the crowd comes to life.

Shoving match to start, which doesn't go well for Shawn. Shawn uses his speed to send Sid to the floor. They brawl and Michaels escapes a press slam with a poke to the eye. Back in and Sid powerslams him for two. Chinlock follows. Shawn escapes and gets tossed to the floor. Sid rams him back-first to the post. It gets two. Surfboard and extended bearhug work the back of Shawn. Legdrop gets two. Shawn comes back with a slam and flying forearm. Flying elbow, and Shawn warms up the band. Sid blocks the superkick and dumps Shawn to the floor, then powerbombs him there.

*Back in, ref bumped. Chokeslam, no ref. A second ref runs in to count two, so Sid decks him. Shawn grabs the camera from ringside and nails Sid (in retaliation for Survivor Series) and that gets two. Sid's up, so Shawn warms up the band again and hits sweet chin music for the pin and his second WWF title at 13:52. Sid carried the match, oddly enough. ** ½*

At this show, HHH debuted new bodyguard Curtis Hughes, a stereotypical big black gangster who was going to act as muscle for him. Sadly, the relationship came screeching to a halt when Hughes was discovered moonlighting at an S&M bar shortly after. Some things you just don't WANT to know about people.

In fact, the heelish edge that Shawn Michaels had been displaying for a good month before this show suddenly disappeared, and Shawn became a full-fledged, squeaky-clean babyface again, which puzzled a lot of people, myself included. Not much else of note happened at the *Rumble*, as Shawn's running buddy HHH retained the IC title against Goldust, Ahmed Johnson beat longtime rival Faarooq in their only PPV meeting, and midgets were everywhere. As it turned out, Shawn's de facto face turn at the *Rumble* had a more sinister downside, which would reveal itself a few weeks after that show.

Meanwhile, on the financial side of things, the WWF was basically screwed. *RAW* was getting firmly spanked in the ratings by *Nitro*, landing in the low 2.0–2.5s week in and week out, and whispers began among informed fans and insiders that USA wasn't going to put up with these kinds of ratings for much longer. Vince was always a fighter, however, and his solution was to fight head-on against the *Nitro* monster by requesting another hour of television, making *RAW* into a two-hour show. Furthermore, it was felt that the increasingly stale nature of *RAW* was largely a result of four-week television taping cycles, wherein the show would be live for one week and then taped for the next three. Later ratings trends would indicate that in fact this was untrue, but it sure sounded convincing at the time so it was decided that beginning in March, *RAW* would be a two-hour live show, every week.

Okay, great, but wrestling is the kind of entertainment form that lends itself to big, dramatic gestures, so on February 13, they cancelled the regular edition of *RAW* on Monday and replaced it with a two-hour live show on Thursday, aptly dubbed *Thursday RAW Thursday*. Within the industry, the joking nickname was "Titan Strikes Back," in reference to Vince mounting his first offense against the *Nitro* juggernaut in quite a while. The main event was scheduled to be Shawn Michaels defending (and losing) the WWF title back to Psycho Sid in preparation for Sid v. Undertaker at *Wrestlemania*.

Now, Vince had gotten lucky with Shawn in November '96, asking him to drop the title to Vader and somehow getting talked into Shawn dropping the title to his friend Sid, instead. Considering Shawn's dubious-at-best record of title losses in the ring, many were shocked Shawn would even agree to do the job for someone in such a manner. However, apparently asking him to lose the title *again* to the same guy only a few months later was too much for poor Shawn to handle and he suddenly developed a crippling knee injury and decided to forfeit the title on national TV instead of losing it. Funny how the timing on that worked, isn't it?

Also, probably not coincidentally, Shawn was in line to lose to Bret Hart at *Wrestlemania* in return for beating him at the previous one. So Shawn simply took his ball and went home, but not before hogging the spotlight for twenty minutes by delivering the famous "Losing My Smile" speech, talking about how much he loved the fans and gave 110 percent in every match and couldn't continue doing so with this devastating

knee injury he had suffered. In fact, he said, he might even have to retire. Those in the know simply waited for the miraculous comeback a few weeks later (May of 1997, to be exact) and shook their heads. Karma happened to nail Shawn with the knockout punch a few months later, but we'll get to that in 1998.

SCENE TWO
Lost—One Smile. If Found, Contact S. Michaels

So Shawn gave up the title, and as a result the main event of the next PPV, *Final Four*, was a four-way match between Bret Hart, Steve Austin, The Undertaker, and Vader. The deal was that Austin had eliminated those three guys to win the *Rumble* in January, and since he had cheated to do so, the result was considered null and void and this match would settle who would get the shot at *Wrestlemania* in March.

When Shawn vacated the title, the match simply became a match for the vacated title, and Sid would get the first shot at the champion the next night on the first two-hour *RAW*. Fate then threw another monkey wrench into the WWF's plans as Austin was booked to win the match and title and then lose it to Sid the next night. Here's my review:

WWF Title Match:
Vader v. Undertaker v. Steve Austin v. Bret Hart

Consider this a mini-Rumble where pinfalls count. Vader and UT pair off, as do Austin and Hart. Vader takes a chairshot early and starts gushing from around his eye. Meanwhile, Bret kills Austin.

Back in and we switch as Austin hits a fluke Stunner on UT for two. Vader opens up on Bret as Austin and UT brawl on the floor. Vader takes out UT, so Austin goes after him, too, dropping the stairs on his head. They engage in a wild brawl as Vader bleeds all over the place.

Switch again, Vader brawls with Bret and Austin takes UT in the ring. All four end up outside, then back in. Hart piledrives Austin for two. Vader misses the Moonsault on UT. Austin and Bret try to throw each other out. More carnage. Bret and Vader have a wild slugfest that ends with Bret punching him right in the bloodied eye to knock him down. Ouch. Austin nearly pushes UT out to the horror of the crowd. UT tries to return the favor, then Bret does the deed himself, dumping Austin out about eighteen minutes in.

Bret and UT slug it out, and Vader clips UT. Vader and Bret then go at it, and that goes badly for Bret. Vader goes upstairs and gets superplexed. Sharpshooter, but UT saves. Steve Austin limps back out to assault Bret some more. Meanwhile, Vader goes for the pump splash and UT sits up and casually pushes him over and out about twenty-one minutes in. That leaves Bret and UT.

Chokeslam, but Austin is back again. UT tries to tombstone Bret, but Austin pushes them over. Bret snaps and goes after Austin, then UT goes after them both, and Bret sneaks out and pushes UT over and out to capture his fourth WWF title at 24:01 ****½

It was quite the match for everyone involved, and indeed Austin's knee injury early in the match caused the title to be put on Bret Hart instead. However, this was no big deal as the goal was to get it back on Sid the next night anyway, so it just meant that Hart would get to do the job instead of Austin. And that's exactly what happened when Steve Austin interfered to give Sid the belt and kick the Bret v. Austin feud into overdrive. Undertaker challenged Sid to the title match at *Wrestlemania*, while Austin and Hart both wanted a submissions-only match to settle *their* score.

So everyone was happy.

Well, pretty much.

Okay, Bret was still unhappy.

See, back in 1996 when Vince had signed him to this huge, twenty-year deal for millions of dollars and large amounts of respect and front-office power and stuff, Bret was under the impression that he wouldn't be used to, you know, make new stars and transition the world title to Sid and stuff that mid-carders generally did. And here was the biggest show of the year approaching, and Bret was stuck in a mid-card feud whose entire purpose was to make a huge star out of Steve Austin at Hart's expense, and furthermore, his heroic character was turning into more of a whiny bitch by the day. Even the fans were picking up on the character change, harassing him at every opportunity about his constant complaining.

> **M**ore cynical folks than myself have suggested that Vince gave Bret his whiny persona so that when he screwed him over months later, Bret's credibility would take a hit. This explanation is so ridiculously petty and paranoid that I can only conclude that it's completely true.

Meanwhile, Shawn Michaels got to escape all of this by faking a knee injury and hiding at home for six weeks or so. So Bret made a decision that would ultimately end his career in the WWF: He wanted a full-blown heel turn, but only in the U.S., and he wanted his family to be elevated along with him as the monster heels of the WWF. Vince agreed, and things were set in motion that would turn into the biggest soap opera ever seen in the wrestling industry.

But let's catch up on some other business before we get there.

Back to *Thursday RAW Thursday* for a moment. Hunter Hearst Helmsley was cruising along as intercontinental champion and preparing to defend the title against Ahmed Johnson at the next show, *Final Four*. However, once Shawn "lost his smile," the bookers were forced to shake up the card. Specifically, Hunter's routine title defense against jobber Aldo Montoya was changed to a defense against under-card "sensation" Rocky Maivia. And just to try a mega-push of the new-comer, they actually put him over the more established Helmsley in a huge upset. The back-lash was immediate and decisive, with the fans chanting "Rocky Sucks" at the poor kid due to the overpushing of the obviously green (but potentially good) new star.

> **I**f I could give prospective wrestlers one piece of advice, it's this: Take good care of your hair. Without that vital third of the equation, you're not going anywhere. Trust me on this.

However, in the WWF's eye, Rocky had three things going for him that generally guaranteed success in the WWF: Height, a developed physique, and a full head of hair. Hunter, who was practically a zen master of the third one, in the meantime went in a completely new direction as a result of the loss, acquiring female bodyguard Chyna at the *Final Four* show in a victory over Goldust. For those who knew her back then when she had a huge, masculine jawline and no breasts, it was harder to believe her later claims that she never had facial surgery done. But then she also felt that she was in line for shots at the WWF title before she was fired a few years later. (And still, her book was a *New York Times* bestseller. There is no justice.)

Amazingly, her presence at ringside actually gave Hunter some heat for the first time in his career as he strayed away from the "Connecticut Blueblood" image and just acted like a jerk instead. Hunter's career didn't really go anywhere until later, but he was still around and doing stuff, and also had the most well-conditioned hair in the business, bar none.

Speaking of being around and doing stuff, *RAW* underwent a cosmetic change almost as drastic as Joanie (Chyna) Laurer's boob job. The March 10 episode saw the venerable *Monday Night RAW* evolve into the louder, brasher, and more obnoxious *Raw Is War*, complete with barbed-wire graphics, darker lighting, and Marilyn Manson theme song. Obviously Vince wasn't messing around any longer. And with only two weeks to hype the shit out of a sluggishly selling *Wrestlemania*, it was about time he did something.

SCENE THREE
Hero of the Day

The March 17 *RAW* featured another major step in Vince's changes when Sid defended the world title against Bret Hart in a cage match, immediately causing much hand-wringing and second-guessing among the online community as to whether Vince actually had the grapefruits to switch the main event from Undertaker/Sid to Hart/Austin with only a week to go before the show. It turned into a moot point as Sid, in fact, retained the title by beating Bret in that cage match, but the match ended up having a more interesting side effect. Vince McMahon came into the ring to interview Bret and find out his feelings on the loss and all that stuff, but Bret snapped on live TV and cursed out the then-saintly McMahon, declaring that "it was bull-shit" and the entire WWF was engaged in a giant conspiracy against him. The effect was instant and convincing as far as fan sentiment went: Bret was now a hated villain and Steve Austin was slowly becoming the hero of the day with his upfront attitude and everyman personality.

The USA network also had an instant reaction, putting *RAW* on a seven-second tape delay from then on so they could bleep out any naughty words; a tradition that continues to this day, even after the show moved to TNN in 2000.

As a side note to that match, it was Bret's suddenly paranoid attitude change and whiny disposition that led some conspiracy-minded writers (such as myself) to suggest that Vince may have had the Montreal screwjob in mind months before it happened, and quite possibly had decided to establish the character Bret would need to have in order to convince enough people that Montreal was a work.

And so we come to *Wrestlemania*, biggest show of the year, and indeed the headline match as far as everyone in the know was concerned with Bret Hart v. Steve Austin. The curiosity over how they'd book it and who would end up looking better carried the buildup for the match better than the WWF's hype could.

UFC washout Ken Shamrock, beginning a budding wrestling career after a few years as an indy worker previous to his UFC days, was the special guest referee, although many questioned how one can referee a match with no rules. And indeed, the question was answered, and the booking was most interesting. Here's my review:

Submission Match:
Bret Hart v. Steve Austin

Ken Shamrock is the guest referee.

Brawl outside the ring to start, with Austin crotching Hart on the STEEL railing and clotheslining him to the floor. They brawl into the crowd and Austin rams Bret into the boards and pounds on him. Hitman comes back and they brawl up the stairs. Back to the ring, and Hart takes a MAN-SIZE bump to the stairs. Austin clotheslines him off the apron. Austin tries to use the steel steps, but Bret kicks them out of his hands. Austin rams Bret to the post. We actually go to the ring.

Austin stomps on Bret, but Bret pulls out a neckbreaker and an elbow off the second rope. Vince starts badmouthing Bret, noting that he'll probably have an excuse if he loses. Wow, I mean, WOW, this shit is brilliant in retrospect. I stand in awe of Vincent K. McMahon.

Bret works on Austin's knee viciously. Austin suddenly hits the Stunner out of nowhere, but can't capitalize fast enough. Big Austin chant. Bret goes back to the knee. The ringpost figure four makes its PPV debut to a monster pop. Bret grabs the bell and a chair and opts to try the Brian Pillman Maneuver on Austin, to a big pop. Austin gets loose and WHACKS Hart with the chair, to a big pop. Another monster shot and a monster pop. Crowd is INTO Austin, big time. Austin with a slam, cross-corner whip, and a suplex. Elbow off the second rope. Austin hits a Russian legsweep and applies an odd cross-armbreaker. Crowd is fifty-fifty.

Boston crab from Austin to a big pop. Bret makes the ropes, so Austin goes for a Sharpshooter instead.

Jerry: "Wouldn't that have been incredible, to have to submit to the Sharpshooter?"

Vince: "Hey, it could happen."

No shit. Bret escapes and Austin tosses him to the floor. Whip reversal sends Austin crashing into the timekeeper. Austin rips open a huge gash on his head. Now that's some high-quality blading. Austin gets rammed to the stairs and the ringpost. Austin is literally dripping blood onto the ring. Hart drops an elbow and stomps away. Crowd doesn't feel so good about Bret now. He grabs a chair and smashes it into Austin's knee. You can almost feel the crowd changing sides. Bret goes for the Sharpshooter, but Austin blocks. Bret pounds Austin in the corner, but Steve counters with a Greco-roman ballshot. Austin whips Bret to the corner, then does some stomping of his own. Austin with a superplex. Austin's face is literally covered in blood. Austin grabs a cable from ringside and chokes out Bret, but Bret grabs the bell that he had brought in ten minutes earlier and rings it on Austin's head. Sharpshooter. We get the famous shot of Austin bleeding all over the ring and screaming in pain. Austin fights the pain and powers out . . . but Bret hangs on.

Bret reapplies the move and moves to the center of the ring. Austin passes out and Shamrock stops the match. Crowd is less than thrilled. Austin is DEAD. Bret soaks in some cheers, then goes back to pounding on Austin. Shamrock takes him down and gets a big pop.

Hart leaves to huge boos. Austin leaves to the crowd chanting his name. * * * * *

And now the stage was set, with Austin officially a huge, babyface, main-event star, and Bret Hart as the whiny jerk who was bitter about everything. Not far from the truth, either, depending on whom you ask.

Further, the barbaric nature of the whole match set the stage for Austin's main-event wrestling later on, taking a rather large page from the ECW playbook.

Ah, ECW.

ECW = Extreme Championship Wrestling, Paul Heyman's Philadelphia-based labor of love and blood. Known for wild brawls and ridiculously overblown story lines, the WWF stole their concepts and wrestlers for years, honing it into Attitude. Everyone felt sorry for Heyman, until years later when bankruptcy proceedings revealed secret payments from the WWF to the ECW totaling into the millions. Oops.

SCENE FOUR
Reunited and It Feels So Good

Those who heard Paul Heyman and the ECW crew in the WWF during the InVasion story line of 2001 probably didn't realize that there was a time when an "ECW invasion" was a pretty big deal. In fact, in February 1997 the WWF was so short of talent for an episode of *RAW* during their Germany tour that they actually gave the time slot to ECW for the most part! It was a taping in New York, which was near enough to the ECW home base in Philadelphia that Paul Heyman was able to provide the WWF with a bunch of his workers and stage some matches live on *RAW* with them. It didn't help in the ratings or anything, but the style was

so drastically different and new that Vince's son, Shane (who was a big fan of the little promotion), actually started suggesting things for the WWF that he had seen on ECW TV. Soon, more and more of the Paul Heyman booking philosophy began creeping into the WWF product.

Steve Austin honed his beer-drinking badass persona (copied liberally from ECW bigwig The Sandman) during his run in ECW, and Vince adapted it, and other facets of the promotion, to his own product.

For instance, Bret Hart and Steve Austin would seemingly engage in an anarchic dressing-room clearing brawl on a weekly basis, which was thanks to the ECW philosophy of violence and chaos over story line. The WWF simply added a little more story line to that formula and less violent, misogynistic beating of females, and it worked wonders. But Bret, badass heel as he may have been, needed backup for the war with the Rattlesnake, and he knew just the people to call: his younger brother, Owen, and brother-in-law Davey Boy Smith (aka the British Bulldog).

Owen Hart and Davey Boy Smith had been tag-team champions for the better part of a year at that point, and they were only kept from splitting up by Bret Hart's numerous backstage interventions on their behalf. At *Wrestlemania*, they were supposed to drop the tag-team titles to the unlikely duo of Vader and Mankind, but Bret asked that they be allowed to keep the tag titles for later on. Before that, Bulldog had been matched up against Owen in the finals of the first-ever European title tournament, and his win caused what seemed to be an irrevocable split between the brothers-in-law. And again, they seemed poised to split for good when Bret intervened, this time in much more dramatic fashion: during a rematch between the two on *RAW* in April. While the two men were engaged in an increasingly vicious brawl for the European title, Bret Hart interrupted, called for peace in the family, and let them both know that he loved them and wanted to see all three reunited as a family again.

Sniff. Now I'm all *verklempt*. Talk amongst yourselves.

Well, okay, so the fans didn't exactly get overwhelmed with sentiment for the reunited Hart family, but it was a pretty big deal in Canada, which is what made the heel turn so unique: Fans in the U.S. booed the sentimental Hart, while fans in Canada treated him as a reborn hero. The possibilities were endless, and Vince seemed to know that as well because, before too long, he had added Hart family sympathizers Jim Neidhart and Brian Pillman to the mix, thus creating 1997's most deadly heel stable . . . the Hart Foundation.

Oh yeah, you just knew the shit was gonna hit the fan now. The first casualty proved to be Rocky Maivia when he dropped his intercontinental title to Owen Hart.

Funny story: While Vince was attempting what later came to be thought of as The Rocky Maivia Experiment in the WWF, over in WCW they had a similar idea: Blueblood-snob Steve Regal dropped his TV title to Polynesian nonsensation Prince Iaukea (himself the grandson of a legendary star of the '50s and '60s—King Curtis Iaukea) in order to duplicate whatever the hell the WWF was shooting for with Rocky. Of course, both experiments ended up being spectacular failures, and a short time after the WWF gave up on Maivia, WCW also gave up on Iaukea. It just goes to show that one constant of the universe is always there: WCW picks the stupidest ideas to copy. Of course, in 2001 they decided to copy the AWA and went out of business with a whimper.

But I digress . . .

Bret and Austin spent much of April antagonizing each other, launching sneak attack after sneak attack (including a notable ambulance hijacking by Austin after he had already attacked Bret to the point of injury), until Bret was forced to temporarily withdraw his onslaught due to a serious knee injury. You could tell both guys were having the times of their lives, though, and although the ratings didn't reflect it, momentum was slowly shifting the WWF's way as a result of the endless war. And I mean you *really* couldn't tell from the ratings because *Nitro* was just laying an unholy ass-whupping on *RAW* the likes of which no one had ever seen before.

Speaking of endless wars, though, the real interesting one was never seen on TV, only backstage. This was a more personal and spiteful war between Shawn Michaels and Bret Hart. Shawn was back from his crippling, career-ending knee injury a record six weeks after announcing his retirement, and seemed fine. In fact, his mouth was at 110 percent capacity and he made sure to make smart-ass remarks to Bret Hart backstage every chance he got. The real-life tension stemmed from Bret accusing Shawn of lying about his injuries to duck him, and Shawn responding by accusing Bret of having an affair with Tammy "Sunny" Sytch. The situation was getting so tense that Vince McMahon started putting them out there in the ring to have twenty-minute-long debates and get it out of their systems, and those interview blocks eventually became a standard opening segment for *RAW*, albeit without all the real-life animosity these had.

Bret had his last match for a while at the *Revenge of the Taker* PPV, losing to Steve Austin by disqualification, and interfering earlier in the night to allow his brothers to keep the tag-team titles against the returning Legion of Doom. He still made appearances on *RAW* after that, but was confined to a wheelchair with a cast on his leg, which somehow annoyed the fanbase even more than usual. During one gab session, which actually ran long due to Bret's extensive speech,

Shawn Michaels even superkicked him out of his wheelchair, actually earning a babyface reaction for Shawn! Nope, people just plain couldn't stand Bret Hart's new attitude, and Vince loved every minute of it. Bret was less thrilled at the success of his obnoxious new persona since he'd always fancied himself a hero of wrestling and couldn't quite deal with being a full-time bad guy. Still, you do what you have to do for the money, and Bret was the best at his job.

By May, Bret was healing, but still unable to wrestle, so the Austin-Hart feud was refocused a little and Shawn Michaels made his comeback late in the month and was immediately made into Austin's partner for the feud against the Hart Foundation. This ended up in a tag match on *RAW* in which Austin and Michaels captured the tag titles from Owen and Bulldog in a ****¾ classic encounter that featured the supposedly crippled Michaels bouncing around the ring like a Ping-Pong ball.

Bret, as usual, took exception to the ludicrous nature of Shawn's comeback, and got into his face backstage, resulting in a fistfight that took nearly the whole locker room to separate. Suddenly, everything on the booking sheets was thrown into disarray again as Shawn and Bret were both sent home for a while to cool off, and a match that had been signed between the two at the *King of the Ring* PPV was changed into an Austin-Michaels match at the last minute.

This was clearly becoming a delicate situation, and Shawn decided to take some time off and reevaluate his character and life while Bret was eased back into story lines again with the July PPV approaching. Everyone was just waiting for the inevitable explosion between the two, and wondering how they could even exist together in the same promotion much longer. The answer would come sooner than most thought.

SCENE FIVE
Canadian Stampede

Anyway, the July PPV was *Canadian Stampede* and emanated from the Calgary Saddledome in Canada, providing for one of the most unique atmospheres in WWF history. Remember how I was mentioning that Bret was a villain in the U.S. and a hero in Canada? Well, Calgary is his hometown, and as the show approached (with a main event pitting the entire Hart Foundation against Austin, Goldust, the Legion of Doom, and Ken Shamrock in a ten-man tag match), the city of Calgary was practically going into throes of ecstasy for the returning hometown heroes. Bret's appearance at a burger stand to sign autographs drew a line of fans that was literally a mile long. Signs and banners were plastered all over the city heralding the return of Bret Hart and his team, and they probably could have committed murder and gotten away with it during that week in Calgary.

Five years later, and ⅗ of the Hart Foundation (Pillman, Owen, and Bulldog) are all dead as a direct result of their involvement with wrestling. Pillman in particular was close to death at this point and probably would have lived longer had he spent his last few months at home recuperating instead of pushing himself on the road night after night.

In fact, the fans were so supercharged for that show that every match was boosted quite a lot thanks to the energy of the Calgary crowd, and everyone gave just a little bit more for their matches. The result was one of the greatest wrestling shows ever put on by any company, featuring classic matches up and down the lineup. The main event more so than all of them, including a ten-minute standing ovation for the Hart Foundation as they came out to take on the (now) evil Americans, led by Steve Austin. Austin was used to playing a heel, so he relished the chance to temporarily drop the babyface act and made sure to throw every obscene gesture and bit of foul language at the ringside fans he could that night. Here's my review:

Main Event:
Goldust, Ken Shamrock, The Legion of Doom, and Steve Austin v. Brian Pillman, Jim Neidhart, British Bulldog, Owen Hart, and Bret Hart

Everyone from the U.S. team got SERIOUS heel heat. Steve Austin was nearly booed out of the building. The Hart Foundation was introduced one-by-one, with the ovation building with every guy, until the roof was nearly ready to blow off the place when Bret came out. It gave me a lump in my throat to watch it. Austin and Bret started.

Oh, by the way, the announcer made mention of a little documentary being shot at ringside. Something about "wrestling" and "shadows" or something like that.

Bret beats the hell out of Austin, drawing INCREDIBLE face heat in the process. The crowd literally boos Austin's every move. I mean, literally, when the guy MOVES they boo him. Austin quickly gets the cobra clutch, and they do the reversal spot in the corner for two. Austin misses the rope run, and Anvil tags in. Austin gets the Thesz press and tags Shamrock in.

Zen sighting number three: He gets my masterpiece, "What's kayfabe?" on screen for a good chunk of time, and then had it confiscated by Adam (of George and Adam fame) about ten seconds later.

Shamrock controls easily, so Pillman tags in. He uses a blatant cheapshot and gets CHEERED for it. I know wrestlers always say that they like playing a heel and riling up the crowd, but Pillman had a grin about four miles wide on his face the entire match because of the babyface heat he was drawing.

Backbreaker gets two. Shamrock hits a belly-to-belly, and everyone tags out. Owen and Goldust go. Enzuigiri gets two for Owen. Crowd starts with a VERY loud "Austin sucks" chant, and Austin wisely plays off it for fun. Hawk comes in with a legdrop on Owen for two. Flying splash gets two. Owen quickly comes back with the Sharpshooter, but Animal breaks. Big heel heat. Bulldog comes in with a hanging suplex and powerslam for two. Bret and Animal go next, and Bret kicks his ass. Goldust comes in and gets his ass kicked, too. Then he gets caught in the corner and a mass-beatdown results and the crowd is rabid and I'm nearly standing up and cheering even now.

Owen comes in and hits the post on a blind charge, but comes back with a leg lariat on Animal and a missile dropkick. Rana is reversed into a power-bomb and powerslam. The LOD hits the Doomsday Device for two, and another brawl erupts. Austin posts Owen and smashes a chair into his knee, then takes a shot at Bruce Hart in the front row. The crowd lets Austin know how much he sucks as Owen heads to the back for medical attention. Austin gets pummeled in the corner to the delight of the crowd, but he fights free. Austin and Pillman go and a fast Stunner ends that fight pretty quickly. Bret bails him out and posts Austin, then smashes a chair into HIS knee and applies the ringpost figure four as the announcers gasp in shock at the bloodthirsty crowd.

Back in the ring, Bulldog crotches Hawk on the top rope for two. Austin heads to the back for medical attention, too. Animal and Anvil get into a test of strength. Anvil wins and the Harts double-team Animal. Bret gets caught in the corner, but Shamrock plays to the crowd and Pillman sneaks in and clotheslines him. Hey, Ken, you're a HEEL here. Shamrock then gets caught in the Hart corner and sent to the floor, where Pillman gleefully launches him into the Spanish table. Pillman is just having the time of his life out there. Sadly, this would be the last great match of his career. It's nice to actually see a smile on his face for an entire match, ya know?

Hart gets the Russian legsweep for two. Bulldog comes in and pulverizes Shamrock, but a low blow turns the tide. Ah, now you're catching on, Kenny. Goldust comes in to clean up with a bulldog on Bulldog and the Curtain Call, but Pillman interferes again. Goldust goes aerial and gets superplexed down for two. Austin makes his return.

It's Bret v. Austin again, and Austin wins this round. Suplex gets two. Bret DDTs him and goes for the FIVE MOVES OF DOOM. Sleeper is escaped with a jawbreaker, and it gets two. Bret comes back and gets the Sharpshooter, but Animal saves, and the crowd is PISSED. Austin does his own version, and Owen returns now to make the save. Austin clotheslines him out to the floor and they fight there. Austin takes a shot at former referee Wayne Hart, and they end up brawling as Wayne jumps the railing. Bret comes over and nails Austin for hitting his brothers, then rolls him into the ring. Austin has some choice words for Bret, which lets Owen roll him up for the pin at 24:30. Like you need to ask what this gets. * * * * *

Well, now everyone was on a roll thanks to this. Bret Hart was undeniably becoming the biggest and hottest heel in all of wrestling as the days went by, Steve Austin was now set up to challenge Owen Hart for the IC title at *Summerslam*, and Bret also was ready to take the WWF title back for a fifth time as he challenged Undertaker.

SCENE SIX

Austin Finds Himself

But again, we go back to Shawn Michaels. He saw a clear chance to regain some heat, and he wanted into the swing of things. So Shawn got inserted into the forthcoming title match as the special referee, with the caveat that if he failed to referee the match in a totally impartial manner, he would be banned from wrestling in the WWF for good. This eventually set up the finish to the match when Shawn accidentally nailed

Undertaker with a chairshot intended for Bret, and he was thus forced to count Bret's title-winning pinfall on the Undertaker. Undertaker was, to say the least, not happy with Shawn's misfire, and suddenly they became the new hot program, leaving Bret out in the cold.

> During the filming for the *Wrestling with Shadows* documentary, Bret commented before the match against Undertaker that Shawn would probably try to do something to steal his heat while acting as referee. He just didn't know how MUCH Shawn would do.

Steve Austin, for his part, was immediately separated from all the political backbiting going on between Bret and Shawn, and instead put into a program with Owen Hart with the intention of taking his career away from Bret's and onto a different track entirely. Steve Austin and Shawn Michaels had won the WWF tag titles from Owen and Bulldog on that *RAW* in which Shawn's knee underwent a faith healing, and were playing the "Wacky Mismatched Partners" team that would get beaten into the ground as a concept over the next few years. Shawn, who of course was the king of diplomacy and a role model for children everywhere, got into a fight with Bret Hart and was suspended as a result, leaving the WWF with no tag champions for the time being. So a tournament was held in July '97, with the winning team meeting Steve Austin and a partner of his choosing to crown the new WWF tag champions. The tournament was won by Owen Hart and British Bulldog, and after weeks of heartfelt campaigning on Mankind's part, Austin decided to choose . . . no one.

Or so he thought.

Now, I'm assuming everyone has already read Mick Foley's book *Have a Nice Day* and knows the whole story here, but basically lovable ex-heel Mankind had done an interview exposing his past as Cactus Jack, and even further back his cheesy tryout video where he played a smooth-talking ladies' man named "Dude Love." Well, count on Vince McMahon to pick all the truly stupid ideas out of a given bunch, because on the night of the tournament's final match on *RAW* for the titles, Mick Foley was talked into resurrecting Dude Love as a permanent alter ego for himself, and indeed he inserted himself into what was a two-on-one match to save his buddy Steve Austin. The two even-more-mismatched partners beat Owen and Bulldog to win the WWF tag titles.

Steve Austin and Owen Hart clearly had an issue to settle now, and a match was set up at *Summerslam '97* for Owen's IC title with the stipulation being that if Austin didn't win the title, he would have to kiss Owen's ass live on PPV. These days, that's practically a rider in every contract, but for the time it was heavy stuff. The match was terrific, but ended with the moment that would change Austin's life and career forever. Here's my review:

Intercontinental Title Match:
Owen Hart v. Steve Austin

The match that changed everything.

Owen goes right after the oft-injured knee of Austin, but Austin retaliates quickly. The little differences Austin shows in movement and wrestling between then and now are very noticeable. Owen is massively over as a heel by proxy, thanks to Bret Hart.

Austin counters the flip and flop out of the wristlock by poking Owen in the eye. Out of the ring and Owen tries to break Austin's hand by slamming it onto the steps and stomping on it. Ouch. Owen bites. That's an action statement, not a personal feeling. Owen spends way too much time on Austin's fingers. Austin comes back with a powerbomb and clothesline over the top, so Owen runs. Austin beats him up and drags him back. Have I ever mentioned that Owen has the best belly-to-belly suplex in the biz?

They trade clotheslines and Austin tries the Sharpshooter, but it gets blocked. Owen nails a German suplex and "injures" Austin's neck, which is why many people wondered if the eventual injury was real or a work, since Owen proceeds to go to work on Austin's neck. A snap DDT reinforces this point.

Sleeper by Austin, reversed by Owen, countered with a jawbreaker. Slows down again with a side headlock by Owen, which he thankfully turns into a heat segment by putting his feet on the ropes. Austin and Owen trade punches, Austin goes for a tombstone, and Owen reverses for his own, and then it happens: Austin's head hits the wrong way and he's left paralyzed.

Owen stalls for time while Hebner checks with Austin, and somehow Austin crawls over and does a weak cradle on Owen to win the intercontinental title. I have no idea how Austin managed to even get off the mat. Still, weak ending aside, it was an excellent match. ★★★★

Austin went to a series of specialists and got a second, third, fourth, and fifth opinion until he (and the WWF) got the opinion they wanted to hear: while it was best for his long-term health if he retired then and there, it might be possible to work through the injury after some recovery time and have surgery done at a later date. So, of course, that's what he did, taking three months off and recuperating while Vince phased him out of the immediate story lines and signed independent wrestler Del Wilkes to play his famous Patriot character to oppose Bret Hart.

Patriot debuted on *RAW* in September of 1997 and scored an immediate upset win over Bret to set him up as the new number-one contender to the WWF title and give Bret something to do at the upcoming *Ground Zero* PPV while Shawn Michaels was occupied with the Undertaker.

Now, Del Wilkes is a nice guy and a heckuva wrestler, but this was becoming distinctly suspicious behavior for the WWF head office,

Personally, I was disappointed that they didn't also sign Patriot's evil nemesis, the appropriately named Dark Patriot. It's always amused me that wrestling could be so shallow as to slap a mask on a guy, call him the "Dark (whatever)" and expect the money to roll in. But I digress.

especially considering Bret's contract status. That status didn't come out until later so the general fanbase didn't really know why Bret was suddenly being treated like a second-class citizen and feuding with perpetual mid-carder Del Wilkes, but after coming off his hottest feud in years, this seemed like a distinctly anticlimactic next step, to say the least. But Bret was a pro and he knew his job, so he went out and gave The Patriot a pretty good twenty-five-minute match for the title at *Ground Zero* and ended up winning in the end. Well, that was fine and dandy, but Shawn and Undertaker were booked to tear the house down with an insane brawl that spilled all over the arena, and that's exactly what happened. In the main-event slot, no less.

On the same show, Steve Austin returned to surrender his half of the WWF tag-team titles to reigning commissioner Sgt. Slaughter, and ended up taking out his frustrations with the bureaucracy on Jim Ross with his Stone Cold Stunner. This actually proved to be an interesting turning point for the character, as his hatred for Bret Hart was now rechanneled into a hatred of authority figures in general, and suddenly the WWF found a story line that the audience could connect with. Austin began Stunning everyone up and down the WWF power hierarchy, including recently "outed" WWF owner Vince McMahon at a historic *RAW* in Madison Square Garden. Up until that point, Vince had merely been the wishy-washy babyface announcer as far as the fans were concerned, although it was only the really dumb fans who couldn't figure out that

Vince was the man behind the curtain. Hell, even the WWF's own in-house magazines acknowledged his ownership openly.

SCENE SEVEN
Things Fall Apart

The Bret Hart situation was becoming increasingly strange, however, as he was again de-emphasized in favor of Shawn Michaels, this time getting stuck in a tag match with brother-in-law British Bulldog against Patriot and Vader at the next PPV, *Badd Blood*. Meanwhile, Shawn took the main-event slot again, facing Undertaker in the first-ever Hell in a Cell match. The whole Shawn-Undertaker feud had another interesting side effect, however.

The feud had started at *Summerslam*, as mentioned, when special referee Shawn Michaels cost Undertaker the WWF title to Bret Hart with a wayward chairshot. Soon after on *RAW*, however, the on-screen WWF powers-that-be decided to "punish" Shawn by putting him in a tag match against the Undertaker, teaming him with snobbish Hunter Hearst Helmsley against Undertaker and Mankind. The match was two-fold irony: on one level, the flamboyant Michaels was being "forced" to team with the uptight Helmsley, but on another, Shawn and Hunter were best friends in real life, and the teaming was a wink to those who were aware of their off-screen relationship. Shawn and Hunter ended up meshing well as a team, and in fact brutalized Undertaker with a chair afterward to really get him good and pissed off. Shawn hired "insurance policy" Rick Rude as his new bodyguard, and the three men became inseparable.

For his part, Hunter triggered the onset of yet another personality change in Mick Foley. They had been fighting each other ever since *King of the Ring*, when Hunter beat Mankind to win the crown. They had another match at *Canadian*

Shortly after, Rick Rude jumped to the WCW in a completely meaningless move, resulting in the magic of videotaped *RAW*s providing the first-ever occurance of one person appearing on both *RAW* and *Nitro* at the same time. In addition, tapes of him in the ECW were still circulating in syndication, providing a record THREE appearances at once that will likely never be touched again.

Stampede, this one with an indecisive finish. Then again at *Summerslam*, this time in a cage match in which Foley had prevailed by morphing from Mankind into Dude Love mid-match and dropping an elbow off the top of the cage in tribute to his hero Jimmy Snuka. They met yet again at the *One Night Only* PPV in England in the opener, when Hunter faced the Dude Love persona and prevailed. Finally, this led to the MSG *RAW*, where Hunter was set to face Mankind in a street fight, only to be shocked and horrified when Foley emerged with yet another facet of his personality . . . Cactus Jack, the psychotic brawler. Needless to say, Hunter lost that match, but Cactus would return a few months later, though Mick Foley changed back into Dude Love in the interim.

The Bret Hart v. Shawn Michaels on- and off-screen war suddenly flared up again when the WWF went to England for their first-ever UK-only PPV, dubbed *One Night Only*. The main event was going to feature the British Bulldog defending his largely meaningless European title against Shawn Michaels and winning, but Vince made an odd offer to him at the last minute: put Shawn over in that match, and when they returned to Britain in a few months, he could get his win back in the rematch.

Now, you have to understand, there was absolutely no viable reason for making this request outside of the excuse given by McMahon about doing a return match. The title itself was mostly just a trophy belt for the Bulldog, and would do nothing to help Shawn Michaels. Putting Michaels over the worshipped-in-England Bulldog would likely enrage the crowd and might even hurt future box-office monies. And, worst of all, it would likely piss off Bret Hart and give him that much more ammunition to gripe about. However, in the end, Shawn won the title in a great match. Here's my review:

European Title Match:
The British Bulldog v. Shawn Michaels

Bulldog had his lying hosebeast of a wife and his cancer-ridden sister Tracy at ringside, so you'd THINK he'd win, right?

Shawn decides to do some stalling to start. Bulldog wins a shoving match in dramatic fashion, and Shawnie throws a tantrum. Shawn walks the ropes during a lockup, so Bulldog tosses him off the top and onto his face. Bulldog dumps him. Shawn takes a walk again, but when he jumps onto the apron, Bulldog rams him into both turnbuckles and then inverted-suplexes him into the ring again. Press slam and abdominal stretch follow, but Shawn escapes. He stomps away, but Bulldog casually tosses him and Shawn takes a dramatic bump to the floor. Bulldog slingshots him back in and works the arm. Shawn uses the cheapshot and eyepoke combo, but he goes for a rana and gets SMOKED with a powerbomb for two.

Back to the arm. Shawn reverses, but Bulldog slams him and tries a Rita Romero Special. His shoulders are down, however, giving Shawn two. Bulldog screams at the ref about this, allowing Shawn to cheapshot him again and pound away. Bulldog suplexes him, but Rick Rude shows up as Bulldog gets a rollup for two. Rude pushes them over, and Shawn gets two. He trips up Bulldog and Shawn tosses him, allowing Rude to ram him into the post for good measure. Shawn nails Bulldog off the top and pounds on him on the floor.

Back in, Shawn drops an elbow and goes to the sleeper. Bulldog eventually suplexes out of it and gets two. Shawn whips him into the corner, however, and hiptosses him into a short-arm scissors. Bulldog does the "power out with the other guy on your shoulders" spot that has been ruined for me since 1993 when I saw Bob Backlund do the same thing to Jeff Jarrett at a house show. They collide on a criss-cross for the double-KO, and HEEEEEEEEEEEEERE'S Hunter.

Bulldog comes back and clotheslines Shawn, and catapults him for two. Blind charge misses and Bulldog eats post, however. Shawn goes up and drops a pair of elbows, and warms up the band. Bulldog ducks the superkick and goes for the powerslam, but Rude grabs his leg. Shawn gets dumped and they brawl, but Bulldog slips and hurts his knee, and the future D-X pounces on him three-on-one while Chyna distracts the ref.

KICK WHAM PEDIGREE on the floor, and they toss him in. Shawn pulls off Bulldog's knee brace and tosses it at his dying sister, once again proving himself to be the classiest guy in the business. Figure four, using the ropes, Hunter's hands, and a Mack truck parked three blocks away with a rope leading to the arena for leverage. Bulldog makes the ropes, but Rude nails him, and he finally has no choice but to black out at 22:53. The crowd is, shall we say, less than enamored with the decision. This was undoubtedly Bulldog's last great, or even good, match. ****

To show you what a classy guy Shawn Michaels was, he demanded to go over Bulldog, even after Bulldog had dedicated the match to his younger sister, Tracy, dying of cancer and the biggest British Bulldog fan in the world. She sat ringside, watched her brother submit to the figure four and lose the title, and died soon after.

Owen and Bret chase off the heels after Shawn endears himself to the crowd further by telling Diana that the win was all for her. In retrospect, this was a very sad match to watch because it was entirely political. Given Vince's plans for the future, there was no justifiable reason to change the title here except to get it off

of Bulldog and humiliate the Hart family in the process to lead up to Montreal. When Bulldog had it, it was a trophy title, but at least it was still a title. Once Shawn got it, it became a prop, something never defended and treated as a joke by both himself and HHH until it had finally lost all meaning midway into 1998. It was a great match, but knowing what we do now, it's a very sad match to watch and Shawn looks like even more of a pathetic, whiny, petulant, lying primadonna, albeit a talented one.

As much as I'm sad to see a great talent like Shawn retired early, no one deserved such a fate as much as Shawn did, and I'm glad he's miserable and hated by everyone in the business now because he earned it, and he has no one to blame but himself.

Bret Hart, for his part, defended the WWF title against Undertaker in an excellent match that was ignored during the buildup for the PPV and then cut off the commercial tape, despite being a ****½ classic. This was clearly treatment unbecoming of one of the biggest stars the WWF had ever produced, and Bret's unhappiness with the product and his own treatment was starting to show in his work and interviews. Despite that, people were still largely anticipating an eventual showdown between Bret Hart and Steve Austin for the WWF title at next year's *Wrestlemania* show.

Then came another one of those weird things that changed the business in ways no one could have anticipated.

SCENE EIGHT
Suck It!

Shawn and Hunter, still without a team name, were beginning to act increasingly juvenile and rude on TV, tormenting rookie interviewer Michael Cole on a weekly basis and flaunting their behavior at commissioner Slaughter. This antiauthority attitude struck a chord with fans, much like Steve Austin, except in a negative way, and they began doing bizarre "shoot" angles where they were trying to get themselves fired so they could move to WCW and join the New World Order.

The most famous incident occurred when they hijacked the video truck and had the footage of the infamous "MSG Incident" shown on live TV to try and force Vince McMahon's hand in firing them. This was a tactic completely unlike anything seen before, and soon after they were solidified as a team when they started calling themselves "D-Generation X." The difference between the family-friendly WWF of the mid-'90s and this new era was striking, as D-X used an alternative-rock theme song, quick-cutting video effects, weird green lights, and interviews filled with as much profanity and sexual innuendo as the censors would tolerate.

This was clearly a team that was about to define wrestling for the next century, and suddenly Bret Hart looked like a fuddy-duddy by way of comparison, a dinosaur who represented men in their underwear rolling around on the mat. To Vince, D-X was SportZ Entertainment in all its glory (you need to replace *s* with *z* to be extreme, you see), the in-ring product secondary to the out-of-ring high jinks that were starting to give the WWF a slight sign of a pulse in the ratings. However, it was a different Vince who had his finger on that pulse: Vince Russo.

man" on the show and turn it into a WWF-focused show. Then, once the show was finished for good, Russo became the editor of *WWF Magazine*.

Russo, a fan of lowbrow B-movies and soap operas, brought a weird edge to the magazine and wrote an even weirder "insider" column under his alter ego, Vic Venom. As Russo's influence over the magazine increased, he began asking to sit in on booking meetings so he could know where the story lines were going and adjust his writing accordingly. McMahon agreed, and Russo became a familiar face backstage from 1996 on. In fact, Russo occasionally chimed in with an idea or two. McMahon took some of those ideas, and when they worked, Russo earned himself another audience. And another. And another. In fact, by mid-1997, the current booking team was under so much stress, thanks to the poor ratings, that McMahon essentially put Russo in charge of writing all of the WWF TV and decided to see if he would sink or swim with the job. Suddenly, gone were the cartoonish characters and skits of the past, and in were more realistic characters like the punks of D-X and the redneck Steve Austin. The WWF production team began circulating a new ad campaign focusing on the athletic backgrounds of their stars, stressing that there were real people in the ring. It was called "WWF Attitude."

(Cue ominous music here . . .)

INTERLUDE

Vince Russo, a video-store owner in New York, was the cohost, along with John Arezzi, of a call-in sports program that focused on wrestling. During the steroid trials of 1992–94, Arezzi hammered mercilessly on Vince McMahon's private life on-air until finally a desperate McMahon did the only thing he could to shut him up: He hired Russo to be a sort of "inside

SCENE NINE
That's Gotta Be Kane!

Bret Hart was clearly becoming the odd man out in this whole situation, and after *Badd Blood*, Shawn Michaels was once again the number-one contender for the WWF title, and a match was signed for *Survivor Series* between the two.

(Cue even more ominous music here . . .)
Interest in the show was fairly high, partly be-

cause of the long-standing, unresolved feud between the two men since *Wrestlemania XII*, and partly because those who followed things online knew about the real-life animosity and were curious to see if they could work a match together without killing each other.

But first, we need to cover some other ground. Specifically the tragic end to the life of Brian Pillman, which occurred the night before the *Badd Blood* PPV.

Pillman, dubbed the "Loose Cannon" as a nickname and gimmick, unfortunately chose to live that life in and out of the ring, partaking in excessive use of drugs and alcohol. However, in the end it was a simple heart problem that got to him. He was found dead in his hotel room in Minnesota after a house show. Sadly, Pillman's death wasn't a shock to most, since it was largely expected that his deteriorating health and accelerating self-destruction would catch up with him sooner or later. The show went on as planned, albeit with a short and somber speech from McMahon to open it, which related Pillman's death, and a couple of match replacements.

> **I**n one final, weird, cosmic insult, Pillman's scheduled match was replaced by a midget match. I have no idea what that means, karmically speaking.

Pillman had been scheduled to face Dude Love in a street fight, with Goldust having a chance to win his wife, Marlena, back if Dude won the match. That story line was supposed to end with Marlena turning on Goldust and leaving with Pillman instead for good. This story line would actually have been a precursor to those pioneered by the Val Venis character in later months, and ironically Terri Runnells (Marlena's real name) left her real-life husband, Goldust, soon after this story line was prematurely ended. In story terms, the poor guy cracked up and turned

into a performance artist known as "The Artist Formerly Known as Goldust" as a way for McMahon to take creative potshots at the world of "high art."

> **G**oldust's new character demonstrated one of the main principles of Vince's philosophy in life—if you don't understand it, mock it.

One story line that no one can possibly accuse of ending prematurely, however, was that of The Undertaker and his estranged brother, Kane. Glen Jacobs, who was selected to play the character of Kane, is an interesting case study in how to get ahead in the WWF. Namely, you should try to:

a) Be tall.
b) Be muscular.
c) Have a full head of hair.

Given these qualifications, it isn't terribly hard to get and maintain a job within the WWF, and indeed, after failing miserably as Dr. Isaac Yankem DDS (Jerry Lawler's personal dentist) and the Fake Diesel (as if playing a second-rate Kevin Nash could mean anything but disaster), Jacobs was given one more kick at the can. The story line itself was fairly straightforward . . . well, as compared to a Coen brothers movie, I guess.

In April '97, Undertaker's former manager, Paul Bearer, had Mankind hit UT in the face with a fireball on an episode of *RAW* to lead up to the *Revenge of the Taker* PPV, when Undertaker would be defending his WWF title against Mankind. Mankind attempted to use an acetylene blowtorch to one-up Bearer's idea the night following the PPV, but thankfully cooler heads prevailed there. At any rate, they had the big match, and Undertaker not only won, but threw a retaliatory fireball into the face of Paul Bearer to take him off TV for a while; until they found something new to do with him. And indeed, a few weeks later he started making dramatic reappearances with blond hair and a scarred face, claiming that "he" was alive. No proof or explanation was given for a while, just Paul making wild claims about someone out to get The Undertaker.

Then, in June '97, Paul escalated the game as he blackmailed Undertaker into taking him back as manager by holding the secret over his head. Once Undertaker got fed up with Paul and punked him out, the "dark secret" was revealed with Bearer now stating that Undertaker's brother was still alive. Given that we as fans knew nothing about his home life, this wasn't exactly earth-shattering news, but you take these things as they come.

Then, into August, came a name: Kane. Or, at that time, Cain. They changed their mind a lot before the debut. Most felt it would end up being Kane, however, because that was Undertaker's original name in the WWF: Kane the Undertaker. In fact, all the stalling was mostly to allow the memories of the Fake Diesel to disappear from peoples' minds and Glen Jacobs to grow out his hair a lot longer. Remember: full head of hair, very important.

Finally, as *Badd Blood* approached, the full backstory of the Undertaker's brother emerged as Paul revealed how the young Undertaker (one had to presume that he wasn't named "Undertaker" at the time, or else it would have made his days in school more than a little awkward; that being said, "Kane" isn't actually a common name, either, so maybe their parents had more problems than we were led to believe) was playing with matches, and Kane would always tag along with him. One day, however, UT played with one match too many and burned down their house, killing their parents and trap-

ping Kane in the fire and leaving him scarred beyond recognition. However, this being a freakish family that obviously lived on top of a nuclear waste dump, young Kane grew up to be superhumanly strong and possessing the same powers of the undead that his big brother had, all the while being raised in a mental hospital with Paul Bearer as a surrogate father.

But wait!

Later on, even more lurid details were revealed when it came to light that in fact Paul Bearer was Kane's *real* father, having gotten Undertaker's mother pregnant, so they weren't really brothers—they were half-brothers. How then could Kane possess the Undertaker's powers of the undead and his ability to no-sell mid-card offense? How could Undertaker possess those powers in the first place? It's probably best not to think about it.

On the bright side, before Kane debuted at *Badd Blood*, Undertaker and Shawn Michaels had a hell of a match, one that won "Match of the Year" honors across the board for 1997. Here's my review:

Hell in the Cell:
Shawn Michaels v. The Undertaker

This was the final result of Summerslam '97, when Shawn had reffed the UT-Bret title match, and ended by fucking up and hitting UT with a chair to give Bret the WWF title. They had a wild match at Ground Zero, and then Shawn was forced into a tag match with HHH, and D-Generation X was formed. After another couple of weeks of incredibly obnoxious antics on Shawn's part, this match was signed. And the general consensus was that Shawn was dead meat.

D-X tries to accompany Shawn, but gets sent back. Shawn tries to avoid UT, who slowly stalks him around ringside. He runs into the ring and right into a big boot. UT rams him into the turnbuckle, and again, which Shawn sells big-time. UT goes for the choke-

slam, but Shawn kicks him in the shin and hammers away. UT shrugs it off and reverses a whip, sending Shawn crashing to the corner. UT with a wristlock, and he slams into Shawn's shoulder a few times, then does the ropewalk. Shawn oversells again. UT with a head-butt and choking. Slam and legdrop for two. Michaels is dazed, and UT backdrops him to the heavens.

Shawn gets up so UT knocks him on his ass several times, and then tosses him over the top rope in a wicked bump for Shawn. He chokes Shawn against the cage, prompting Shawn to try to climb out of the cage. UT pulls him down to the floor, another wicked bump. Front row starts yelling "Make him bleed," thus demonstrating how much Shawn was despised at this point. UT whips him into the cage, and then tears his head off with a clothesline coming back. Again. Great bumping by Shawn. The announcers are totally selling the idea of UT taking his time and destroying Shawn bit by bit.

Taker tries a piledriver onto the floor, but Shawn flips up and hammers on his head. UT calmly smashes the back of Shawn's head into the cage and drops him onto the floor. Ouch. To the steps. UT hammers away on Shawn, and rams him back-first into the ringpost, then to the cage, then to the ringpost, to the cage again. Crowd eats it up. This, folks, is a shitkicking of the first order.

Shawn tries to push UT into the cage, but UT simply clotheslines him on the way back. He smashes Shawn into the stairs. UT whips Shawn into the cage, but Shawn uses the momentum to nail UT on the way back, giving himself the advantage.

He wisely rolls back into the ring to escape The Undertaker. He nails him a few times on the way back in, but UT snaps Shawn's neck on the top rope on the way down. Shawn comes back and knocks UT off the apron into the cage. UT keeps coming. Shawn tries a tope suicida, sending UT crashing into the cage, then he climbs halfway up the cage and drops an elbow to UT on the floor. UT keeps getting up, so Shawn clotheslines him off the apron. Shawn, getting desperate, grabs the stairs and rams them into UT's back a few times. He piledrives Taker on the remains of the stairs and rolls back into the ring to escape again. He comes off the top rope with a double-axehandle to UT on the floor.

Shawn finds a chair under the ring before returning. A shot to the back puts UT down again. UT gets up, so Shawn knocks him down again. It gets two. Notice the story. UT controlled for the first portion, while Shawn had to use his brain and every advantage possible to come back. UT tries to come back, but gets caught in the ropes and pummeled by Shawn. Shawn charges and eats a boot to the mouth, and charges again and gets backdropped over the top, onto a cameraman. He nails the cameraman (a local worker) and injures him. The medical crew opens the cage to give the guy assistance as Shawn hits UT with the flying forearm back in the ring. Shawn with the Randy Savage elbow, and he cues up the band. Superkick, but UT sits up. So Shawn runs out the door.

UT follows and they fight in the aisle. Shawn drop-kicks UT, but on a second attempt gets caught and catapulted into the cage. If you go in slow motion, you can see Shawn rip the blade across his forehead in midair. It's not noticeable, though, otherwise. UT rams Shawn into the cage a few times like a battering ram. Shawn kicks him in the nuts to counter. Shawn climbs the outside of the cage to escape the increasingly crazed UT, and UT follows. They fight on the roof, and Shawn attempts a piledriver, reversed by UT to a big pop. UT grates Shawn's face into the mesh as a neat camera angle from below lets us see it. Taker military presses Shawn onto the cage, then nails him, sending Shawn scurrying to the edge to run away. He starts to climb down the cage, so UT stomps on Shawn's hands until he crashes to the table below.

Like the Terminator, Undertaker follows and biels Shawn onto the French table, then press slams him to the remains of the Spanish table. Shawn is just bleeding all over the place. UT literally kicks Shawn's ass around the cage, and tosses him back into the ring. Clothesline, then he puts Shawn on the top rope and chokeslams him off. UT finds his own chair and smashes it into Shawn's face, then calls for the tombstone . . . and the lights go out.

The now-familiar music and red lights start, and Kane makes his first appearance. He rips the door off the hinges, does the pyro thing, and tombstones Undertaker, then leaves. Michaels pulls his blood-soaked carcass off the mat, rolls over with his last ounce of strength, and covers for the pin. D-X drags him out of the ring before The Undertaker can wake up and finish killing Shawn. Ending deducts ¼*, but make no mistake: This is THE match of the year. ****¾

The winner of that match, Shawn, was then scheduled to face Bret Hart in Montreal at the *Survivor Series*, and we're getting there, but hold your horses for right now. First I want to talk a bit about the New Age Outlaws.

SCENE TEN
Dogg-Ass

Generally considered a pimple on the ass of wrestling these days, the Outlaws were a fairly big deal back in their early days. The team came about due to a bigger botched angle months before, and the story goes like this . . .

The Honky Tonk Man, former "greatest intercontinental champion of all time," reentered the WWF in late 1996 and began searching for a new protégé to lead to that belt and groom as champion. He began doing color commentary on *RAW*, explaining his epic quest and "scouting" various mid-carders as the one to lend his guidance to. Well, this was all well and good, but the WWF had no real idea who the protégé was supposed to be—it was just an idea that Honky floated out there and they let him go out and shoot his own angle, so to speak. And in fact, this angle dragged on for *months*, with no movement or clear idea of where the hell this was supposed to be going.

> **D**isco Inferno's luck went from bad to worse when he was allowed to return to the WCW on the condition that he do a job to female wrestler Jackie at the *Halloween Havoc* PPV. Jackie was later signed by the WWF, while Disco never made it there, even after the sale of the WCW to the WWF.

Most people assumed that estranged WCW jobber Disco Inferno was perfect for the role, but he couldn't get out of his contract and the WWF didn't appear to be interested anyway. So finally, in April of '97, Honky announced that he had found his next superstar . . . ex–tag champion and current jobber-to-the-stars Billy Gunn, fresh off splitting up the Smoking Gunns and going nowhere. However, Gunn turned him down and left him to be beaten up by "Double J" Jesse Jammes. Honky announced that his *real* protégé would debut at the *Revenge of the Taker* show against Jammes, to avenge that beating. The show came and . . . from my review:

"Double J" Jesse Jammes v. The Honky Tonk Man's Protégé

Yes, HTM spent months hyping his newest find, and we get . . . Rockabilly Gunn. Oh, you didn't know that this match sucked? Your ass better call somebody!

Honky does a quick interview to explain the nonsensical Gunn turn. The crowd is just gone, not caring a whit about either guy. Astonishingly, Gunn and Jammes would be tag champions by the end of the year, and the most over tag team in WWF history within another six months.

Rockabilly gets a two off a Rocker Dropper. This match made the Netcop Busts compilation for the sheer historical value of the stupidity. Massive stalling and showboating from both guys here. Jesse makes the big comeback with a bunch of punches. Rockabilly goes for a suplex and Jammes reverses to a small package for the pin. An awful match with an ending that made zero sense on several levels. On the bright side, it sowed the seeds for the New Age Outlaws. DUD.

So poor Billy was left to limp along for much of 1997, feuding off and on with the equally lame singing cowboy Jesse Jammes until, finally, the real-life friends turned on Honky Tonk Man on-screen and complained to Vince McMahon off-screen that they were better off as a tag team. Vince agreed, and in October '97, Jammes turned himself heel and started calling himself the "Road Dog," as a play on his former roadie persona when he was Jeff Jarrett's bodyguard, while Rockabilly simply became "Bad Ass" Billy Gunn. The duo began using every cheap, heat tactic known to man and mouse to get the people in the arena booing them.

Really, Billy Gunn had little to worry about, careerwise, as even five years later the WWF is still trying to push him as something meaningful due to his size and build.

As an experiment, the WWF put the tag-team titles on them, having them beat the Legion of Dinosaurs . . . er . . . Doom, on an episode of *RAW* in November via a cheap finish. They then ambushed and shaved off Hawk's Mohawk over the next few weeks, while Jammes developed his mike skills by never shutting up. Their finisher was generally hitting the guy over the head with a championship belt and then laughing about it. Their alternate finisher for a while involved a poor, abused boom box, stolen from the Head-bangers, which exploded upon impact on the skulls of their opponents. Sadly, they couldn't even let the poor thing die in peace as they instead rebuilt it with duct tape and used it week after week. Talk about your cruel and unusual punishments.

Shakespeare, it ain't, but it was effective at tapping into the cynical younger crowd who saw these two guys as hip and cool and saying what they wanted to say: The Legion of Doom were old and stale and if it took a guy who used to be called "Rockabilly" to point that out, then so be it. And as the year closed, the Outlaws were still the tag champions, with no signs of losing the belts anytime soon. They even had their own customized introduction, as performed by the Road Dogg (whose name had been changed slightly for trademark reasons). You've probably heard it before:

"Ladies and gentlemen, boys and girls, children off all ages, the WWF is proud to present to you it's TAG-TEAM CHAMPIONS OF THE WOORRRRRRRLD . . . the Road Dogg Jesse Jammes, the Badd Ass Billy Gunn, the New Age Outlaws!"

Not many thought they could last as a team. But then these were the same people who had considered "Rockabilly" a good career move.

SCENE ELEVEN
What Happened Before Montreal

Speaking of bad career moves, by November '97, it had become public that Bret Hart wanted to go to the WCW.

Now, you have to understand something here, and this is something that Vince McMahon was either unwilling or unable to accept even after years of having Hart in his promotion: Bret Hart is a national hero in Canada, on the level of Michael Jordan in the U.S. On top of that, the WWF has always been the only game in town, wrestlingwise, as the WCW was never able to even get a foothold into the Canadian market outside of Toronto. So you can imagine how devastated many Canadian wrestling fans were when they read on the major Web sites one morning early in November that Bret Hart had apparently quit the WWF and was going to the WCW. Imagine, if you will, being nine years old and waiting for Santa Claus to arrive for Christmas, only to have your parents inform you that he wouldn't be coming because he had been gunned down by the Easter Bunny Posse in a drive-by shooting two days earlier.

Yes, I know, it's only a wrestler changing promotions, but Bret Hart and the Hart family meant so much to Canada that it eclipsed even Vince McMahon's relatively petty and short-sighted view of the nationalistic monster he had created earlier in the year. Bret Hart, when he went on national TV early in 1997 for his "heel turn," ended up listing all the great things about Canada that we, as Canadians, are deeply proud of, and it struck a chord with the entire population of wrestling fans in Canada. It wasn't just a wrestling angle for us, it was a way to finally express our own unique form of patriotism by living vicariously through Bret, who was saying the things that no one in Canada had had the opportunity to say before.

Bret has since apologized for saying that if someone ever wanted to give America an enema, they should stick the hose in Pittsburgh. You can see how this could be taken out of context.

When Bret and the Hart Foundation arrived in Calgary for the *Canadian Stampede* PPV in July '97, they were greeted like the Beatles arriving for the Ed Sullivan show in the '60s, and the roar that was maintained by the Calgary crowd, and the one in Edmonton the next night at *RAW*, wasn't just for Vince's little one-ring circus and third-grade level story lines, it was because we *cared* about Bret—and as long as he was with the WWF, we cared about wrestling in general.

Vince never understood that—he apparently saw the Bret Hart heel run as further testament to his own self-proclaimed genius and didn't look deeper into it than that.

So after the news of Bret's impending departure leaked out, the WWF Canada sent out a desperate statement of denial, which was in fact a bald-faced lie, but Bret himself went on the TV show *Off the Record* to announce that indeed he had given his notice and was "exploring other options," that is, going to WCW.

But why? Years later, both sides are still sniping at each other over the subsequent events, and when it comes right down to it, no one is still 100 percent certain of what Vince's thought process was in jettisoning one of the WWF's biggest draws of the modern era. There are two prevalent theories as to what set in motion the events that would change wrestling history forever:

1) The Shawn Michaels Theory: Shawn Michaels was a well-known McMahon suck-up who used his political clout and backstage connections to influence his way up the front-office ladder until he was giving suggestions to Vince directly. However, with his two main sources of backup, Scott Hall and Kevin Nash, off to the competition, Shawn was left without 50 percent of his support base and needed a direct line to McMahon himself in order to maintain his position at the top of the promotion.

To do this, he had to somehow get rid of the one person who always saw through his bullshit games and maneuvers and was the only other threat to his position as the number-one heel in the business for the big-money feud against Steve Austin. So in the end, it came down to "this town ain't big enough for the both of us" between Bret and Shawn, as most figured it eventually would, and Vince sided with the one guy who was perfectly suited for the raunchy, edgy direction that he wanted to steer the Good Ship Titan toward in the months to come. Bret became the stodgy old veteran, pushed out by the younger, healthier, and hipper Shawn.

Funnily enough, if this theory is true, then Bret got the last laugh because he was good for another three years of solid matches for WCW, while Shawn would be retired from the business only six months later.

2) Money: Vince had signed Bret to an impossibly long twenty-year, guaranteed contract, and he may have simply decided that he no longer wanted to honor the agreement he had made with Bret in desperation a year previous. If so, this would reinforce the many claims Bret made about Vince being a liar and a cheat in the months following Montreal. The justification here from Vince's end of things seems to be that part of the deal involved Bret becoming a sort of lieutenant booker under Vince, basically answering only to him. Vince (at the behest of his son, Shane, and Shawn Michaels) wanted to move the business more toward the smut and filth that eventually became the Attitude Era, a movement that Bret Hart wanted nothing to do with. Thus, Vince needed out of the contract so he could get rid of the one thing standing in the way of the new direction.

Either way, Vince had his reasons, and he told Bret that he would be intentionally breaching Bret's iron-clad contract, and that Bret was free to sign with WCW if he could do so.

The *Survivor Series* was approaching quickly, however, and Vince began harping on the idea of having Bret do the job to Shawn Michaels in

In fact, after raising the prices of the former *In Your House* PPVs from $19.95 to $29.95, the WWF was very much profitable again and Vince could easily afford to pay Bret Hart everything promised. Vince, of course, conveniently leaves this out whenever he tells the story.

Montreal. Bret felt the opposite should occur—he would go over in Montreal, and then do the job for Shawn at the next PPV, in Springfield, Massachusetts, in December. Shawn, for his part, took the attitude that if Bret was leaving, then he didn't see why it would make any sense for him to put a future WCW star over, and furthermore, the $64,000 question was "Will Bret turn up on *Nitro* with the WWF title belt the night after *Survivor Series* regardless?"

Given those two conditions, I can sort of understand where Shawn was coming from. With that being said, Shawn's place as a WWF employee was *not* to go around questioning every booking decision, but rather to do his job to the best of his ability. And in this case, his job probably should have been a "job," if you will.

Anyway, after much back-and-forth yelling and screaming between Bret and Vince, it was eventually decided that indeed Bret would go to WCW at the end of November, and the match at *Survivor Series* would end in a DQ finish, with Bret surrendering the WWF title the next night on *RAW* and letting Vince do with it what he would.

Bret, as a point of fact, actually offered to drop the title several times well *before Survivor Series* if his intentions about the belt were a concern to Vince, stating for the record that he was willing to lose the belt to anyone from Vader all the way down to the Brooklyn Brawler if Vince so desired. Bret's concern was merely that he didn't want to drop the title that night, in that city. However, Vince reasoned that interest in the show might decline if Bret wasn't champion going in, so he wanted the belt up for grabs and denied all of Bret's requests to lose the title leading up to the show. So that's all well and good, the buy rate was going to be up because of interest from the fans in the "last match ever" between Bret and Shawn, and it was a hot Montreal crowd in a completely sold-out arena.

SCENE TWELVE
What Happened in Montreal

Vince's intentions for the future of the promotion were starting to come out in the spin control, however, as he issued the following statement to counteract the rabid anti-WWF sentiment that was building on the Internet once Bret's contract situation had been revealed:

Over the past few days I have read certain comments on the internet concerning Bret Hart and his "alleged" reasons for wanting to pursue other avenues than the World Wrestling Federation to earn his livelihood. While I respect the "opinions" of others, as owner of the World Wrestling Federation I felt that it was time to set the record straight. As it has been reported recently on line, part of Bret Hart's decision to pursue other options is allegedly due to his concerns with the "direction" of the World Wrestling Federation. Whereby each and every individual is entitled to his, or her, opinion, I take great offense when the issue of the direction of the World Wrestling Federation is raised. In the age of sports entertainment, the World Wrestling Federation REFUSES to insult its audience in terms of "Baby Faces" and "Heels".

In 1997, how many people do you truly know that are strictly "good" guys or "bad" guys? World Wrestling Federation programming reflects more of a reality based product in which life, as well as World Wrestling Federation superstars, are portrayed as they truly are—in shades of gray . . . not black or white. From what I am reading it has been reported that Bret may be concerned about the morality issues in the World Wrestling Federation. Questionable language, questionable gestures, questionable sexuality, questionable racial issues. Questionable?

All of the issues mentioned above are issues that every human being must deal with every day of their lives. Also, with that in mind, please be aware that Bret Hart has been cautioned—on numerous occasions—to alter his language by not using expletives or God's name in vain. He was also told—on numerous occasions—not to use certain hand gestures some might find offensive. My point is: regardless of what some are reporting, Bret's decision to pursue other career options IS NOT genuinely a Shawn Michaels direction issue, as they would like you to believe!

In the personification of D-Generation X, Shawn Michaels' character is EXPECTED to be living on the edge—which I might add, Mr. Michaels portrays extremely well. The issue here is that the "direction" of the World Wrestling Federation is not determined by Shawn Michaels, OR Bret Hart for that matter. It is determined by you—the fans of the World Wrestling Federation. You DEMAND a more sophisticated approach! You DEMAND to be intellectually challenged! You demand a product with ATTITUDE, and as owner of this company—it is my responsibility to give you exactly what you want!

Personally, I regret the animosity that has built up between Shawn Michaels and Bret Hart, but in the end, it is the World

Wrestling Federation that is solely responsible for the content of this product—NOT Bret Hart—NOT Shawn Michaels—NOT Vince McMahon for that matter. May the best man win at the Survivor Series!

To the WWF's shock, this merely made a lot of things worse. For instance, it was pointed out, while many people deal with "racial" issues every day, not many deal with a gang of caricatures loosely based on the Nation of Farrakhan on a daily basis. Or a group of South African white supremacists called "The Truth Commission" for that matter. Or an undead zombie with an estranged supernatural half-brother, come to think of it. In fact, Vince's whole problem seemed to be that he wanted things both ways—by presenting his product as "reality based" to cater to the whims of the Jerry Springer, white-trash audience while at the same time seeming more highbrow for the legitimate media. While almost everyone immediately saw through this line of crap for what it was, it did give the WWF an important new direction and a new catchphrase: WWF Attitude.

All was not wine and roses backstage, however.

While Bret and Shawn cooperated as professionals leading up to the match, many of Bret's friends backstage came up to him and warned him about being double-crossed, telling him to make sure to kick out at one instead of two, and not to get put into any submission holds. Bret was suspicious, but his thinking was that surely this *was* the dawn of the twenty-first century, and not the sleazy yesteryear of the 1920s where mafia-connected slimeball promoters would send in a ringer to take care of a troublesome wrestler, right? This was Vince McMahon running things, the friendly and jovial announcer who bravely had fought off the millionaire good-old-boy promoters' clubs in the '80s to forge an empire under Hulk Hogan and Americana and apple pie. This was Vince McMahon, the now struggling "last independent promoter" who was waging an expensive war of attrition with the seemingly bottomless pockets of Billionaire Ted and his corporate empire. This was Uncle Vince, who gave millions to charity and hung out with "the boys" in the back to share laughs. Surely, of all people, Bret could trust Vince, right?

But Bret at that point wasn't quite the jaded cynic he is these days, so as one last fail-safe in case there really *was* some funny business going on, Bret went to his longtime friend and confidant referee Earl Hebner, and asked him to personally make sure that Vince didn't pull anything on him. Earl solemnly swore to Bret, on his children's heads, that he wouldn't double-cross him. Bret and Shawn planned out the match as their slot on the show approached, still unsure of what the finish would be. Someone, with most sources saying Pat Patterson, stooged to Vince that Bret wanted a spot where Shawn would put him in his own Sharpshooter about fifteen minutes in, and the stage was set.

> **S**hawn has since admitted that he was fully in on the double cross, even though everyone pretty much suspected that anyway, what with him being a huge liar and all.

Vince was missing from his usual commentary position that night, and he hasn't returned since then. Bret and Shawn did a very good match for the first twenty minutes, including a long brawl into the stands so that the fans could see Shawn "get his" for all the things he had said about Bret on TV leading up to the show. Then, backstage, Bruce Pritchard (a WWF front-office guy) started yelling that they needed more security, which would seem to run contrary to the simple DQ finish Bret was told it would be. Bruce has since claimed he wasn't in on it.

In the ring, Earl Hebner was knocked out by an errant shot from Michaels, and Shawn put Bret into his own finishing move as planned, but the backstage director started screaming into Hebner's earpiece that it was time to get up already. Hebner did so with superhuman speed (for a referee), and with Bret on the mat in his own submission hold, called for the bell. Vince McMahon, sitting next to the poor timekeeper, elbowed him hard in the ribs and yelled "Ring the fucking bell!" and it was all over for Bret. Earl Hebner sprinted like a coward for a waiting taxi and went back to his hotel room to hide, while the officials at ringside hastily shoved the belt into Shawn's hands and sent him on his way back to the dressing room.

From the perspective of the fans watching at home, we had never experienced anything even vaguely like this before, and we had no way to reconcile what had just happened with the truth. To us, it was just a strange-looking finish, and we were thinking that someone must have messed up. In fact, the next day at work, many people who had seen the show asked me about it, confused as to what exactly had happened, and many were disappointed at the abrupt finish, as though it had been just part of the show.

In fact, it was anything but, as everyone started finding out soon afterward. Stories started circulating about Bret Hart punching out Vince McMahon after the show, and that it was a shoot on Bret by Shawn Michaels. Things were cleared up fairly soon as more and more nasty details of the whole affair started leaking out. The *RAW* on Monday was a disaster, with some wrestlers boycotting the show and the Canadian crowd chanting "We Want Bret" off and on for the entire two-hour show. Shawn immediately took up the cause of burying Bret Hart in earnest, trotting out a midget dressed as Bret on a show soon after the *Survivor Series*, and then beating him up. Vince cut a famous interview in which he explained his side of the story, much of it scripted to make him sound like the bad guy, and now the cracks in the façade that once was benevolent announcer Vince McMahon were starting to show, and the true nature of the beast, Mr. McMahon, was emerging.

After Bret punched Vince's lights out, Vince was out like a light and broke his ankle on the way down. Vince has since revised history to state that he gave Bret a free shot, and then fell backward into Gerald Brisco, who stepped on his ankle and broke it. Vince also generally omits the entire locker room threatening to boycott *RAW* and Undertaker threatening to kick Vince's ass six ways from Sunday. But that would probably hurt his image.

SCENE THIRTEEN
What Happened After Montreal

In fact, we still haven't met the "real" Vince McMahon as even the Mr. McMahon character is a very exaggerated version of his backstage persona. But not by much, most feel. And with that interview, Bret Hart was now a dead issue in the WWF because the WWF was completely past Bret's departure and had forgotten all about it, excepting of course for every other show, when they'd take potshots at him on air and reuse the Montreal finish to rub that in his face for the next four years. I personally think that Vince's last words on his deathbed will be "Pull the plug, pull the fucking plug!" but time will tell on that one.

From here on in, pencil in Vince for a Stunner every month or so.

Vince's new evil character, a millionaire owner who was willing to screw over his biggest star without blinking an eye, seemed to be a desperate last gasp to intimidate WCW into backing off, instead it proved to be the spark that turned the company around. But while Vince was the spark, Steve Austin was the fifty-megaton bomb with a fuse just waiting to be lit.

Austin had regained the intercontinental title at *Survivor Series*, winning it from Owen Hart in a subpar match (due to his still-severe neck injury), but Austin was a rabid competitor and could no longer sit on the sidelines nursing his neck. This, in fact, became a focal point of the on-screen character, and in October, a semi-evil Mr. McMahon demanded Austin sign a waiver absolving the WWF of any liability should Austin be injured due to his neck problems. Austin signed it and delivered the Stone Cold Stunner again to McMahon, and Vince didn't forget it.

On the *RAW* following *Survivor Series*, the fans groaned to see hated ingenue Rocky Maivia positioned as the next big challenger to Austin's throne. Rocky, who had been a critical and popular disaster early in 1997, had returned in August of that year with a heel turn on Brian "Chainz" Lee to join the Nation of Domination, the resident, militant, black-supremacy group in the WWF. But while Rock's idiotic babyface persona was better left in the '70s from whence it came, his goofy heel shtick, complete with superhero muscle poses and interviews so self-centered that he made me look modest by comparison, struck a chord with the jaded fanbase, and he started becoming cool. And now the chants of "Rocky Sucks" were actually encouraged by the WWF brain trust, which helped matters somewhat for him.

The whole Austin-Rocky thing came to a head at the *D-Generation X* PPV in Springfield (the show that was originally supposed to feature

Bret dropping the title in a four-way match, in what seemed like a lifetime ago), where they did a match for the intercontinental title that was all brawling and goofy spots and that set the stage for the main-event brawls that would define the company and Steve Austin over the next few years. The show also featured Shawn Michaels defending his ill-gotten WWF title against Ken Shamrock, but the less said about that the better. Well, perhaps I *could* mention that Shamrock was known to yell out spots so audibly that people watching other TV programs could hear him across the spectrum, but that would just be mean.

S hawn Michaels may share in the blame for Shamrock's spot calling, with stories circulating of Shawn specifically telling Ken to call the spots nice and loud. Shawn was that kind of guy.

Anyway, the next night on *RAW*, Vince McMahon called "shenanigans!" on Austin's disputed win over Maivia (for the usual reasons—unconscious refs, off-road vehicles running over competitors, someone pulling a scale model of the Sears Tower out of their kneepad . . . you know, the usual) and asked, nay, *demanded*, that Austin surrender the title back to the WWF by the end of the show. This in fact stemmed from Vince's having asked Austin in real life to drop the title to Maivia that night, but Austin had refused, and Vince wrote the confrontation into the story line. Rocky was quite obviously Vince's pet project, as the months following this angle would prove. At any rate, Austin decided to compromise with Vince: He indeed surrendered the title to the WWF (which then gave it to number-one contender Maivia), and then beat the hell out of Vince, allowing Rocky to give his first quotable line in the

Act Three

Austin v. McMahon (1998)

"Tuesdays are no fun anymore."
     —WCW President Eric Bischoff, complaining about winning the ratings war
     too handily in February 1998.

Champions as the year began:

WWF Champion: Shawn Michaels

Intercontinental Champion: The Rock

Tag-Team Champions: The New Age Outlaws

European Champion: Hunter Hearst Helmsley

Light Heavyweight Champion: Taka Michinoku

If, God forbid, there is ever a nuclear holocaust that wipes out most of North America, it seems safe to say that the only things to survive will be cockroaches and the WWF. Sure, they'll have to swing their demographics wildly toward the 18–34 insect population, and the quarterly investor conference calls would be lot less newsworthy, but knowing Vince, he'd still keep plugging along right up until the end of civilization as we know it. "Change or die" is the motto of wrestling in recent years as it's survived everything from steroid trials to sex scandals to the worst thing of all: public apathy. Ted Turner and his, to quote Vince McMahon, "dubya-see-dubya" promotion fall somewhere in-between those crises. However, as 1998 showed, a little toilet humor can go a long way.

SCENE ONE

Shawn Michaels Gets His

And did I mention that Steve Austin was pretty darn popular? I probably should, because it's quite important to note that. Vince knew that, which is why Austin won the *Royal Rumble* for the second year in a row, this time by eliminating The Rock cleanly with no controversy. With Bret Hart gone and forgotten already, the WWF's new meal ticket was readily apparent in the form of the Rattlesnake.

The *Rumble* also proved that God indeed has a sense of humor, as Shawn Michaels faced the Undertaker in a somewhat subpar casket match, and at one point Shawn hit his back on the corner of the casket and ruptured a disc. He didn't even realize it until two days later when he could no longer get out of bed.

The match was also interesting because Undertaker had "reunited" with his brother, Kane, the week before this match when Kane had a sudden change of heart and decided to side with The Undertaker. See, after Kane debuted, Undertaker spent weeks telling everyone how he didn't want to fight his brother. This feeling echoed the sentiments of most of the smarter fans at the time, very few of whom particularly wanted to see that match, either, albeit for different reasons.

During the casket match, Shawn had a bunch of his goons attempt to attack Undertaker in tribute to the 1994 casket match where ten men shoved Undertaker into the casket to give Yokozuna the win. This prompted Kane to make the save (to a huge ovation), only to then turn on his brother and chokeslam him into the casket, giving Shawn the win. I think that, perhaps, a five-year-old, illiterate, redneck yokel in Southern Mississippi who was watching wrestling for the first time that day *may* have been fooled by this turn, but the rest of us pretty much had that one pegged right away. To make matters worse, Kane locked his brother in the casket and set it on fire. Talk about your dysfunctional family. Fear not, though, Undertaker would be back.

Sharp-eyed viewers (well, maybe the totally blind might have missed it) probably noticed a trapdoor in the casket through which Undertaker slipped under the ring to escape a potential cremation. The same trick was also done in 1996 at two PPVs—*Beware of Dog* and *Mind Games.*

On that same show, things turned around for good for the WWF, although in an unexpected way. Mike Tyson was a special guest of the McMahons and was being interviewed in their skybox. He declared that his favorite wrestler was "Cold Stoned" Steve Austin, and darned if those sentiments didn't apply to the rest of America, as well. Austin used the inspiration to win the *Rumble* and earn the title shot for *Wrestlemania* against Shawn Michaels, but Mr. McMahon wasn't really happy about it. But then Vince's

new on-screen persona wasn't terribly happy about much those days.

Somebody who was reasonably happy was Mick Foley, who was shifting personalities as needed, and was spending most of his time at that point playing Dude Love, the fun-loving hepcat. His fun was interrupted when he was about to beat Billy Gunn on *RAW* and got attacked by Gunn's partner, the Road Dogg, and you just knew it was going to lead to him finding a partner and seeking revenge at some point. So in Long Island, Foley again underwent the Incredible Hulk–like transformation back into his socially maladjusted Cactus Jack persona, and this time brought the equally dysfunctional Terry Funk with him, playing Chainsaw Charlie in a masked role that fooled no one.

Speaking of Funk and Foley, a bizarre sort of male-bonding occurred between them in the ECW, when Funk accidentally lit him on fire with a flaming branding iron. My theory is that Foley decided to become lifelong friends with him after that because, really, if that's the sort of thing that Funk does to his FRIENDS, you wouldn't want to be his enemy.

February sucked, so we'll skip over most of it.

Okay, there were a few cool things that happened—for instance, Austin was annoying Vince quite a lot more than Vince would have liked. Despite earning the title shot fair and square, Vince seemed apprehensive about getting behind Austin as his champion, and finally said so in an interview on *RAW* that defined the feud for months to come. Austin's feelings were, of course, hurt by this, and he decided to confront Vince about it at the worst possible time—during a quasi–press conference in the ring when Vince was introducing Mike Tyson as the special referee for the big *Wrestlemania* match between

Austin and Michaels. Austin triggered a pull-apart brawl between himself and Vince, and we viewers who had stuck with the program over *Nitro* through thick and thin could feel the tide start to turn with this. Many thought the Tyson segment, which was given massive mainstream coverage and tons of hype, might have been enough to score a win over *Nitro*. It didn't happen, but that ratings pop would come soon enough.

SCENE TWO
Dumpsters and Boxers

Things would actually get worse for poor Vince when he managed to convince Tyson to return for another try at announcing the referee gig, only to have Shawn Michaels interrupt the segment this time and trigger his own brawl . . . and then reveal that Tyson had, in fact, decided to ally himself with D-Generation X. Michaels didn't do much in-ring stuff at that point because he was basically crippled and taking frequent injections of painkillers just so he could walk upright. In fact, he skipped the February PPV (albeit with a legitimate medical excuse this time), and the WWF hyped a surprise entrant in the main-event, eight-man tag match to take his place—which ended up being Savio Vega.

That's generally the nature of "surprise" partners in the WWF. On the bright side, at least it wasn't Jimmy Snuka.

A word on surprises in wrestling, if I may: They suck. Okay, that's two, but I bet you were surprised. Anyway, whenever a promotion promises a "mystery partner" or a "big surprise" for a show, forget it. If they had anything worthwhile they'd be advertising it. Mysteries and surprises indicate that the promotion either doesn't know yet who they have, or doesn't have confidence that that person will sell tickets. So you

get a situation like the infamous *Survivor Series '90* egg fiasco, where a giant egg was hyped for weeks on end before hatching at the PPV to reveal . . . The Gobbledygooker, a giant, dancing turkey. Or *Survivor Series '96*, which featured a much-hyped mystery partner that turned out to be decrepit retiree Jimmy "Superfly" Snuka, brought in for a nostalgia pop from the New York crowd. Both are frequently cited as examples of the WWF's generally bad track record when it comes to surprise guests.

> **T**he Gobbledygooker, perhaps the worst gimmick of all time, was played by Hector Guerrero, older brother of current star Eddy Guerrero and uncle to Chavo Guerrero, Jr.

Speaking of the February show, titled *No Way Out*, WCW actually attempted to sue the WWF on the grounds that the show's initials—NWO—would fool viewers into thinking that the show was presented by WCW's own nWo group. Perhaps keeping the mean intelligence level of most fans in mind, the show was hastily renamed *No Way Out of Texas* in a very un-Vince-like capitulation.

> **I**ronically, four years later the real nWo would join the WWF ranks at . . . No Way Out.

Back on *RAW*, sportz entertainment reared its ugly head in the form of one of the first of Vince Russo's patented worked-shoot segments, based on the previously covered Enzuigiri of Doom angle in 1995. Cactus Jack was facing Chainsaw Charlie in a street fight that they'd decided to have just for fun. A few minutes into the match, Jack dropped an elbow onto Charlie from the Titantron screen . . . into a Dumpster.

Yeah, they just happened to find a Dumpster backstage, and by a shocking coincidence, it was filled with packing peanuts. I guess someone really wanted to get rid of them or something. Anyway, after dropping the elbow, the New Age Outlaws made their dramatic run-in and shut Cactus and Chainsaw into the Dumpster, then sent it flying off the stage with our heroes in it. They spent the better part of half an hour focusing on the fake-looking "injuries" sustained by the babyfaces, an effect that was further ruined when they did a run-in at the end of the show after "escaping" from the local hospital. However, the interesting thing about the segment wasn't this dog of an angle, but rather a comment in the fake, backstage area made by Michaels and Helmsley to the Outlaws.

Note: The real key to the success of the WWF in the late '90s was, I feel, due to the moving back of the magic curtain. In the '80s, fans were only allowed to see the ring and arena, and longed to see backstage so they could feel like they were getting a peek behind the curtain. So Vince (Russo or McMahon, it doesn't matter which) came up with the idea of filming segments "backstage" (really a staged set in the real backstage) so that fans who wanted to be considered smart could see what the rest of the world was "missing." This was quite brilliant because, of course, they were still in total control of what was being shown, but the illusion of *not* being in control was put forward and proved to be irresistible to wanna-be insiders. On the downside, you ended up with endless segments of people walking down the hallway before their match, but I guess you can consider it a necessary evil.

So anyway, my point (and I did have one) was that in the fake, backstage area, D-Generation X (who had been associating with the Outlaws on-screen here and there) pulled them aside and let them know that they did the right thing, because Controversy = Ratings, and the farther they pushed the envelope (presumably by pushing larger amounts of people off bigger stages into smellier Dumpsters), the higher the ratings would go. Whether the Outlaws took this advice to heart, we'll never know, but it certainly proved to be prophetic advice for the WWF in general, thus proving HHH to be the smartest man in wrestling years before anyone realized it might indeed be true.

On the flipside around this time, Kane shot lightning bolts at helpless lighting techs until Undertaker returned from wherever undead zombies go when they've been unsuccessfully cremated by their close relatives, and boy was he pissed. So much so, he made a dramatic entrance with a microphone clipped to his zombie costume during a Kane interview and walked through pyro effects in order to hammer home the point that he would walk through hell itself in order to face his brother, presumably in keeping with Vince McMahon's promise from the year before to deliver a more intellectually challenging and/or sophisticated product. If Undertaker really wanted to walk through hell, he should have just waited for the inevitable Undertaker-Kane matches like everyone else. But the rubes ate it up, so what can ya do?

SCENE THREE
Eric Bischoff Does Something Stupid(er)

Wrestlemania was at least set up with three, intriguing, main event–type matches: Shawn defending the WWF title against Steve Austin in a special "foregone conclusion" match; Undertaker facing Kane for the first time (but not the last . . . O dear God in heaven, not the last by far . . .); and the Outlaws defending the tag titles against Cactus Jack and Terry Funk in the charmingly conceived Dumpster match.

Prior to the match, Shawn Michaels was wandering around the dressing room telling anyone who would listen that he would not, in fact, do the job because Steve Austin hadn't paid his dues yet. Undertaker calmly taped his fists up in a menacing manner, and that was all the persuasion Shawn needed.

The fans were similarly intrigued, as *Wrestlemania XIV* had one of the largest buy rates in history and the Fleet Center in Boston was insanely rabid for Austin the whole night. Sadly, the match itself was considered a huge disappointment after the weeks of hype and months of build up for Austin, but at least Michaels did a clean job for once. Here's my review:

WWF Title:
Shawn Michaels v. Steve Austin

Mike Tyson is YOUR special enforcer and he mugs like a mark in the ring. Steve Austin's pop is . . . uh . . . Austin-like. You've gotta feel for Shawn knowing now what he was going through. Shawn stalls, and Austin isn't impressed, and lets his fingers do the talking. A chase follows, and Austin unloads on him and literally kicks his ass. A backdrop puts Shawn out, but Hunter attacks Austin to buy time. The ref tosses HHH and his man-beast Chyna, so we're one-on-one. C'est juste.

Shawn keeps on Austin in the interim, and they brawl up the ramp and Shawn uses the D-X band's drums as a weapon. Wonder if that's cymbal-lic of anything? Ahem. Back in, Austin catches Shawn coming off the top and sends him into the corner with a bump that fucks up his back so badly that I can feel it years later. It gets two. Austin works a wristlock and gets a stungun for two. Stunner is blocked, but Shawn flies out and hits a table. He looks in SERIOUS pain from that Flair flip in the corner.

Back in, Austin gets the FU Elbow for two. Austin hits the chinlock as they powwow about the back injury. Shawn jawbreakers out and wraps Austin's knee

around the post, but Austin pulls back and reverses on him. More brawling, but Shawn backdrops Austin into the crowd and then Tyson ignores a bell to the head. They head back in, but Shawn can barely walk and you can see the pain on his face with every step, literally. He keeps pounding away as best he can, but Austin spears him down and tosses him. I have no idea how Shawn can do that stuff in his condition. Shawn wraps Austin's leg around the post, however, to take control.

Shawn works the knee, but the back is getting so bad that he can't bend over and has to stop between moves to rest on the ropes. Austin bails, but gets dropkicked into the table. Tyson helps him back in (giving him a wedgie in the process) and Shawn clips him viciously. Figure four gets some near-falls with the help of the ropes, but Austin reverses. Austin slugs back and catapults him for two. Shawn grabs the sleeper, but the ref gets Stinkfaced and bumped. Austin stunguns him and tosses him around, but Shawn gets a grounded version of the forearm and he amazingly manages to kip up. Good God.

He goes up for the Shane O Mac elbow, no ref. Sweet chin music is reversed to the Stunner, reversed to the superkick, reversed again to KICK WHAM STUNNER for the pin and the title at 20:00 as Tyson makes the count and then turns on Shawn. Say what you will about Shawn, but mad props for his last match. Interestingly, this match was slagged by many in a sideways manner (as in, good but disappointing), but I think it was just WAY ahead of it's time since Shawn was forced to tone down that high-flying shit and go to a more mat-based style that ended up being a precursor to the stuff HHH and Rock were doing in 2000. Everything from the heavy psychology to the brawling in the crowd to the triple-reverse finish hadn't yet migrated to the main-event position because Austin hadn't changed the style yet. This definitely warrants a higher rating considering all the injury factors involved. * * * *

So that appeared to be that for another month. Also on that show, The Rock once again escaped from Ken Shamrock to retain his intercontinenal title, Jack and Funk won the tag titles from the Outlaws (albeit with controversy over whether they had used a legal Dumpster or not), and Undertaker pinned his brother after three tombstones.

Meanwhile, over in WCW, Eric Bischoff did a very dumb thing. Okay, that's probably kind of an obvious statement, but specifically Bischoff ended up being responsible for turning the whole shebang around for the WWF in April 1998. See, part of the really big humiliation for the WWF around that time was seeing random WWF guys show up on WCW programming to denounce their former employer. From the Hogan Love-In in 1994 to Luger and Madusa in 1995 to Hall and Nash and Syxx in 1996 to Bret Hart and Rick Rude in 1997, the cool factor resided in Atlanta thanks to the guaranteed contracts and guerilla negotiating tactics that Bischoff used. Of course, Vince himself had done all the same things years before, so some (myself included) felt it was just karma getting her licks in.

To be perfectly fair, Bischoff may have topped his stupid decision list when he told a room full of WCW wrestlers that the only people in the company who ever "put asses in seats" were Hulk Hogan, Randy Savage, and Roddy Piper. That one sure boosted morale.

But back to Bischoff. Late in 1997, Sean Waltman (the former 1-2-3 Kid who had become the nWo's buddy "Syxx" in 1996) suffered yet another neck injury in a long series of them over his career. Sean wasn't generally happy with the way he was being used by WCW at that point, which was more as a cruiserweight bully than a legitimate heavyweight threat, and was about to get even more

unhappy. Sitting home recuperating from the injury, he received a Fed-Ex from Bischoff's office in March 1998 letting him know that his services would no longer be required by WCW.

A word on Eric Bischoff, if I may: In May 1998, Bischoff went on WCW TV and actually challenged Vince McMahon to a street fight, presumably to settle who the better promoter was. Instead of simply ignoring this like the meaningless grandstand challenge that it was, the WWF made the mistake of actually issuing a statement denying that McMahon would be at the *Slamboree* PPV to face Bischoff. Later on, the WWF sued over WCW's on-air reading of this letter because pro wrestling fans are trained to think that when a promotion says someone will not be somewhere, they actually will be there, and thus the statement was intended to mislead fans into thinking that Vince would be at the PPV, QED. The whole matter was later settled out of court.

And to think people were complaining that nothing was happening in wrestling in the weeks before *Wrestlemania*.

The WWF immediately signed Waltman to a long-term contract (pending his rehabilitation and ability to stay clean) and the night after, *Wrestlemania* became the official start of the Attitude Era for the WWF. Hunter Hearst Helmsley, who had retained his European title over Owen Hart the night before and was now actively going by "Triple H" as his professional name, came out with Chyna to cut the most shocking promo of his career to that point: He was firing Shawn Michaels from D-Generation X for "dropping the ball" against Austin. His replacement? The returning Sean Waltman, prompting a nation of wrestling fans to sit up in shock.

See, outside of the online fans and dirt-sheet readers, no one had any clue Waltman had even been fired by WCW. Sean (who would eventually be dubbed "X-Pac," as a play on his former Syxx-Pac nickname in WCW) ended up cutting a scathing promo on WCW, noting that Bischoff's head was "so far up Hogan's ass that he could see what he had for breakfast." And at the end of the show, HHH and X-Pac interfered to allow the New Age Outlaws to win the tag titles back from Cactus Jack and Terry Funk, and a newer and hipper D-Generation X was born.

This was *huge*. Over in Turner-land, the nWo was getting more stale by the day and the new bad boys of D-X over in the WWF called to rebellious teen punks like a siren calls a sailor. But the ratings still didn't reflect this change in momentum as *Nitro* held on, now by the slimmest of margins. But one thing happened that changed that trend for good.

SCENE FOUR
Four Point Six

On the same show as X-Pac's debut, Vince McMahon presented Steve Austin with a brand-new WWF title belt to replace the one that had been in use since 1988. The old belt was showing its age, plus Vince didn't want third-party belt makers putting out their versions of the redesign and the WWF alone now held the copyrights on them. However, Vince's presentation of the belt had a caveat for Austin: Vince wanted a cooperative, ass-kissing corporate champion (like Michaels was in some sense), and Austin could either comply the easy way or the hard way. Austin's answer was to give McMahon another Stunner and be on his way.

The next week was a taped show, featuring McMahon dressing Austin in a tailored suit, only to see it get ripped off in dramatic fashion by the end of the night. Also, Cactus Jack gave a sulking interview in which he blamed the fans for chanting Austin's name when he was getting beaten up, and promised to retire the Jack persona for a long time. This show also lost to *Nitro*, but not by much.

Finally, with only a couple of weeks until Austin's first title defense at the *Unforgiven* PPV against an unnamed opponent, Austin challenged Vince to a one-on-one match at the end of *RAW* to settle things once and for all. Vince then tricked Austin into accepting a stipulation whereby Austin would have one hand tied behind his back. They spent the show building up the match, including skits with Vince's longtime stooges Patterson and Brisco as they showed him how to block the kick to the gut that precedes the Stunner. With instruction like that, how could he lose?

After much hoopla, the match happened, but seconds into it, Mick Foley ran in, back in his Dude Love persona again, and stopped things before they could get started. He took a chairshot for Mr. McMahon, and suddenly they had their main event for *Unforgiven*. Dude beat the shit out of Austin to further that angle.

And, more important, *RAW* finally beat *Nitro* in the ratings. *Nitro* came back to crush them again the next week, but the remarkable eighty-two-week winning streak on WCW's part was finally over.

Other things began taking shape around this time as well when developmental projects Sean Morley and Adam Copeland graduated to the big leagues as ex-porn star Val Venis and troubled youth, Edge, respectively. Vampire fanatic Dave Heath was brought in as the blood-spewing Gangrel to spruce up the mid-card. The multinational Nation of Domination was reorganized when The Rock stepped up to have longtime leader Faarooq removed, and he began making overt threats to D-X. D-X themselves began the most ambitious character makeover ever seen, going from generic thugs to edgy loudmouths, and the WWF filmed them in military fatigues showing up at a *Nitro* event that was happening in the same state as *RAW*. Suddenly the anti-WCW forces of D-X underwent a 180-degree turn in the fans' eyes almost overnight,

The WCW's legal department didn't really like D-X's antics, which is why they stopped pretty quickly.

becoming clear babyfaces for opposing the WWF's greater enemy, WCW.

So we came to *Unforgiven*, where Steve Austin faced his first challenge from Mr. McMahon in the form of corporate turncoat Dude Love. Here's my review:

WWF Title Match:
Steve Austin v. Dude Love

This was round one, as Vince had withheld the identity of Austin's opponent until a week before the show and then turned Mick Foley into his corporate zombie.

Dude jumps Austin, but gets his ass kicked and bails. Back in, Thesz press and elbow as Ross takes a shot at Bischoff for declaring that a guy in black boots and tights could never get over. Spinebuster and elbow, and Dude bails again.

They brawl as Dude tries to run, only to get viciously clotheslined from behind by Austin. They head to the stage (a popular spot tonight), and Austin casually tosses him onto the bare concrete six feet below. Back to ringside, the slaughter continues. Austin drops an elbow off the apron, and back in we go. Austin misses the rope straddle and Dude bulldogs him. Elbowdrop and Dude punishes him in the corner. Dude works the neck with a body scissors as Vinnie Mac joins us at ringside.

Austin breaks the move and yells at Vince, but Dude rolls him up for two. Austin posts Dude as Vince "observes" from ringside, near the timekeeper, wink, wink. Dude bails and Austin tries a piledriver, but as usual he gets backdropped. He hurts his knee and Dude leaves for the ring as Vince taunts Austin. Austin stalks him, but Dude returns the favor on that clothesline from behind. Dude tries a suplex in, but Austin blocks, so Dude necksnaps him to the floor. The ref counts, but Vince tells Austin to "be a man and get

back in," and that the ref is fired if he reaches ten, so Austin beats the count.

Dude hooks the ABDOMINAL STRETCH OF DOOM (with which he got past the awesome challenge of Steve Blackman, though under dubious circumstances) and Vince goes crazy, telling the timekeeper to ring the bell. Austin reverses the move, and Vince goes equally crazy, telling him to ignore everything he just said. Funny stuff.

Brawl outside, and Austin suplexes Dude onto the stairs. They fight into the crowd and Austin dumps him back in, and into the ring. Dude comes back with a neckbreaker. Sweet chin music is blocked, and the ref gets bumped. Stunner is blocked with the Mandible Claw, and Vince revives the ref . . . unsuccessfully. This would actually become a story line point as Vince declared the ref unfit and took the job himself at the next PPV.

Austin dumps Love, but scuffles with Vince. Love charges with a chair, but gets it back in his face. Austin chairshots Vince out cold, and heads back in for a little KICK WHAM STUNNER action, and counts the pin himself at 18:48. It was later decided to be a DQ win for Dude Love, justifying the rematch at Over the Edge '98. Great brawl that got a little overwhelmed by the story line at times. The next month, they would solve that problem by making the story the focal point of the match and building on it. ****

Vince and the Dude regrouped while a rematch for the next show, *Over the Edge*, was signed between Steve Austin and Dude Love. This time, Vince announced that he would personally referee the match while Pat Patterson would handle ring announcing and Gerald Brisco would do the timekeeping honors. Here's my review:

WWF Title Match:
Steve Austin v. Dude Love

Words can't even describe how brilliantly and meticulously scripted this must have been. Finkel reads off glowing words about Pat Patterson . . . on cue cards . . . to introduce him. Then Patterson kisses Gerald Brisco's butt, including the name, address, and phone number of the Brisco Brothers bodyshop (the number was spraypainted on the prop cars by the entranceway, too) and then introduces Mr. McMahon and Dude Love. He refuses to introduce a "bum" like Steve Austin, so Austin gets no intro. Undertaker then makes a surprise appearance as the troubleshooter.

They start with a normal wrestling match, and then the genius of the booking kicks in. They get outside the ring and Dude takes control with some illegal moves, so Patterson suddenly announces that "This is a reminder that this match is No-DQ." Austin slams Dude right onto the timekeeper's table, knocking over Brisco (he holds up the hammer to show that he's still ready to "ring the fucking bell"). Dude takes a mammoth clothesline off the railing to the concrete and they brawl over to the car-wreck section of the entranceway. Patterson announces that "This is a reminder that this match is falls-count-anywhere." Brilliant stuff.

McMahon counts a few two-counts after some crazy bumps by both Love and Austin, swearing out loud each time Austin kicks out. Brisco, Patterson, and Undertaker follow them over, and Brisco is still carrying the bell! Too funny. Austin nicks himself on the forehead and bleeds all over the place. More crazy bumps from Love, then they head back to the ring. Austin with the Stunner, but McMahon won't count the pin. He screams at Patterson to throw a chair in and Austin argues with him. Dude swings at Austin, who ducks, and McMahon takes a monster chairshot and is out cold. Stone Cold Stunner on Dude.

Another ref runs in and counts two . . . but Patterson drags him out of the ring and slugs him. Dude gets the Mandible Claw on Austin and Patterson slides into the ring to count 1 . . . 2 . . . but Undertaker drags him out! Then he chokeslams him through the announcer's table! The crowd is just nuts at this point.

Brisco slides in, counts two, and UT drags him out and puts him through the Spanish table! Austin fights off the claw, kicks Dude in the nuts, and Stunners him, then drags McMahon over and physically forces the unconscious McMahon to count three as Austin retains the title in one of the most emotionally exhausting matches I've ever seen. ****½ The crowd is just cheering Austin nonstop as we end the show.

SCENE FIVE
Look Out Below!

So now the plot was starting to thicken, as Undertaker (after making an appearance during that match) was thrust into the main-event scene again. The D-X v. Nation feud was also starting to heat up as the Nation (with new member Owen Hart) beat D-X in a six-man on that show, making the collision between The Rock and HHH seem all the more inevitable. Vince, meanwhile, was upset with Dude Love, feeling that Mick had let him down on two straight PPVs. So he fired Dude Love, and in fact that character has not been seen since. But at the end of the show, a new and improved Mankind (complete with shirt and tie) saved Vince from an Austin beating, and Foley was once again back in Vince's good graces.

Well, sort of. Because for *King of the Ring*, while Austin was scheduled to face Kane in what was basically a no-win situation (whoever bled first would be the loser, and Kane had no exposed skin to bleed), Vince wanted to punish Undertaker for interfering in his business, and test Foley's loyalty at the same time. So he put them in the second Hell in a Cell match, and hoped for the worst. And he got everything he had hoped for out of it. Here's my review:

Hell in a Cell II:
Mankind v. The Undertaker

Mick said in a later interview that his biggest mistake was asking Terry Funk for advice before this match. Funk's wisdom: "Start on top of the cage." So they did as Mick goaded UT into climbing up the cage. It should be noted that all the squares of fencing on the top were loose, so it wasn't just that one.

So UT tosses Mick off the top of the cage onto the Spanish table, and to be brutally honest, it lacks the same impact as when you're bombed and not expecting it. I mean, it was a nice bump and all, but there wasn't anything to build up to it. And on second viewing, Mick guides himself down by holding on to the cage as he falls. I mean, for full points on the dive, you have to free fall. The judges at the Olympics wouldn't allow a dive where the diver grabs the board to guide himself, would they? Anyway, all jesting aside . . . Terry Funk comes out to check on Mick and they stretcher him off, but Mick fights them off and climbs the cage again to a big pop.

Then comes the next Holy Shit Bump when UT gives Mick a half-assed chokeslam and Mick takes a bump sixteen feet through the cage to the mat below. UT goes for the ropewalk, but Foley pushes him off and gives us the famous shot of the tooth sticking out of his nose as his mouth bleeds. They fight to the floor and UT rams the stairs into him. UT goes for a tope suicida, but Mick ducks and UT hits the cage . . . and blades on camera. Doh!

Back in the ring and a Mankind piledriver on a chair gets two. Legdrop on a chair gets two. Double-arm DDT, and Mick rolls under the ring and retrieves his bag of thumbtacks. He puts the Mandible Claw on and UT drops him on the thumbtacks. Chokeslam on the thumbtacks. Tombstone finishes it. Okay, now for the major criticisms and why this is NOT a ****¾ MOTYC.

1. The actual moves done between the bumps were not well executed. The chokeslam through the cage was sloppy, with Mick basically falling backward. UT did a pretty perfunctory tope, and then made the rookie mistake of blading in clear view of the camera. That's just sloppiness. Go back and watch Badd Blood and compare with Shawn's primo bladejob in midair.

2. There were only a few actual wrestling moves done: Legdrop, DDT, Mandible Claw, chokeslam, tombstone. UT v. Shawn, the closest WWF match with which to compare this one, had smaller bumps by Shawn, but more of them and more intense ones, with better wrestling and better brawling in-between them.

3. The chokeslam bump was an accident.

4. Undertaker was working on a broken ankle and was very limited in his mobility.

Anyway, history has already judged this match as Match of the Year for 1998, but I thought Austin-Foley from Over the Edge was a better brawl, and Vince took just as good a bump at St. Valentine's Day Massacre. Foley bumping does not a match make, it just makes more money for the hospitals. My verdict: I'll be more generous than the workrate fanatics and go *, but the "Holy shit" factor from first watching it is totally gone after numerous replays have killed the uniqueness of the original viewing.

There you have it.

Foley spent yet another of his endless nights in a hospital to recover, but not before pulling himself off the stretcher backstage and doing a run-in during the main event when Kane upset Steve Austin to win the WWF title after a wayward chairshot from The Undertaker had busted Austin open. Fans shocked at the title reign ending so soon had little to fear—Austin regained the title, in what I felt was the better match, twenty-four hours later on *RAW*. But a question was now being asked about Undertaker's interference—could he be working with his own estranged brother, or with Vince McMahon, or both?

A title match was quickly signed for *Summerslam '98* between Austin and Undertaker, after Taker won a three-way match against Kane and Mankind for the number-one contender spot by impersonating his brother, but that title match was two months away. In fact, there was still an-

other show in-between—*Fully Loaded*—and the question from the fans became: "Why should we care about this one when the real attraction is still a month away?"

To solve that problem, Vince Russo came up with the next instance of his not-yet-tired formula for these situations: The Wacky Mismatched Tag Champions Who Hate Each Other. In this case, the walking-freakshow team of Kane and Mankind destroyed the now-babyface New Age Outlaws on *RAW* and won the tag-team titles, which was coincidentally around the time that they announced a main event of Steve Austin and Undertaker v. Kane and Mankind for *Fully Loaded*.

> **T**hat's another hallmark of Vince Russo's brilliance—building up a hot babyface team and then squashing them.

SCENE SIX
The Gang Warz Begin

Meanwhile, down in the ranks of the peons, scum, and other mid-carders, the Nation of Domination and D-Generation X were having quite the interesting little war. Now, I can say (and often have said) many bad things about Vince Russo's generally bassackward approach to wrestling booking. Crash TV, endless run-ins, illogical B-movie story lines ripped right out of a Shannon Tweed vehicle, you name it. However, while Russo was rapidly gaining power on the booking team, he was also pushing his philosophy of giving equal time to the "less important" members of the crew, namely the mid-card stars who would need to carry the promotion later on. And the mid-carders he really bestowed this push upon were HHH and The Rock. Sure, the Nation and D-X were along for the ride and some of them were even elevated as a result. But realistically, the WWF knew they had a pair of sure things in HHH and The Rock.

Let's review, shall we: Tall? Check. Full head of hair? Check. Muscular? Check. So with all three demanding criteria of being a top-level WWF superstar fulfilled, they set about crafting the mid-card around them in hopes of getting those two to the next level. Of course, in HHH's case, it just took that much longer for him to catch up to Rocky.

The whole feud between the Nation and D-X started when the usual heated words about who should win the Nobel Peace Prize turned into fisticuffs, and then got promoted on PPV. That's the normal progression of things in wrestling. However, this feud had a bit of a different twist to it: The infamous "Nation Parody."

Borrowing an idea that WCW had for one of their top-level feuds (having the New World Order dress up and spoof the famed Four Horsemen), D-Generation X followed the same formula, albeit in a more tasteful manner. In WCW's case, Arn Anderson had just retired the previous week and given a very heartfelt (and ratings-grabbing) speech that moved the fans. The nWo made a mockery of it, eclipsing Arn's one big moment in the sun and creating a new catchphrase for ringleader Kevin Nash as a result of his mocking of the "Spot" monologue given by Arn. But while that angle had some very deep and real backstage tension behind it, the WWF's version was strictly played for laughs.

But more than that, it had an interesting side effect. Because, you see, in order for the Nation

> **T**he worst part about the "Horsemen Parody" angle was that the original interview segment featured a heartfelt retirement by Arn Anderson when he gave his spot in the team to Curt Hennig (aka Mr. Perfect). A few weeks later, Hennig turned on the Horsemen and joined the nWo, effectively burying the Four Horsemen name for good.

to be effectively parodied, they needed characters *to* parody. Up until then, it was generally just Rock's superhero poses and bravado backed up by three, big, black guys who didn't say or do much. So, leading up to the parody, suddenly we had D-Lo Brown playing a sycophantic weasel who repeated everything The Rock said and waggled his head a lot. Kama Mustafa became a womanizing playboy called The Godfather. And Mark Henry . . . well, he was still deadweight, but some things are too much to ask.

So armed with new and easily identifiable characters to be mocked, D-X went out one week and let them have it. HHH was "The Crock," complete with painted-on eyebrows and self-centered attitude. Road Dogg became "B-Lo," agreeing with everything the Crock said. Billy Gunn did what he did best, standing around as The Godfather and looking dumb. And X-Pac put on his best blackface paint and overstuffed bodysuit and played "Mizark" Henry, a nickname that actually stuck with the real Mark Henry for quite a while. The Nation reacted with the usual disgust and outrage, and pretty soon Rock had challenged HHH to a match at *Fully Loaded*, title v. title, for both the European and intercontinental belts.

Then, a couple of weeks before the show, another twist: D-Lo Brown scored a huge upset over HHH on *RAW*, using Nation interference to win the European title. D-Lo also got lucky in the form of an injury angle—he was beaten handily by Dan Severn around this time and had suffered a tear of his pectoral muscle. Now, normally that wouldn't be a particularly pleasant thing, but in his case it was a relatively minor injury, which he worked through by wearing a padded, chest protector during his matches. Of course, since he was a heel, the amount of time he actually wore the protective gear far exceeded the time needed for the injury to heal, thus annoying the fans whenever he'd use it for

nefarious purposes. D-Lo had his new gimmick. He was thrust into a summer-long feud with X-Pac over that title, while the match at *Fully Loaded* between HHH and Rock would just be for Rock's IC title.

The catch? It was to be best two out of three falls, which immediately made people worry about the potential quality since, in some circles, Rock's not-so-joking nickname was "Chin-Rock," after his tendency to go to a rest hold at a moment's notice. As it turned out, it wasn't the resting but the run-ins that sank the match in the end. Here's my review:

Intercontinental Title Match, Two out of Three falls: The Rock v. Hunter Hearst Helmsley

Both the Nation and D-X were banned from ringside, so that should tip you off to something right away.

Rock beatdown to start, and a lariat gets two. Rock gets some shaky-leg kicks, but walks into a lariat. Chyna nails him. Rock counters the Pedigree, but gets tossed. We brawl. Nothing of note, just wasting time. (Cf. the Iron Man match at Judgment Day where no out-of-ring brawling was necessary.)

Back in, Rock lays the smackdown and gets a lariat for two. HHH gets a desperation neckbreaker to come back. Suplex sets up the regal kneedrop, which gets two. HHH dishes some Connecticut Violence, but gets tossed out. Back out, more brawling. Mark Henry joins us for Run-In number one and splashes HHH on the floor, before Billy Gunn (Run-In number two) saves. Rock adds a shot with the belt, and gets two. Swinging neckbreaker gets two. Punches get two, and Rock hits the chinlock to stall. This first fall is a total write off. Crowd agrees with me, losing patience.

HHH fights out, but Rock lariat gets two. Does he think he's Stan Hansen tonight or something? Back out, AGAIN. Some quick choking results and back in for a Hurricane DDT for two. Back to the chinlock. Sure, it's only a thirty-minute match, why not? Rock rams HHH face-first to the mat for two. HHH comes back and USES THE KNEE. Now Godfather joins us (Run-In number three), but gets cut off by the Outlaws (Run-In number four). Why bother with that?

Rock chokes HHH out. He does some posing to waste more time, and now D-Lo does Run-In number five, but HHH blasts him. HHH turns around and walks into a Rock Bottom to lose the first fall at 20:19. Hunter gets 1:00 to rest (and use up another minute) and we're off again.

Rock tosses HHH out and it's more brawling. Rock slingshots him into the Spanish table, but IT DOESN'T BREAK. Quick, fire the producer. Back in, People's Elbow (now named as such at this point) gets two. Double KO follows as Chyna kills D-Lo. Now X-Pac (Run-In number six), comes in, hits the X-Factor on Rock, and HHH gets two. Chairs get involved and the ref is bumped. Chyna (Run-In number seven) DDTs Rock on the chair and HHH gets the fall at 26:33 to even it up. One-minute rest and we're rolling.

HHH covers the unconscious Rock for two. More brawling outside. Back in, facebuster and lariat get two. Rock Samoan drops HHH for two. Slugfest leads to the Pedigree . . . as time expires at 30:00. Crowd is upset at that one. With five brawling segments, three stalling periods, and seven run-ins, it becomes apparent the booking was more protected than Charlie Sheen before a night with Heidi Fleiss. **

The quality of the match was relatively immaterial next to the larger objective, however: Get both guys over as legitimate threats. HHH always had a perception problem since his career had been predicated on being either the Connecticut Blueblood or Shawn Michaels's Zany Sidekick up until then. HHH, serious main eventer, wasn't something that the fans could easily accept. They did have a headstart, however, as Hunter got an over prematch spiel, if nothing else, by doing a passable Michael Buffer imitation and telling the fans "Let's get ready to suck it!"

A word on profanity, if I may:

That's another thing that Vince Russo was

helping to influence during his rise to power in 1998—a more realistic way of talking. Part of the whole reason that comedians imitate "wrestling promos" is because they're generally clichéd and filled with things that no rational human being would ever say in a legitimate fight situation. People who are 6' 3" and 300 pounds just don't feel the need to censor themselves when trying to express their feelings. If they want to say "ass" and not "butt" or "behind," it was much more realistic to simply let that happen and then bleep them out from the TV side of things.

Thanks to Bret Hart's tirade they were airing RAW on a seven-second tape delay anyway, so why not take advantage of that? Now certainly there were lines that shouldn't be touched upon—explicit sex talk, the f-bomb, or outright racist talk, to name three—but when D-X responded to the taunts of the heels by pointing to their crotches and telling their opponents to "suck it," it left little question as to what their feelings on the matter were. Besides, thirteen-year-old, insecure teenagers ate that stuff up.

Anyway . . .

HHH was now, in a broad sense of the word, over as a babyface. The fans still had no real vested interest in his matches or character, but they thought he was a pretty cool guy and liked him better than The Rock, so it was enough to muddle through the summer with and establish his own identity apart from Shawn Michaels and the Clique. Also, at *Fully Loaded*, Steve Austin and Undertaker successfully defeated Kane and Mankind to win the tag-team titles, although they would lose them back in a four-way tag match on *RAW* a few weeks later under dubious circumstances, which seemed to involve Undertaker lying down for a Kane tombstone and deliberately not kicking out.

SCENE SEVEN
The Brawl for All

The only other real feud of note going on at that point featured Owen Hart taking on Ken Shamrock in a variety of submission-gimmick matches, which only cemented Shamrock's reputation in Canada as a hated enemy. But while Shamrock was a legitimate, real-life badass, the WWF ran with another idea, reportedly from John "Bradshaw" Leyfield, which was intended to create a pretend badass, but as a result nearly sank their main-event program for the next two months. The idea was this: take sixteen of the WWF's perceived "tough guys," give them boxing gloves, and put them into a legitimate boxing/wrestling hybrid competition (ala the UFC) and see who actually is the toughest.

Longtime favorite of the Japanese (and Jim Ross) Steve "Dr. Death" Williams was brought in as a ringer, and the idea was for him to waltz through the tournament, impress the hell out of the cynical fans, and then challenge Steve Austin as Vince McMahon's new rough-and-ready enforcer for the fall programs.

Well, they pretty much went oh for three with those goals. The competition was a disaster of epic proportions, and its name was the *Brawl for All*.

The thinking behind throwing this . . . thing . . . out there on *RAW* every week was that big,

strong guys in the wrestling world should translate to being big, strong guys in the real world—only it didn't. Real-life mat-wrestling specialist Dan Severn was thrown into the field without any knowledge of striking, for instance. Ex-boxer Marc Mero faced the more martial-arts-focused Steve Blackman and got pummeled. The idea behind the tournament may have been solid, but everyone forgot that boxing is not wrestling and vice versa. Wrestling fans chanted "We want wrestling!" throughout the tournament and the competitors fell one-by-one to a staggering series of injuries, injuries that no one had even thought could occur outside of extraordinary circumstances. And that was just the first round.

By the time they made it to the second round, it was an acknowledged clusterfuck by both fans and WWF officials alike. People who lost in the first round were subbed for those they lost to because of the injuries. Mark Cantebury suffered a career-ending back injury, which he worked through until he could no longer perform. But through all of it, the goal was simply to have Steve Williams kick butt and then go on to challenge Steve Austin.

And so, fittingly, in his second-round match, Williams was knocked cold on his ass by jobber Bart Gunn with a left, and to add salt to the wound he had been injured falling down earlier in the match, tearing his hamstring and leaving him on the shelf for months. Gunn went on to win the tournament, easily storming through Kama Mustafa and Bradshaw, but it proved to be worse for his career than losing would have been because Jim Ross wanted nothing to do with pushing him, and instead of getting the career-making boost that his ex-partner Billy Gunn had gotten, he was banished to Japan until his contract expired. No one talks about the *Brawl for All* on WWF TV anymore, for obvious reasons.

Bart Gunn got the last laugh. He's currently one of the biggest stars in Japan, competing as Mike Barton for All-Japan Pro Wrestling.

SCENE EIGHT
Changes Come Around

Things kept steamrolling toward *Summerslam* in the meantime, and they used AC/DC's "Highway to Hell" as the theme song and played it incessantly on every show. The *Summerslam* PPV itself was a tremendous success, drawing a huge buy rate and selling out Madison Square Garden. In the main event, Steve Austin pinned The Undertaker cleanly in quite a decent match, while HHH defeated The Rock in a ladder match to win the IC title. That match would set both men on a path to the main event, although Rocky got there faster. In fact, during the match the crowd changed allegiances due to the hard work of both, chanting "Rocky, Rocky!" in a nonsarcastic manner for the first time since his introduction in 1996.

The New Age Outlaws also recemented their position as the dominant team of 1998 (although there wasn't much competition), beating Mankind in a handicap match to regain the tag titles. This marked the official face turn for Mankind, one from which he never turned back. Also, in a loss that turned out to be a win, Jeff Jarrett was defeated by X-Pac and was forced to shave his long, blond locks off, leaving the short look of a serious upper-card heel instead of a gimmick wrestler. Soon after, he introduced the WCW escapee Debra McMichael as his new manager and finally had a persona that people could almost get into.

The winds of change, in fact, were blowing all throughout the WWF's booking strategy as they were beating *Nitro* more or less on a weekly

The haircut Jarrett received proved to be another one of those tragic wrestling stipulations where no one remembers to bring sharpened clippers to the show, and the resulting in-ring haircut is more of a trim than anything. None of these matches can top Jim Cornette getting shaved in Mid-South, however, as the electric razor broke and Tommy Rogers was forced to shave Jim's head bald with a dry, disposable razor.

basis, but not standing pat. The WWF was still determined to create main-event stars out of HHH, Rock, and Mankind, although HHH was announced to be suffering from a knee injury that would keep him out of action for months to come, thus derailing their plans somewhat.

The Austin Express kept rolling, however, and without Steve Williams to provide the next challenge for him, it was revealed that in fact Undertaker and Kane were working together, and were working with Vince McMahon in order to end Steve Austin's title reign. This was the beginning of the story line most consider to be Vince Russo's masterpiece (in terms of wrestling story lines, of course).

Also around this time, on August 2 to be exact, a new WWF show was launched on the USA network: *Sunday Night Heat*. Intended as a summertime stunt for ratings, it scored such impressive numbers that USA put it on the permanent lineup. The show featured the first on-screen role for Vince's son, Shane, as he played announcer along with Jim Ross, bringing the word "Boo-yah!" into popular use.

Okay, I lied about that last part. But Shane of course figures into our story a little later on.

So with the brothers Kane and Undertaker now working together on the side of evil (which made those who thought the whole underlying story line was a little silly even more convinced

Other Shane McMahon catchphrases that failed the test of time: "My Pops" in reference to Vince, and "Kingfish" in reference to Jerry "The King" Lawler. However, even I use "Shane-O-Mac" to describe Shane these days, so kudos to him on going one for four, at the very least.

of that), Vince booked Austin into what was basically a handicap match at the next show, *Breakdown*, against Kane and Undertaker. The match wasn't exactly what you'd call a mat classic, as both guys pinned Austin at the same time after a double-chokeslam, and controversy reigned. Austin was pissed off, yada yada.

In a truly rare bit of continuity, Vince McMahon claimed the "Smoking Skull" version of the WWF title that was custom-made for Austin, and put it over his mantle as a trophy. It was forgotten about until Austin regained the WWF title in 1999, at which point the writing team actually remembered about the skull belt and had Austin reclaim it to finish the story line.

Meanwhile, a phenomenon was about to be created. The Rock was indeed receiving a good amount of cheers instead of boos, and in fact the rest of the Nation seemed to resent that. And when it was announced that the WWF needed a new number-one contender to the WWF title, and that it would be decided in a three-way cage match between Rock, Ken Shamrock, and Mankind at the *Breakdown* PPV, well, that just made the situation all the worse. Rocky won the match to become the number-one contender and before you knew it, the Nation went and turned on him. Ain't that always the way? Here's my review:

Triple Threat Cage Match: The Rock v. Ken Shamrock v. Mankind

The Rock cuts a promo and then Mankind replies with one of the funniest promos I've ever heard. Shamrock gets booed in Canada as usual. You'd think after getting booed in every city in Canada for the past year that it'd dawn on him that he's not very well liked up here. Rocky gets the mad face pop of the century.

Lots of random brawling to start as Mankind makes the occasional sneaky escape attempt while the other two are fighting. I'm almost afraid to hear how loud the pop for the Elbow will be. Goofy spot as Shamrock puts Mankind in an abdominal stretch and Rock puts Shamrock in one. Double hiptoss spot to break. Rock and Mankind end up teaming up and beating on Shamrock. Then Rock turns on Mankind and he and Shamrock team up. Shamrock goes for the anklelock on Mankind so Rock breaks him up. Then Mankind and Shamrock double-team Rock and the crowd boos like nuts.

Mankind sets up some sort of dancing spot and Rock comes back. DDT on Mankind, spinning DDT on Shamrock. DOUBLE PEOPLE'S ELBOW! The place explodes! Rocky tries to climb out, but gets stopped. Crotch-first to the ropes. Rocky crotches Shamrock and Rockbottoms Mankind for two. Huge "Shamrock sucks!" chant just to rub it in.

Shamrock with the belly-to-belly and anklelock, but Mankind breaks it up. Mankind tries to climb out, but Rocky stops him. Rocky is holding on to him by the hair and gets him to the top of the cage. Shamrock climbs up to join him, but gets knocked off. Rocky gets knocked off and Mankind goes to the top of the cage, but misses the elbow! Everyone is out in the middle until Shamrock crawls for the door. Rocky is busted open. Shamrock gets pulled in by Mankind and brings a chair in with him. Mankind DDTs Shammy and gets the chair, nailing Shamrock to a huge pop. Mankind climbs out of the cage like an idiot while Rock merely rolls over for the pin! Rocky wins! Great match! ****

SCENE NINE
The Sock Puppet Heard 'Round the World

Rock remained embroiled in the self-destruction of the Nation over the next month or so (D-Lo and Mark Henry went their own ways, while Godfather became the fun-loving pimp with no connection to his former team), leaving the world title situation in the hands of Mr. McMahon. And the night after *Breakdown*, he appeared to be ready to solve it, bringing out both Undertaker and Kane in preparation for giving one of them the title.

Astute readers probably noticed that the belt that Vince was going to present was the old version of the title belt, which had been retired months earlier. In fact, their new belt had been damaged and was still being remade, necessitating the use of the "classic" design that night.

However, as usual, Steve Austin felt the need to interject himself, in this case driving an ice resurfacer down to ringside and attacking Vince while the brothers looked on apathetically. Vince immediately snapped and discharged the brothers from his employ, and made yet another match between them as the main event of the next PPV, *Judgment Day*, for the WWF title.

The added twist for that match was that Austin would referee it, and if he didn't declare a winner, he would be fired. The brothers showed their gratitude by turning on Vince and breaking his leg. Soon after, Vince (who was now wheelchair-bound), hired WCW reject Ray Traylor to re-create the Big Bossman character as his bodyguard. But not before Vince was forced to spend a night in the hospital to have the cast put on his leg, an event that spawned a couple of very interesting things.

First of all, Vince was attacked by Steve Austin (dressed as a doctor) and violated with an enema hose after being beaten up with a bedpan. But even more interesting was the dawn of a new relationship between Vince and the increasingly lovable Mick Foley. Having turned face at *Summerslam '98*, Mick was cruising aimlessly through the mid-card and occasionally annoying Vince, most notably by offering him a drink of his (half-finished) Big Gulp as Vince was being loaded into the ambulance following the attack by Undertaker and Kane. And Mick showed up again, visiting Vince in the hospital to cheer him up, this time bringing Yurple the Clown with him as entertainment. Mick also brought a sock puppet with him, which he dubbed Mr. Socko, and which in turn annoyed Vince even more. However, the fan reaction to the sock puppet was astonishingly passionate, and signs and faux-Sockos turned up by the dozens at *RAW* among the fans. So Mick, ever the showman, started amending his Mandible Claw finisher by sticking a sock on his hand, and thus becoming even more over as a babyface as a direct result.

Yurple the Clown is, as far as I know, no relation to Doink the Clown. Despite the staggering coincidence involved in two people being legally named "the Clown."

After being annoyed by Foley to the point of insanity, Vince's next step was to form a stable to help take care of Austin—the creatively named Corporation. And his first inductee was Ken Shamrock, who was frustrated and confused as a babyface. Vince's reasoning was one of the strangest lines I've ever heard uttered by him: "You're the World's Most Dangerous Man, and every corporation needs a dangerous man!" I've gotta wonder who Disney and Microsoft have hiding in their cubicles now. Shamrock's heel turn paid immediate dividends as he blew through the one-night intercontinental title tournament (HHH had to vacate due to his injuries), defeating X-Pac with the anklelock to win.

Judgment Day came and went, and as usual the under-card was junk outside of a decent Shamrock-Mankind match. 1998 wasn't exactly the best year for pure wrestling fans as far as the WWF was concerned, it should be noted. Hell, Mick Foley getting tossed off a cage won Match of the Year, which should tell you something right there. Anyway, in the main event of the PPV, Austin indeed failed to declare the winner, instead choosing to give Stunners to both Kane and Undertaker and then declaring himself the winner. In reality, the fans were the true losers because the match was quite possibly the worst main event in years. An outraged Vince, immediately following Austin's selfish refusal to play along, fired him on the spot and that should have been that.

Austin, however, was nothing if not pesky, and he showed up on *RAW* the next night dressed in hunting gear. And indeed it was for Vince's benefit, as Austin kidnapped his former boss and held him hostage throughout the show, leading up to a rather silly angle where he "shot" him with a prop gun that produced a BANG 3:16 sign from the muzzle, like in a cartoon. Vince, ever the proponent of highbrow entertainment, pissed his pants in fear, literally. The various levels of idiocy involved there aside, Austin then stuck a piece of paper into Vince's pocket, which was presumably his reason for being back on WWF TV one day after being fired. But then it's not like anyone has believed a stipulation in wrestling since 1985, so no one had worried about it too much.

Earlier in that show, Austin was showing his gun off to a cop, who commented, "That's a nice toy." This either shows a staggering lack of intelligence on the part of the story line police, or it was merely a nice bit of foreshadowing toward the payoff. Years of experience with wrestling have taught me that it was probably the former.

SCENE TEN
The Deadly Game

Vince announced a tournament for the WWF title at *Survivor Series '98* with everyone expecting Rock to win it. Shortly after, the official beginning of the McMahon Family Era was seen as *Heat* commentator Shane McMahon revealed that, in fact, it was him who had brought Austin back into the WWF, with a five-year contract no less, and a guarantee for one more title shot, plus a berth in the tournament. It seemed that Shane was upset that Vince had neglected him all those years while he was busy running the WWF and all. Vince, in a show of tough love, busted his son down to lowly referee and disowned him.

But Vince's childless state didn't last long because Mankind took to him like the son Vince now didn't have anymore. Vince was touched by Mick's loyalty (well, as touched as Vince ever gets) and decided to give him a present to reward him: his own title; namely, the hardcore title, in recognition of his years as the Hardcore Legend. Vince let him know that he was like a son to him, which prompted Foley's classic response ("Thanks . . . Dad") and Vince's disgusted double-take. Amazingly, the hardcore title would not only outlive its initial joke nature, but become almost as prestigious as the women's title! Well, almost.

The Rock.
Still the coolest guy
in wrestling.

The Big Cheese himself,
Vince McMahon.

Chris Jericho, the Ayatollah of Rock 'N' Rollah.

The "man-beast," Rhyno, stares down Olympic hero Kurt Angle.

Rhyno attempts to prove that Kurt Angle may be a choker.

Kurt Angle cranks on the devastating Angle-Lock submission hold.

Undertaker, role model for greasy bikers everywhere.

Undertaker and his half-brother Kane—they are friends here, in case you've lost track.

Undertaker gives Test an elbow in the corner.

The lovely and talented Stacy Keibler, who does nothing, but does it really well.

The Rock gives the fans
what they came to see.

Chris Jericho keeps his belt after
another successful defense.

Booker T, 5-time former WCW champion and master of the Spinaroonie.

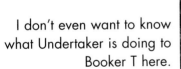

I don't even want to know what Undertaker is doing to Booker T here.

Matt Hardy—the "smart" Hardy Boy.

Jeff Hardy—just hanging around.

Rob Van Dam, the only guy more self-centered than me.

Rob Van Dam likes to get high, as shown here.

Lita pins Ivory after a Moonsault.

Trish Stratus drops Molly Holly crotch-first onto the top rope. Does that even work on girls?

The Rock and Chris Jericho, Wacky Tag-Team Partners Who Hate Each Other.

Vince and Linda McMahon, fresh off the old "drug my wife and have her committed" gag.

Stephanie McMahon, the head writer and most annoying person on TV.

The Rock reacts to a sneak preview of Vince McMahon's new XLL—the Xtreme Lacrosse League.

Lance Storm—hero for the humorless everywhere.

Brock Lesnar—the future savior of the WWE?

Bradshaw wins the European title for all the Texans who live there.

Billy Kidman hits
Tajiri with a DDT.

Billy Kidman, caught in
Tajiri's complex, but cool,
Tarantula move.

Tajiri refreshes Kidman's
memory as to the location
of the ring.

Diamond Dallas Page (DDP) suggests to Kane that he should find a way to channel his anger properly.

This is Kane's solution.

Presumably Mankind won a tournament in Rio de Janeiro to claim the belt legally.

Survivor Series was the first PPV booked entirely by Vince Russo, and it marks the true beginning of his run as the real behind-the-scenes power in the WWF. Mankind, Steve Austin, The Rock, and Undertaker all advanced to the semifinals, and in the Austin v. Mankind match, Russo's booking saw its finest moments. Here's my review:

Semi-Final Number One: Mankind v. Steve Austin

This match was probably the single best fifteen minutes of Vince Russo's entire tenure. Austin kicks Mankind's ass to start, tearing off the tuxedo jacket and leaving Mick in a ragged dress shirt, tie, and pants, a look (and a shirt) that he would retain until only last month.

Vince is wheeled to ringside to ensure Austin gets screwed over. Mick escapes the Stunner and runs away. Austin follows and they brawl down the aisle. Back to the ring, where Mick takes over. Austin fights back and stomps a mudhole in him (but neglects to walk it dry), but goes outside and gets rammed into the post. Mick grabs a chair and DDTs Austin on it for two. Piledriver attempt is reversed and the Stunner gets two because Vince is "miraculously" able to leap out of his wheelchair and punk out the ref.

Disowned son and lowly referee Shane McMahon comes in as Austin hits another Stunner, and it also gets two, because Shane shocks the hell out of everyone by stopping to flip the double-bird to Austin. Austin is so shocked he doesn't notice the Stooges coming in to administer a beatdown and a chairshot, and that allows Mankind to get the pin (with Shane's blessing this time) at 10:23 to advance to the finals. And the Master Plan is thus a success. Good brawl + Good soap opera = Sports Entertainment 101. ***½*

So with Mankind in the finals, Rock advanced past The Undertaker after Kane interfered, causing his brother to be disqualified (thus making Undertaker a heel and Kane a face and causing the writers to change their minds, yet again, on who had started the fire that had burned Kane way back when), setting up Rock v. Mankind for the WWF title, which everyone pretty much expected given Mick's "favorite son" status with Vince as of late. But that would change very soon. Here's my review:

WWF World Title Tournament Final: Mankind v. The Rock

Slow start. Rock gains control, but Mick goes to a chinlock. It was fascinating reading about this in Mick's book, because he admitted that he had absolutely no idea what they were going to do and the entire match was called on the fly from that chinlock. It doesn't make the resulting match any BETTER to know about that sort of thing, but it's always interesting to read about it.

To the floor, where The Rock gets a suplex and goes after Vince, who has joined us at ringside. Rock suplexes Foley into the crowd, where they brawl. Into the ring, back to the chinlock for another planning session. Mick fights out and gives him the Cactus clothesline to the floor, and they brawl again. Mick grabs the stairs, but gets bashed with a chair, then takes another shot in the head with it for good measure. It gets a two-count for Rock back in the ring. Mick comes back and drops a Cactus elbow on him. More brawling. Mick legdrops Rock on the announcer's table, which gives him a two-count back in the ring. Rock gets a fluke DDT and mounts a comeback. He hits the floor again (oy vey!), and Mick launches himself, but misses, and goes through the Spanish table.

Back in, the People's Elbow gets two. Foley comes back with the double-arm DDT and gets the Mandible Sock. Rock counters with Rock Bottom. It gets two. Rock then hooks a completely incongruous Sharp-

shooter, and of course, Mr. McMahon plays his part and tells the timekeeper to "ring the bell." Gee, where have I seen that before?

Rock gets his first WWF title at 17:15, turning heel in the process (although he never really turned face after leaving the Nation, officially) and becoming the Corporate Champion. Quite the swerve there, although the match sucked. *½ Still, it was realistically the third match for both guys that night, so you can't expect too much from them.

It pretty much all went downhill for Russo from here, for those keeping track.

SCENE ELEVEN

This Book Must Weigh 300 Pounds, Then

The next night on *RAW*, Rock defended his newly won title against Steve Austin in that promised title match, and it scored one of the highest ratings in wrestling history as a result, ending in an Austin DQ victory. But Austin had now used up his only title shot, and wouldn't get any more . . . unless he could win the *Royal Rumble*. And before that could happen, Vince McMahon had yet another roadblock for the Rattlesnake—Austin had to defeat Undertaker in a Buried Alive match at the next PPV, *Rock Bottom*.

Meanwhile, Mankind got his rematch with The Rock at that show, cementing his babyface status. Rock retained the title on a technicality (he passed out to the Mandible Claw, but Vince protested that he didn't actually say "I quit" and thus was still the champion—a logical twist that is idiotic on so many levels that I don't have the space to list them all here) and Austin defeated Undertaker in a match so hideously stupid that I just have to include a review here:

Buried Alive:
The Undertaker v. Steve Austin

Michael Cole truly hits his stride as a dumbass in this match when he came roaring out of the gate and into the homestretch by declaring that the headstone beside the grave "weighs in excess of 3,000 pounds" and thus gave me my running gag for this match. He followed up by wondering how Austin could beat Undertaker at his own match. I dunno, maybe the same way Mankind beat Undertaker at his own match and everyone else under Vince Russo always beats someone at their own match?

Brawl outside to start. They fight into the dirt. Cole helpfully points out all the digging tools lying around, like the shovels and hoes. SAVE THE H . . . ah, never mind. Into the ring, Austin gets a Thesz press and elbow. And that's enough of that wrestling crap, so we head out again. Austin slams UT onto the floor and into the 340-pound steel stairs. Taker swats Austin away and into the 765-pound Spanish announcer table, which breaks. Austin tries a piledriver, but it's reversed. Into the ring, UT chokes him. Yeah, way to show that moveset, Mark.

We walk leisurely back to the gravesite (nice of Austin to oblige). Punching and rolling in the dirt follow. Austin nails Undertaker with a 1,200-pound piece of railing, and they struggle over the grave. Undertaker falls in. He hits Austin with a burial wreath, at 220-pounds, and they have a dramatic showdown in the grave. Wow, how Bergman.

Taker grabs a shovel (520-pounds), but Austin beats on him. Austin flees, but gets hit in the knee and crumples. They brawl again, nothing of note. Back to ringside, Undertaker wallops him with a chair (a mere 380-pounds). Cole notes that the crowd "doesn't know what to make of it." That, and "sitting in awe" both translate to "Zzzzzz." You hear both of them a lot during Undertaker matches.

Taker rams Austin into the post, which at 1,459 pounds should knock Austin into a coma, and choke-slams him back in the ring. Well, that's great, dumbass, now you've put him out five hundred feet away from the place you need to. UT leads Austin back to the grave and finds a 349-pound gas can (empty), then tosses Austin into the grave. Cole helpfully points out that it's "six feet deep!" even though both guys were STANDING in it not five minutes before and it barely came up to their waists.

Austin fights out and clocks Taker with the GAS CAN OF DOOM, then hits a Stunner that knocks UT into the grave. End of match, right? No, stupid, Russo is booking. Austin heads to the back as Taker crawls out and hides, then a bad-looking semi-explosion comes out of the grave, followed by Kane. Michael Cole, paranormal philosopher, points out that Kane is "rising from the grave" in the same tones he might ask you to buy a PPV. That just really creeps me out for some reason.

Kane beats on Undertaker (for those, like me, who have trouble keeping score, this was obviously the "hate" portion of their love/hate/love/hate/love/ hate/love/hate/love/hate/love/hate/love/hate/love/ hate/love relationship) and tombstones him into the grave. Yeah, that looked REAL convincing, guys. Austin adds that last bit of idiocy by bringing a backhoe out, which very . . . slowly . . . dumps a load of dirt ("hundreds of pounds" worth in one scoop, sayeth Michael Cole) on UT, barely covering him, for the win at 21:30. Ye gods, what did we do to deserve this? Note to WWF bookers: Next time you want to try something like this, consult a backhoe driver beforehand. –*

So Austin would have his chance to enter the *Rumble* after all, and all was not lost for Mankind, either, because he had bullied Vince and Shane into giving him one last rematch with The Rock three days before the new year in Worcester, Massachusetts. And in that match, with the help of a Steve Austin chairshot, Mick Foley finally lived out his lifelong dream, capturing the WWF title on *RAW* to close out 1998 in fitting fashion.

But I don't think anyone was ready for what happened in 1999.

Act Four

The Russofiction (1999)

"I was dreaming when I wrote this/Forgive me if it goes astray"
—Prince

Champions as the year began:

WWF World Champion: Mankind

Intercontinental Champion: Ken Shamrock

Tag-Team Champions: Ken Shamrock and Big Bossman

European Champion: X-Pac

Light Heavyweight Champion: Gillberg (Duane Gill)

As regular readers of mine know, lots of things bug me. And specifically, lots of things in wrestling bug me. And even more specifically, Vince Russo bugs the hell out of me.

And this chapter will explain exactly why.

See, creativity is a good thing. Speaking as someone with his own nearly unlimited reserves of dumb ideas, I can fully understand where Russo was coming from with a lot of the stuff he tried. However, an equally important part of having ideas is having someone to filter the good ones from the stupid ones, and about halfway into the year Russo lost sight of that important part and began to think he was the sole reason for the success of the product.

The thing you have to understand about Vince Russo is that he wasn't the product of a wrestling background, at least not as much as those who grew up with the business. He was a video-store owner in New York who had become a fan later and gained an "in" by cohosting a radio show in which his cohost, John Arezzi, raked Vince McMahon over the coals about the steroid trials until McMahon basically bought the show by paying off Russo with a job as *WWF Magazine* editor. Russo's tastes in entertainment didn't lie in the traditional in-ring product, but rather in soap operas, bad movies, and action-hero clichés. Now, as a contributor to the overall product this would be a veritable boon, but not as the sole voice on the creative team. Jerry Springer got popular and then flamed out for a reason—the sort of smut being peddled by himself and Vince Russo had a short shelf-life and was mainly confined in appeal to the trailer-park trash demographic.

Jerry Springer is just as fake as wrestling, in case you're wondering. Ironically, the first time this was learned for the most part was via wrestling fans, when former world champion The Iron Sheik took a job playing a wrestler on the show under a different name.

SCENE ONE
The Royal Rumble

But let's start from the start and pick up where we'd left off last time—with the two main, on-going story lines: Undertaker's transformation into a heel and the Mankind v. Rock feud.

Apparently being buried alive at the last PPV of December had a reinvigorating effect on Undertaker because he returned early in January with a newer, darker look, and a big-ass druid cloak, like something fresh out of *The Exorcist*. And hey, that was a pretty cool idea in itself—guy gets buried, goes nuts, gets a darker image. No problem.

But Russo had to take it just *that* much further.

No, see, not only was he a darker Undertaker, but he was now an Undertaker who could actually hypnotize people into becoming his undead servants. The logical leap of faith required here actually made people nostalgic for 1994, when he was limited to mere instantaneous reincarnation and fighting his evil doppelganger.

Oh, and to top things off, he did a human sacrifice on *RAW* using a fake knife to slice open Dennis Knight and turn him into the zombie slave Mideon. Or Midian. Or any other alternate spelling, depending on who was doing the graphics that week. Why anyone would want Phineas Godwinn as their right-hand man is beyond me, but I'd also think that there's better ways of going about it than cutting his wrists open with a butcher knife. Later, the talent pool in his newly named Ministry of Darkness (as opposed to the Ministry of Sunshine, I guess) stepped up the recruiting drive when the Acolytes kidnapped Mabel at the *Royal Rumble* and turned him into Viscera, a hideous act that not only made him evil, but caused him to suddenly grow fake-looking contacts last used by Adam Bomb in 1994. Truly this was a force of unstoppable evil. Much like Rena Mero was becoming.

A word on Rena Mero, if I may.

Brought into the WWF with Marc Mero as his valet in 1996 under the name Sable, she quickly became even more popular than he was, probably more due to her leather catsuits and huge bazooms than her winning personality. By 1998, she was getting into the ring for a feud with Luna Vachon and looking pretty good. By the end of 1998, they had resurrected the dead women's title and put it on her. By the beginning of 1999, they were seriously talking with UPN about creating an entire show based around women's wrestling, with Sable as the lead star. Soon she had signed a lucrative deal with *Playboy* to pose nude, to the delight of drooling fanboys everywhere. Then she made the same mistake that every woman in the WWF has made (and will continue to make as long as Vince is running things): She thought people cared about her and she actually meant something. In-between half-assing her matches and doing media tours to promote her magazine spread, she decided to make a power play and demand more money. Whoops. Buh-bye, Rena, see you in B-movie hell. See also: Chyna and Wendi Richter. Stacy Keibler should also heed this warning. As mean and sexist as it may sound, North American wrestling has no tolerance for women as anything but sex objects or freakshow oddities on the bottom of the card because wrestling is run by sexist pigs with misogynistic tendencies. In this case, we were all getting sick of hearing Rena go on major talk shows and talk about all her "accomplishments"—like pioneering the bra-and-panties match and resurrecting mud wrestling for the '90s, I guess—while keeping a straight face and shilling her latest *Playboy* spread.

> **A**nd seriously, what kind of a born-again Christian poses nude for *Playboy*, anyway? Is there some kind of exemption in the Bible that I missed dealing with this?

But I digress.

The *Rumble* itself would have been largely unnotable had the writers not gone completely insane and suddenly decided that Vince McMahon winning it was a really swell idea. Yes, in 1999 Vince McMahon booked himself to enter the *Rumble* at number two, leave for a good forty-five minutes, return to do color commentary, and then stand around while The Rock interfered and pulled Steve Austin out, giving Vince the win. Have I mentioned lately what a genius that Vince is? On the other hand, that wasn't even the most pathetic act of self-promotion that Vince did that year, so really I have no reason to complain any louder about this one. Here's my review:

Royal Rumble Match:

Austin of course had number one from a rigged drawing the week previous, and Vince had number two. Intervals were ninety seconds this year, give or take, depending on what drugs the person doing the timing had taken over the course of the night. As an addendum, whoever could toss Austin would get a $100,000 bonus from Mr. McMahon.

Austin murders Vince to start. He opts not to toss him because doing so would indicate a desire to win the match, and according to Vince Russo winning and losing mean nothing anymore, so instead he opts to deliver more punishment and continue the oh-so-brilliant and oh-so-well-written story line for the match. This year's Rumble entrants are basically divided into two tiers: the jobbers and the stars. It's pretty easy to divine the pecking order in the WWF at that point by noting who comes in 3–16 and who comes in 18–30. This alone makes the Rumble incredibly lopsided in terms of the believability of those involved.

Golga is number three (see what I mean?), allowing Vince to sneak away into the crowd. Austin quickly tosses Golga, and then chases Vince into the crowd. In any other Rumble, both guys would be eliminated for leaving for that amount of time, but Vince Russo is writing this one, so they return later. MUCH later. Deus ex machina: They want to have Vince enter at number two and be there in the end without actually remaining in the match the whole time, so the rules of the match are rewritten to suit the story line, rather than the other way around. Vince McMahon could just as easily have been thrown out right away, and then return to help another Corporate member (say, Shamrock, for instance) win the thing later on. That would have accomplished exactly the same result without the idiotic, retrofitted, "Oh, you didn't read the fine print" nonsense that followed the next night (Vince Russo used "You didn't read the fine print" as a way to retroactively change his booking decisions about four times off the top of my head, three with Commissioner Michaels and one with Vince's unretirement. Ironically, Russo thought he'd have total control in WCW, but guess what? He didn't read the fine print, either). There was absolutely no justifiable reason for Vince to be there at the end, let alone for what ended up happening.

Droz is number four with no one in the ring to fight. See, now why did Golga have to be eliminated there? That's ninety seconds of dead airtime that could have been used for wrestling. We cut to the back as Austin is beat up by the Corporation. Edge is number five. Gillberg is number six, and he gets eliminated right after his entrance. Steve Blackman is number seven. What star power here, eh? Michael Cole, the Little Goatee-Wearing Bitch calls him a "young superstar," even though Blackman is probably ten years older than Cole. Meanwhile, Austin is being carried out on a stretcher. Dan Severn is number nine. FEEL THE

ELECTRICITY! Although if Severn had ¼ of the charisma that Kurt Angle has, they could have given him that gimmick and gotten him over. Meanwhile, Austin is loaded into an ambulance. Tiger Ali Singh is number nine.

We cut to an exciting shot of an ambulance driving away to really hammer the point home. Yes, Virginia, people actually paid thirty dollars to see an ambulance drive away. It's SPORTZENTERTAINMENT, BAY-BEE! The match is jobber hell right now, and the crowd is gone. Cole the Little Goatee-Wearing Bitch notes that Edge and Droz have been in a long time. Shit, is he THAT hard up for things to talk about that he has to call two guys being in there for a whole six minutes "being in the ring a long time"? Watch some fucking Gordon Solie tapes for once in your pathetic life, Cole, and learn the fine art of when to shut up.

Blue Meanie is number ten. Mosh is number eleven, but Mabel beats him up and takes his place. He dumps Severn, Blackman, and Singh. He's still fat, and he's still not over. Road Dogg is number twelve. Mabel dumps Meanie. Still fat, still not over. Dogg backdrops Edge out. More stupidity follows as the lights go out and the match stops while the Acolytes kidnap Mabel and bring him to Undertaker for reprogramming as Viscera. By the way, he's still fat, and he's still not over. Dogg is left alone, which is dead space number two in this match. Gangrel is, fittingly, number thirteen. Dogg gets rid of him. Kurrgan is number fourteen and destroys Road Dogg. Al Snow is number fifteen. He climbs the ropes to get leverage while trying to force Kurrgan out, so Dogg casually pushes him out. Goldust is number sixteen. Godfather is number seventeen. The crowd wants hos. Kane is number eighteen as we finally break the Jobber Barrier. He's in a bad mood, too, so good-bye Dogg, take a seat Kurrgan, see ya, Godfather, and arrivederci, Goldust. But now the mental hospital workers charge the ring and go after Kane, so he eliminates himself and leaves through the crowd. I guess only Austin and Vince get to go THROUGH the ropes so they can do that and then come back later.

So we get another few minutes of dead space,

since Shamrock is number nineteen and has nothing to do. Vince returns to do color commentary, thus making a total mockery of the match in one fell swoop. Billy Gunn is number twenty, still selling the injury. Shamrock beats the hell out of him. Test is number twenty-one with really bad music. We cut outside as Mabel is being loaded into a hearse, and very conveniently Austin has managed to hijack the ambulance and return it to the arena AT THAT VERY MOMENT. Next time I get beaten unconscious by five thugs, remind me to get THAT ambulance to treat me.

Bossman is number twenty-two as Austin returns to the match thirty minutes after leaving the first time. Austin backdrops Shamrock out. HHH is number twenty-three as the star power rises. Speaking of rising, Val Venis is number twenty-four. Austin kicks Gunn in the ankle and tosses him. X-Pac is number twenty-five. Everyone keeps going after Austin for the money. Mark Henry is number twenty-six. Jeff Jarrett is number twenty-seven. Too many people in there right now. D-Lo Brown is number twenty-eight, and as if hearing me rant, Austin disposes of Test and X-Pac in succession to clear things out a bit.

Owen Hart is number twenty-nine. HHH rids us of Jarrett. Owen and D-Lo double-team Austin. Chyna is number thirty, and she gets rid of Henry right away, but showboats and gets dumped by Austin. HHH dumps Val. Austin waits until HHH turns around, then hits the Stunner and tosses him. D-Lo gets the Lo-Down on Austin and works him over pretty good. Owen gives it a try, but charges Austin and goes bye-bye.

Final Four: Big Bossman, Steve Austin, D-Lo Brown, and Vince McMahon. D-Lo showboats after taking Austin down, and Bossman dumps him easily. Bam, Stunner, good-bye, Bossman. That leaves Vince at ringside, so Austin beats the hell out of him and drags him in. Vince hits a desperation low blow, but takes the Stunner. And heeeeeeeeeere's Rocky. Austin stops to yell at him, acting like a total idiot and breaking character, which allows Vince the chance to sneak up from behind and win the Royal Rumble at 56:34. God bless Vince Russo. The first forty minutes were so bad with all the dead space and jobbers that nothing could have saved this one. **, which makes it the worst Rumble ever.

Also on the show, Mankind defended his newly won WWF title against the Rock in an "I quit" match in which everyone was just sitting back and wondering how they'd weasel out of that stipulation. The answer proved to be lamer than we could have guessed. Here's my review:

WWF Title: Mankind v. The Rock

Rock's sideburns were seriously out of control at this point. I hear they started demanding appearance fees, so Vince McMahon fired them and WCW promptly signed them to a $100,000-per-year guaranteed contract and put them on Lash LeRoux, with promises of winning the TV title later in the year. A lawsuit over merchandising rights may or may not be pending.

Mick hammers on Rock quickly, nailing him with the microphone as Rock tells him that he can kiss his ass. Cactus clothesline takes us to the floor, where Mick eats stairs. Rock stops to do some commentary and Mick cracks a chair over his head. Back in for a double-arm DDT and the Mandible Sock. Rock is out and can't submit. He tosses Rock out and they fight back into the crowd. Rock powerslams Foley back to ringside to come back. He debuts the bell-ringing spot (place bell on head, hit with hammer) and tries Rock Bottom on the Spanish table, but the thing collapses before the move can hit.

Rock goes for the EVIAN SPEW OF DEATH, but that just wakes Mick up. Must have been that new, caffeinated water. And while I'm on the subject, who the hell thought of that one? I mean, Christ, just get a damn cup of coffee if you need a caffeine hit so bad. Or a can of Jolt Cola. The concept of paying for something that covers 75 percent of the earth is stupid enough as it is, but to further add insult to injury by pumping caffeine into it is more than I can take. You just KNOW it was a thirty-something, Kenny G–listening, suit-wearing, stock broker scumbag yup-

pie wanna-be who thought this one up, and probably Nicorette gum, too, just to represent every segment of the population who's in denial about their own ability to function as a normal human being without a medical excuse for their own neuroses. Wouldn't surprise me if it was Crystal Pepsi with the carbonation removed and a new label put on it, too. I mean, hell, if the kind of ingenuity that went into convincing the public that they REALLY need to spend money on bottled water and nicotine-laced gum were to be put into something USEFUL, then maybe we wouldn't be so far away from a cure for cancer or even some of the piddling diseases that kill millions in third-world countries. Anyway, I'm ranting again . . . back to the match.

They brawl down the aisle, where Rock gets a DDT on the concrete. Rock finds a ladder, but takes it in the mouth. Mick drops an elbow onto the ladder, but gets the worst of it. The crowd reminds Rocky that, in case he forgot, he indeed sucks. Contrived spot follows as they climb the ladder to the balcony, and Mick ends up diving into a gimmicked electrical bank, and sparks fly. The lights go out for effect and Michael Cole the Little Goatee-Wearing Bitch does his best Jim Ross impersonation as he declares Foley electrocuted and possibly dead. It's just Foley being a show-off, Michael, you don't have to act like it's a momentous occasion because it only encourages him and it detracts from the truly emotional part of the match later on.

Shane comes out to plead for mercy from The Rock, but no go. Rock drags Mick back to the ring as Michael keeps yelling, "Why won't he ask him if he quits?" Gee, Michael, you Little Goatee-Wearing Bitch, maybe it's because Rock knows, just like everyone else in the audience, that Foley won't ever say "I quit," which was kind of the point before the match of the huge video package highlighting Foley's saying over and over how he'd never, ever say "I quit" unless he was dead; also, by no small coincidence, the point of the very ending of the match itself. Maybe Cole is just jealous that his color commentator gets hotter chicks than he does or something.

Rock finds some handcuffs and cuffs Mick, and the

really sick part begins. Foley kicks and bites as best he can to survive, but Rock hits a clothesline and then grabs a chair. He puts it over Foley's face and drops the Corporate Elbow, which Michael Cole the Little Goatee-Wearing Bitch declares may have "smashed his skull in." Yes, Michael, I'm sure that dropping an elbow on a chair is enough to generate the necessary pressure needed to crush a man's skull, of course. Now, I'm all for announcers getting into the match, but sometimes a LITTLE professional detachment and/or ESPN-ish irony is needed to keep from wrecking the really nasty stuff later.

And nasty stuff follows, because Foley won't quit, so Rock just absolutely bashes his head in with two chairshots. Mick won't quit. Three more, and the crowd is growing noticeably squeamish. Foley rolls out to the floor for sanctuary, but Rock follows and delivers three more. Foley won't quit. NOW Cole's hyperbole is apropos, and of course now he has nothing left because he fired all the shots in his Interjection Six-Shooter earlier in the match. Premature interjection is always a tragic thing among young males. Foley staggers down the aisle, and Rock nails him from behind with an absolutely sickening shot to the back of the head that knocks him clean out. Rock sticks the mike in his face, and someone (the same guy who raised the briefcase, hit Austin with a cinderblock, and then ran him over at Survivor Series) plays a tape of Foley screaming, "I quit!" from Heat, and Rock wins the WWF title back at 21:44. Knowing the condition that Foley ended up in after this match was over, this was pretty scary to watch again. ★★★½

Mick later revealed all sorts of nasty details about the match and how he felt Rock was taking liberties with him, but never fear . . . they had a rematch soon after. It was called Halftime Heat, an experiment by the USA network in which they would run a match during the halftime show of the Super Bowl as competition. In this case, it was an empty-arena match between The Rock and Mankind. They started in the ring with no fans (much like WCW at the time) and

proceeded until there was a winner. The idea was inspired by a similar match from Memphis between Jerry Lawler and Terry Funk in the '70s. They ended up brawling into the stands, through the concession and kitchen areas, and into the back, where Mick used a forklift to "pin" Rocky under a pallet (complete with dramatic and physically impossible aerial camera angle) to win the title back. To my irritation, it did a monster rating, although thankfully the WWF has not been tempted to try anything like it again.

SCENE TWO
HHH's Larger, Twin Brother Returns

But back to the Vince-Austin soap opera for a moment. The night after the *Rumble*, Vince went on *RAW* to give up his spot at *Wrestlemania* in the main event, presumably to one of his Corporation members. Good thing, too, because otherwise we might have been forced to watch Vince wrestle (and maybe win) the WWF title. Ha ha ha ha! That'd just be silly and insulting to the intelligence of every man, woman, and child watching the product. Never happen. Nope. So clearly getting out of this stipulation would require going that extra mile to screw the paying fans out of the result of the show they had paid thirty dollars to see. And if there's one thing Vince has always been about more than anything, it's making sure that when the paying fan gets screwed, they get screwed by the best.

So anyway, newly appointed commissioner Shawn Michaels (okay, he was appointed in 1998, but no one cared), live via satellite from his home in San Antonio and clearly pounding back one too many drinks, declared that if the winner of the *Rumble* gave up his spot, then the runner-up would assume the slot in the *Wrestlemania* main event. So basically the WWF was now being conducted under beauty pageant rules and Steve Austin had backed into the

Wrestlemania main event. But Vince had one last try at regaining that slot for one of his men—he would face Austin in a steel-cage match at the next PPV, *St. Valentine's Day Massacre*, and if he won then he got his spot back. Of course, only Vince McMahon would presume he could stand a chance against the biggest star in the business in a cage match, but it's not like that sort of logical leap surprised anyone at the time.

Also around this time, the WWF began their first (of many) fanatical pushes of Billy Gunn as a singles "star," because (let's review) he's tall, muscular, and had a full head of hair. In keeping with the lowest-common-denominator booking strategy at the time, he also dumped the Billy Gunn name entirely and started going by the much-more dignified Mr. Ass. Some were cruel enough to dub him "Mr. Gass" in response, but I assure you that I'm above such cheap humor, unless of course I'm the one who thought of it.

Another rather historic happening occurred at this time when HHH returned from his knee injury with another seventy-five pounds of muscle miraculously packed on during the rehab period. But remember, the WWF tests extensively for steroids, so I would never make such an accusation, even if they were walking around with cans of Miracle-Gro in their gym bags and more needles than a cancer ward. At any rate, HHH signed a new, long-term contract around this time, and there were whispers that they wanted to make him world champion by the end of the year. HHH? World champion? Preposterous, everyone (myself included) said. But remember: tall, muscular, full head of hair. And so the insane super-push of HHH began in February 1999, amidst snickers from everyone. The first step was to turn his valet and real-life honey, Chyna, against him, because it would have that much more impact when they turned her back a month later, I guess. So Chyna joined the Corporation and started hanging out with Kane (who was being brainwashed into working for

Vince), leading to The Feud that No One Wanted to See: Kane v. HHH.

> **O**ne rather witty angle carried this feud: HHH dressed up as Goldust and shot a giant confetti bazooka into Kane's face. HHH seems to have a lot of angles centering on phallic symbols or the size of his manhood. Just saying.

So the second PPV of the year, *St. Valentine's Day Massacre*, came and went, and Steve Austin shocked everyone by getting a pretty decent cage match out of a fifty-year old man. Paul Wight, formerly the Giant in WCW, made his debut in that match on the way to turning heel and face 700 different times over the next two years as The Big Show. For the moment, however, he was a member of Vince's Corporation.

Speaking of the Corporation, I would be remiss in not pointing out that someone actually thought it would be a good idea to start a feud between the Corporation and the Ministry of Darkness, which resulted in Big Bossman v. Mideon actually being a match on a PPV. No, honest. We had to pay for it and everything. Later in the show, ex–porn star Val Venis won the intercontinental title from Ken Shamrock with the help of fast-counting guest referee Billy Gunn, whose issue with Shamrock had been transferred to Venis because of an argument about Shamrock's story line "sister," Ryan.

Funny story there: Ryan Shamrock, played by ex-stripper Alicia Webb, was having an affair with Val Venis (as captured in the avant garde cinema piece *Saving Ryan's Privates*), which naturally offended the brotherly sensibilities of Ken. While that would have been a fine story by itself, Vince Russo wanted to take it one step closer to the edge by having Ken be in love with his sister and thus be jealous of Venis. Ken was completely disgusted with this idea and immedi-

The angle began with Billy Gunn hitting on Ryan, and getting shot down. By the end of the angle, he was the only one who HADN'T scored with her, story line–wise. I mean, hell, even freakish quasi-homosexual Goldust (who was, at that point, engaged in a bizarre relationship with the Blue Meanie) got to get freaky-deaky with Ryan. No wonder Billy ended up playing half of a gay tag team two years later.

ately refused to do the story line, and in fact quit to join the Pride mixed–martial arts organization a few months later. But as of this writing, he is romantically linked to Alicia Webb, aka Ryan Shamrock.

SCENE THREE
Russo Screws Up Wrestlemania

So the march to *Wrestlemania XV* began as the WWF title bounced around *again*. Foley, with his widely publicized dream of main-eventing a *Wrestlemania*, went to a bullshit double-knockout finish with Rock at *St. Valentine's Day Massacre*, and then lost the title to Rock on *RAW* the next night in a ladder match with help from Paul Wight. Didn't matter so much, though, because Rock-Austin was the big money match and everyone wanted to see it anyway, no matter how much they loved Foley. And Foley's a very lovable guy, so that's saying something. And while the build for the main event was relatively idiot-proof, even for Russo's booking standards, unfortunately the rest of the card was definitely not.

Take the hardcore- and intercontinental-title matches. Please.

So here are the setups: "Road Dogg" Jesse Jammes of the New Age Outlaws wins the hardcore title early in 1999 and defends it against

Al Snow in a good series of matches. Snow fails to win, until Jammes is injured and the title is put up for grabs between Snow and perennial jobber Bob Holly at the February PPV. Holly wins and dubs himself "Hardcore Holly," a name that has stuck until this very day. So a three-way match between champion Holly, challenger Al Snow, and returning Jesse Jammes is signed. No problem so far, right?

Okay, so then you have the intercontinental-title situation, with Val Venis as the champion being chased by Shamrock, who got screwed out of the title by Billy Gunn. There's another three-way match signed. So far, so good. I guess that was too easy, because soon after, Goldust gets involved in the intercontinental-title situation for no good reason other than Ryan Shamrock's becoming a whore and moving from Val to Gunn to Goldust, and so it becomes a four-way match. And then, Russo's masterstroke: Two weeks before *Wrestlemania*, he switches the Outlaws (Jammes and Gunn) and has them challenge for the opposite title, and has Jammes win the intercontinental title from Venis, while Gunn wins the hardcore title from Holly.

So now the hardcore-title match at *Wrestlemania* is Gunn v. Snow v. Holly, a match that not only sucks the meat missile, but makes no sense from a story line standpoint. Further, the intercontinental title four-way is now Jammes v. Goldust v. Shamrock v. Venis, and again the entire lynchpin of the Venis-Shamrock feud (Gunn) is in a totally different match! My personal theory is that since the match was only booked to go ten minutes, by the time people watching actually might stop to try and figure out who hates whom and why, the match would be over.

Don't laugh, it's not called "Crash TV" for no reason.

Speaking of which, Vinnie Ru's fabled "Crash TV" was really starting to rear its ugly head around this time when *RAW* changed from a wrestling program into a series of two-and-a-half-minute "matches" (and I use that term loosely) interspersed with bad acting and comedy skits. The actual theory behind it, and stupid as it sounds you can't argue with success, is that if you throw thirty pounds of shit at a giant fan, but don't give viewers the chance to change the channel, they'll keep watching just to see how bad it can get. This is the car-crash mentality, and although ratings were high for a good stretch, the backlash would be ten times worse later on, which we'll get to in due time.

Although Austin won the WWF title from The Rock in a pretty good match in the main event, the real head scratcher of the show was a little further down the card, in the X-Pac v. Shane McMahon match. Shane had won the European title from X-Pac in a tag match (don't ask) with a move that just impressed the hell out of all the fans who were cynical and jaded to begin with. Never mind that Shane wasn't even a wrestler or particularly in shape, he was a McMahon and he'd get a title and make top talent job for him, by God!

Everyone thought this one would be pretty cut-and-dried: Shane steals the Euro title from X-Pac, a rematch at *Wrestlemania* is signed (which it was), and X-Pac gets his revenge and beats the holy hell out of Shane to win the title back. Well, not quite. Here's my review:

European Title Match:
"Stone Cold" Shane McMahon v. X-Pac

Common sense and fan sentiment said that X-Pac kills Shane here and goes on to have a successful European title reign. But of course, SWERVES HAVE ATTITUDE, BAY-BEE!

X-Pac survives the assault of the Stooges to start, then chases Shane around the ring. Shane runs away like Vince Russo runs from good ideas. Back in, X-Pac kicks his head off and tries a broncobuster, but Test pulls Shane out. He posts X-Pac for good luck. Shane-O-Mac works him in the corner and then drops . . . the

Greenwich Elbow. X-Pac moves, but Shane low blows him anyway. Belt-whipping follows, but Shane gets bumped over the top and X-Pac hits a pescado. In this case, the total opposite of the Kane one. It makes contact and everything. X-Pac takes out the Posse, but Test gets in a cheapshot to drop him.

Back in, Shane drops a second rope elbow, but gets dropkicked down from the top and superplexed. Test saves the pin, but gets taken out. X-Pac lays in his own shots with the belt, leading to the broncobuster. Test sneaks in and KOs him with the title belt, however. It gets two. Shane misses his own broncobuster, and Test is in again. He gets a broncobuster for his troubles as HHH and Chyna are out to even the odds. However, HHH turns on X-Pac as Chyna distracts the referee by turning from face to heel fourteen times in succession, and Shane retains his title at 8:41. *** * ***

However, it turned out to be an important story line development because, without this match, Shane could never have gone on RAW and officially retired with the title after his first match. Of course, both Shane and the title were unretired by Summerslam, but this is wrestling, and logic rarely enters into things. Eric Bischoff said so on Meltzer's radio show between double-talk, so it must be true.

So indeed, the next night on *RAW*, Shane McMahon came out and retired the European title. But that's not the big point here as this match was HHH's big heel turn, intended to spring him into the main event. He was repackaged as the leader of the Corporation, complete with fruity chainmail vest and new music, the original mix of which sounded vaguely like seagulls being tortured with hot pokers. And suddenly Jim Ross spent every match telling us what a technical marvel HHH was, despite all his matches being filled with punching and kicking.

A quick word on Jim Ross, if I may.

In December 1998, JR suffered a relapse of his Bell's Palsy, the effects of which are roughly the same as having a stroke, and in fact it occurred during a PPV broadcast for the United

Kingdom, leaving him to suffer through a paralyzing attack while trying to do commentary. It left the left half of his face paralyzed and he took some time off to recover, leaving Michael Cole to act as lead announcer for the WWF. Well, since Cole is widely regarded as an incompetent git by the fanbase, the fans were demanding the return of Jim Ross.

Ah, but Vince Russo, rapidly gaining power, didn't like Jim Ross, probably because Ross saw through Russo's façade of "creativity" for the joke he was eventually revealed to be. So Russo crafted a masterful story line whereby the rather pathetic-looking Ross would come out and cut bitter promos against Vince McMahon and commandeer the *RAW* broadcast with the help of badass best friend Steve "Dr. Death" Williams in scenes reminiscent of his bitter tirades against the WWF in 1996, which led to the emergence of the "Fake Diesel and Razor" angle. Trust me, you don't even want to get me started on that one. At any rate, this story line, amazingly, was supposed to make the fans *boo* him. Instead, they chanted his name even louder and booed Michael Cole even more incessantly. Finally, Vince McMahon stepped in and gave JR his job back, starting with *Wrestlemania*, and relegated Cole back to the B-shows, where he belonged.

At any rate, from April '99 onward, the entire WWF somehow became geared toward one goal and one goal only: make the fans buy HHH as a badass number-one heel. So Ross started playing up his alleged technical skills, later calling HHH the "Cerebral Assassin," even though he wasn't particularly smart about his attacks and hadn't yet assassinated anyone.

Typical HHH master plan: Lure babyface out to the ring alone. Hit him with a sledgehammer. Repeat as needed.

SCENE FOUR
UP YOURS, Corporate Ministry!

But back to *Wrestlemania* for a quick stop-off, as I know that you, much like the entire fanbase at the time, are just waiting on the edge of your collective seats to find out the next chapter in the fascinating Ministry v. Corporation feud. And indeed that step proved to be more than many could handle, as Undertaker faced Big Bossman in the ever-dangerous Hell in a Cell. In this case, the danger was gnawing your own arm off to avoid having to watch it since the two guys wrestling barely made contact and moved more slowly than a congressional hearing. And after Undertaker put Bossman (and us) out of his misery to win the "match," the Ministry's resident teen-screams, Edge and Christian (in the days before they were funny), rappelled from the ceiling and tried to kill Bossman by hanging him from the rafters. Here's my review:

Heck in the Cell:
Big Bossman v. Undertaker

This one had "bad idea" written all over it as plain as the eyebrow on Vince Russo's forehead, but that's never stopped them before. Punchy-kicky to start. And that goes on for a good long while before they fight outside. Absurdist line of the night, from (who else), Michael Cole the Little Goatee-Wearing Bitch, who declares that Hell in a Cell is dangerous because you can get your fingers caught in it. Lawler does me proud by responding to that one for me.

Bossman cuffs Taker to the cell as a spontaneous "boring" chant starts. Undertaker does a bladejob best described as a polite concession to the expectations of Philly fans and the match format. Bossman gets rammed to the cage and joins the Gig Club, although really it's about 0.0000004 Muta between them and I've seen menstrual flows that were more inspiring.

Someone get these losers some aspirin and a "Best of Muta" tape, STAT.

> **"Muta"** refers to a subjective scale of bleeding used by hardcore wrestling fans to describe how bloody someone has gotten. It is based on a jaw-droppingly repulsive bladejob done by Keiji "Great Muta" Muto in Japan in 1991 against Hiro Hase, wherein the ring, the ref, his opponent, his tights, and parts of the front row were covered in his blood by the end of the match. 0.0000004 Muta is not very much blood at all.

Meanwhile, the ongoing saga of which side of the arena can do a bigger "boring" chant continues. Sadly, I'm not sitting close enough to the rear speakers to make an informed judgment on the matter. UT mercifully tombstones and pins Bossman at 9:46. Call it −***½, and that's generous.

The Brood rappels from the ceiling and HANGS the Bossman, which was of course forgotten by the next night, because CRASH TV = RATINGS.

And then they cut to an interview backstage. That, my friends, is Crash TV. Because Lord knows many people switch channels during a forty-dollar PPV.

But back to Undertaker, because there wasn't really anything else of note during April '99 to talk about anyway. . . .

Russo, long a proponent of more "realistic" story lines, came up with one for Undertaker where he'd go after Vince McMahon (by setting a mysterious teddy bear on fire) in order to attempt to take over the company. You see, the teddy bear belonged to Vince's never-before-seen daughter, Stephanie. And Stephanie would provide Undertaker with just the hostage he needed to take advantage of Vince. In fact, Vince began doing interviews explaining how

Undertaker was scaring him because he was getting "too far into his character," thus admitting that it was all story lines. But not *this*, this was real.

That's the Russo philosophy in a nutshell: Everything you see is fake, except for what you're watching right now, which is real. Apparently this philosophy even carried through to the end of the *Backlash* PPV, when Stephanie was seen getting into a limousine, only to discover that Undertaker was driving it, giving fans the all-time Bad Dialogue Champion at that point: "Where to, Stephanie?" Maybe it was the delivery, I dunno. But the point was, Vince McMahon and The Undertaker really, really, *really* hated each other within the confines of the story line, what with Undertaker kidnapping family members and terrorizing Vince every show and trying to kill his henchmen and all. This becomes important in a little bit, so I just wanted to stress it.

Things changed a lot for the WWF the week after that *Backlash* PPV, as the fledgling UPN network gave them a pilot for a new wrestling show—*Smackdown!* The exclamation point is theirs, not mine. Wanting to put their best foot forward in their first shot at network TV since the cancellation of *Saturday Night's Main Event* on NBC and FOX years before, the writing went into hotshot overdrive, as they redebuted Owen Hart as the Blue Blazer, and in the most ridiculous and nonsensical story line twist since . . . well, maybe ever, Shane McMahon's Corporation merged with the Undertaker's Ministry to form . . . The Corporate Ministry.

See, Shane had "fired" his father from the Corporation and took it over himself when Vince was getting too wrapped up in The Undertaker kidnappings, which works fine as a plot twist if the point is that they were really working together all along to oust Vince. But later on, well, it got a little trickier.

By this time, the winds of change were also blowing in other directions as the WWF could no longer reasonably keep The Rock on the evil side of the ledger due to the overwhelmingly positive fan response, and they finally caved in and turned him babyface as a result. He never turned back. Meanwhile, in totally the opposite vein, a group of hodge-podge babyfaces opposing Shane's new entity formed up, consisting of Mankind, Test, Ken Shamrock, and The Big Show. The last three were former cronies for the Corporation who were fired for whatever flimsy excuse for a face turn that the WWF needed on that given week. But the best part was their name—the Union of People You OUghtta Respect, Shane. Or UPYOURS, for short. Ho ho ho, the hilarity boggles the mind. Thankfully, most people just called them the "Union" for short until the inevitable self-destruction once Russo got bored of actually writing story lines for them. Actually, scratch that last part—the *best* part was that the WWF music guys recycled the whistle from Tugboat's old WWF music and gave it to the Union. *That* was the best part. Or not. Really, no one cared anyway, so it's a moot point.

Test's initial push saw him frequently wearing a shirt with the slogan "Guns don't kill people, I kill people," which I think wasn't the worst thing in the world toward getting him over as a babyface in the South, if nothing else.

Anyway, there was one minor story line point with the Union that does actually make them warrant inclusion here rather than the creative oblivion that I would normally write them off into, but I'll get to that later.

SCENE FIVE
Over the Edge

By May of 1999, Undertaker was in line for another title shot at Steve Austin, and it was delivered for the *Over the Edge* PPV, with Vince McMahon being the special referee. Oh, and further down the card, The Godfather was scheduled to defend his intercontinental title against faux-superhero the Blue Blazer, really Owen Hart playing a goofy gimmick in an attempt to get him over as a mid-card threat again.

Owen Hart had originally debuted as Blue Blazer in 1989 when he came over from Stampede Wrestling, a "secret" that was not particularly well hidden from wrestling fans. It did nothing for Owen's initial career, and by 1999 the WWF had wanted to do a nostalgia-type deal for longtime fans. However, almost the entire fanbase had turned over in 1997, so there was only 5 percent of the remaining fans, maybe, who even remembered 1989. But it went through anyway because that's the WWF for you. The idea leading up to this was that Owen and partner Jeff Jarrett would take turns playing the "Blazer," with each one showing up while the "Blazer" was around in order to verify that in fact it wasn't them. This led up to Blazer finally getting a title shot at the *Over the Edge* PPV, where he would rappel dramatically from the ceiling, but "accidentally" fall off the harness about five feet above the ring, causing him to land face-first on the mat to the amusement of all. That, of course, is not how it turned out.

Now, all attempts at objectivity aside, Owen Hart was my favorite wrestler, ever. He is one of those wrestlers of whom I can say that I have seen nearly every match in his career, starting from his debut match in Stampede all the way up to a house-show match that he did here in Edmonton a week before the *Over the Edge* show.

Debate rages about whether or not Owen was being punished for refusing to do a marital infidelity story line. It really depends on which side of the lawsuit you're on: according to Martha, the Blazer was a punishment. According to the boys in the back, he asked for the gimmick. Either way, he's still dead.

I have been a supporter and rabid fan of his since day one, and watching him grow up as a person and a professional was truly something special to behold. He had started as a nervous kid in 1987, doing backflips off the top rope to compensate for what he lacked in the basic psychology of wrestling, and only got better from there every day of his life. I watched in horror as he jumped to the WWF in 1989 and got stuck with the stupid "Blue Blazer" gimmick, then watched as he was made to look like a jobber by people who I knew weren't even one-tenth as naturally talented as Owen was.

The bright spots, like a great match with Curt Hennig at their concurrent *Wrestlemania* debut in '89, gave me hope for his future, but soon he was fired and in WCW for a short stint. I truly believe that had he stayed there, he would have found his niche and been huge, but for whatever reason the WWF lured him back again in 1991 and stuck him in a tag team with Jim Neidhart, hoping to recapture the magic of the original Hart Foundation, except with big, puffy pants. Owen became "The Rocket" Owen Hart, giving me no hope for his future. They replaced Neidhart with Koko B. Ware, and gave them even bigger pants and even more jobs on TV, until Owen seemed doomed to opening-match job duties against the Headshrinkers for the rest of his career.

By the end of 1993, even Owen was ready to quit the business and become a fireman, but his brother Bret talked Owen, and the WWF, into staying for one last try, this time in a main-event-level run against Bret in which Owen would turn on him and challenge him for the WWF title. This, thankfully, entrenched Owen into a solid spot on the roster, leading to him winning *King of the Ring* and the tag-team titles, among other things.

I think, however, the one gimmick that was so prototypically Owen was the Slammy gimmick. See, in 1995, after the "Enzuigiri of Doom" angle with Shawn Michaels, Owen went on to "win" a Slammy award for the most disgusting act of the year. He, of course, took that as a compliment and went around showing his award to everyone who would look. The next year, not nominated for an award, he ambushed the awards show and accepted the "Best Bowtie" award on Bob Backlund's behalf, thus becoming "Two-Time Slammy Award Winning" Owen Hart and making sure to carry both trophies around with him in every match from then on. That was the Owen I always want to remember when I think about him, not the guy who jumped from failed feud to failed feud, or the guy who was treated like dirt before that—just the guy who could legitimately hang as a wrestler with anyone in the promotion, but wanted to have some fun out there and entertain you.

And so, on May 23, 1999, Owen played along with the Blazer gimmick, but something happened to his harness—what, exactly, we'll never know—and he fell to a grisly death in the ring below, breaking his neck and dying backstage. They didn't even stop the show. In fact, they ended the show with a guy named The Undertaker winning the WWF title in the main event, and they made Owen's partner and good friend Jeff Jarrett wrestle in a ridiculous mixed-tag match freakshow against weightlifter Nicole Bass and Val Venis right after the fall from the rafters. Call me cynical, but I have found it particularly hard to be entertained by the WWF since that point. While I may have disrespected

Vince McMahon for turning the sport of wrestling into a circus and held a grudge against Vince Russo for booking ludicrous angles with no payoff, I can truly say that I hate both men for killing the greatest wrestler I had ever had the pleasure of watching in the name of a stupid gimmick that no one had cared about anyway. I still watch the product, and I still count myself as a wrestling fan, but I hope there is an afterlife and I hope Vince McMahon burns in hell forever for stealing Owen Hart from me and everyone else who counted themselves as a fan of his. And that's all I'm going to say about that matter.

Okay, not quite. The next night on *RAW*, the regular show was postponed for a week in favor of an Owen Hart tribute show. It featured a series of literally meaningless matches put on as exhibitions, interspersed with vignettes from various WWF wrestlers talking about how much Owen meant to them. Now, without naming names or calling anyone a liar, to my eye and ear it sounded like roughly half of those vignettes were put together solely for political reasons rather than for any genuine affection for Owen. The show ended with Steve Austin toasting Owen with a beer, which struck me as hypocritical after he had made the decision never to work with Owen in a main-event program following the neck injury sustained at *Summerslam '97*. But the show did over an 8.0 rating, which stands as the high point for *RAW*, and probably Vince Russo's peak as a creative writer, so I've gotta give them credit for that at least.

But we came crashing back down to earth the next week.

SCENE SIX
The Lamer Power

It all seemed kind of silly following Owen's death—a very real tragedy—to go back to the usual goofy WWF story lines, but that's exactly

what happened. Undertaker had been yapping about a "Higher Power" that he answered to ever since the creation of the Ministry of Darkness. Now, with the merger of the Corporation and the Ministry, the only step left was to reveal who that Higher Power was. So, on May 31, a mysterious figure in a black cloak (who was now being called the "Greater Power" for some reason) waited for the Corporate Ministry to subdue Austin, at which point he revealed his face to Austin alone, leaving a cliffhanger for the next week's *RAW*.

Well, that was all well and good, but they didn't actually have anyone to be the so-called Greater Power and there were now only six days left before the big payoff. The choices came down to one logical choice and two illogical ones. The logical one was Mick Foley, who would be reenergized by a heel turn and programmed again with Steve Austin in the main event. However, Foley didn't want to be a heel again with no buildup, so he declined. The next choice was Steve Austin, and considering that he was standing right there when the Greater Power appeared and was supposed to be his biggest enemy . . . well, I won't even finish the thought because logic rarely entered into anything involved in the WWF's 1999 story lines. Needless to say, there was only one real choice left, no matter how dumb it actually ended being in retrospect: Vincent K. McMahon.

Not like it was a big secret or anything. In fact, on *Nitro* just before the big revelation, Eric Bischoff was doing commentary and flippantly remarked that it was pointless to watch *RAW* because the Greater Power's initials were "VKM." And while he had no advance knowledge of this, anyone with half a brain could have figured it out by that point. And indeed, it was Vince, and indeed it made no sense and rendered the last six months of story lines completely silly and pointless. But they rushed ahead and decided just to forget that whole plotline and move on to something else, which was a smart move in hindsight.

So less than a minute after Vince gave his big speech as the Greater Power, including another all-time lame-o catchphrase ("It was *me*, Austin! It was *me all along!*"), his wife, Linda, came out to name Austin the new CEO of the WWF and a match was quickly signed between Austin and the Vince/Shane tandem for *King of the Ring*, with the entire ownership of the WWF on the line in a ladder match. Well, this didn't exactly set the world on fire, and neither did the field for the actual *King of the Ring* tournament itself. See, the advertising heavily featured Big Show in a prominent role, and he was making huge money after being stolen from WCW, and it would have made sense for him to crush the competition and win the tournament, so instead they had Billy Gunn win in a shocking swerve.

A word, if I may, on shocking swerves. There is the theory, primarily championed by Russo and his minions, that a story line is not enough because wrestling fans are more intelligent than your usual TV viewer and thus demand surprises and twist endings. However, at the same time the theory says that these story lines cannot be too long or complex, because wrestling fans are less intelligent than your usual TV viewer. There is, of course, an inherent contradiction there, and that's the main problem. Russo's entire plan was to deliver high-impact, low-thought television while at the same time trying to please the intellectual crowd.

However, Russo was not himself the intellectual type, so instead of well-crafted stories you got the Greater Power or Vince's Family Turns on Him Again. By mid-1999, they were no longer even story lines, but more "a bunch of stuff that happens from one week to the next." Russo was literally booking things on a napkin three hours before show time, as he admitted in an interview shortly before his departure from the promotion. Chyna would waffle between heel and face every week, and often would change sides during the same show! When she was with HHH, she was his tough bodyguard who hit guys in the groin and cheated like nuts, but earlier in the card she would be challenging woman-hating heel Jeff Jarrett and acting as a babyface. It was simply impossible for fans to rally behind someone who couldn't decide from segment to segment which side he or she was actually on.

So that line of thinking brought us to *King of the Ring*, where the advertising was focused on Big Show in an effort to make fans think that he would win, and thus they would be surprised when Billy Gunn emerged as the WWF's next big star. Of course, the fans were so annoyed at Billy Gunn winning *anything* that any potential value his push may have had was completely negated by the total lack of fan response to his win.

Further, the New Age Outlaws had just split up and Billy had just beaten ex-partner Road Dogg at the fateful *Over the Edge* show in May, so the natural final to the tournament was looking to be Gunn v. Dogg when both made it to the semi-finals of the tournament, against Kane and X-Pac, respectively. However, again it was a swerve, as Road Dogg was quickly eliminated by X-Pac, who in turn was quickly beaten by Billy Gunn in the finals. The question was, if X-Pac was going to lose in the end anyway, why not just have him lose in the semi-finals and do the final that the fans really wanted to see? Even worse, "Badd Ass" Billy Gunn had now been shortened to simply "Mr. Ass," and his gimmick was that of someone who was apparently obsessed with his own ass. He even had a new theme song done—"Assman." Yeah, that's *really* what all the kids are looking for in a T-shirt. Needless to say, the latest attempt at a Billy Gunn push was not the smashing success they were hoping for.

And speaking of things not being smashing

> Sample lyric from Assman: "A nice tight one can stop me on a dime . . . the best surprises always sneak up from behind."

successes, another PR nightmare, of a different kind, started rearing its ugly head during the summer of 1999. Coming back to The Undertaker's ill-fated Ministry of Darkness character again, his latest character trait was to take a giant Undertaker symbol (closely resembling a cross, in fact) and then tie his victim to it in a crucified position and then raise the "symbol" to the rafters.

Well, this immediately outraged certain members of the moral minority who were already looking for any excuse to nail the WWF for advertising to kids and then sending them antireligious messages, and the incidents were later dubbed "Russofixions" once it became apparent which creative genius was behind them. But this stuff would end up having much, much larger consequences later on, which ironically were predicted by Eric Bischoff long before they had happened. For, you see, there was a right-wing fundamentalist group called the Parents' Television Council that was watching closely now that the WWF had ties to network TV in the form of their upcoming *Smackdown* show on UPN. And with characters like the fun-loving pimp Godfather, porn star Val Venis, the satanic Undertaker, and woman-hating Jeff Jarrett running around the WWF, they would have plenty of ammunition at the ready when they struck.

But we'll get to them later.

SCENE SEVEN
The Magic Briefcase

To finish with the atrocity that was *King of the Ring* '99, I'll just point out that Shane and Vince

McMahon indeed defeated Steve Austin in the ladder match thanks to the so-called Magic Briefcase angle. Here's my review:

Main Event:
Steve Austin v. Vince McMahon and
Shane McMahon

With a year of hindsight, video packages, time for contemplation, and explanations from those involved, I STILL don't see how this story line can possibly be considered to make the least bit of sense in any way. Vince tries to intro Steve Blackman as Shane's replacement, but that darned GTV reveals that Shane is fine after all, and he gets dragged out and into the match again.

We go brawling down the aisle right away, then back in for some ass-whooping from Austin on both. Shane gets posted, then the McMahons finally get smart and double-team Austin. Vince goes for the ladder, but Austin kicks his ass. Shane saves, then goes flying up the ladder-themed entranceway thing and back down again. Austin tosses the McMahons into the ladder-based supports one-by-one, until the whole thing topples down on them in a neat spot. Austin hauls the official ladder into the ring, nailing Shane with it and sending him flailing into the announcer's table. Austin sets up the ladder outside and elbows Shane through the Spanish table, a spot that came off looking flat somehow. He goes back up, but Vince pushes him over and into the U.S. table. Another flat spot.

Vince climbs the ladder back into the ring, but gets knocked off by Austin. Austin clobbers Shane with the ladder in the corner. He slingshots him into it, then stomps a mudhole in Vince. Austin climbs for the briefcase, but the ladder gets knocked over. The McMahon clan tries two alternate methods of reaching the case (alley-oop and chicken fight, to be precise) but neither works. Stunner 1, Stunner 2. Austin climbs, and of course we are witness to one of the stupidest deus ex machina endings in wrestling history as the briefcase moves up and down by the hand of some unknown Corporate Ally, allowing the McMahons the chance to knock Austin off again.

Vince and Austin fight on the ladder, and Shane dumps both off, then climbs up and grabs the case for the win at 16:55. **¼ for Match of the Night honors. The result ended up meaning nothing to the story lines, since Vince was "retired" by Austin at the next PPV, thus making the whole exercise pointless. Much like this entire show, which featured a tag wrestler winning King of the Ring when everyone (except the WWF) knew that his push would fail, Undertaker successfully defending his title only to lose it the next night and never get close to winning it again, and a confusing story line (How DID Linda and Stephanie get their 50 percent back, anyway?) in a main event as stale as, well, 2000's main event.

So Vince was once again head honcho of the WWF, and Austin was once again his number-one nemesis fighting against the corporate menace. To compensate Austin for doing that job to the McMahons, he was given the title back the next night on RAW in a match against reigning champion Undertaker that, as of this writing, still stands as the highest-rated match in the history of that show. However, the saga unfortunately didn't end there, as Undertaker was given a rematch at the next PPV, Fully Loaded, with first-blood stipulations and another one added on: If Austin lost, no more title shots ever, and if Undertaker lost, Vince is off WWF TV forever.

Well, no one bought either stipulation as being even remotely probable, but they tried it anyway. And, long story short, Austin won the match and Vince was taken off WWF TV forever. Except, of course, for the next night on RAW where he gave his big farewell speech, one night after losing a match where he would never appear on TV again, ever. I guess we didn't read the fine print or something.

For those keeping track of things like these,

Chris Jericho jumped to the WWF from WCW at this point, none too soon to escape the total breakdown of the promotion, and immediately shot to the top of the ranks as a babyface, even though he was supposed to be a heel. Perhaps debuting him with an elaborate pyro display and new music during a Rock interview segment may have somehow convinced the fans that Jericho was something special when in fact they were supposed to think that all new stars should "pay their dues" and all that nonsense, but regardless, Jericho immediately broke through sluggish booking to become a much bigger star than was ever intended for him.

> Over in the WCW, Raven commented on a WCW-run call-in show that if he had Jericho's entrance, maybe he could have gotten over, too. He quit the promotion days later.

Meanwhile, Austin was slowly breaking the news to the WWF that he had serious complications from his neck injury in 1997 and needed surgery, now. So what the WWF needed was a fresh face at the top of the card—a main-event threat for the new millennium. Truly, a man with a nose big enough to carry the weight of the world on it. That's right, HHH, the Cerebral Assassin. The truly "insane" part of his insane push to the top began at Fully Loaded, as he defeated The Rock in a strap match to determine who the number-one contender for the WWF title at Summerslam would be.

Yes, hell had indeed frozen over, HHH was now going to main-event the second-biggest WWF show of the year against Steve Austin. Slight problem: Vince Russo had the attention span of an eight-year-old and started changing his mind leading up to the show. We got goofy stipulation matches on RAW in the weeks before, the end result of which was that, two weeks before the PPV, the main event stood at Steve Austin v. Chyna for the WWF title thanks to ridiculously convoluted booking gymnastics with which I will not insult your intelligence here. The point is that the show was rapidly approaching, to be held in Minneapolis with Governor Jesse Ventura as the special referee for the title match, and they didn't even know for sure what the match would be.

They had no confidence in HHH to carry a match like that himself (rightly so), and no confidence in Steve Austin to be healthy for the match (also rightly so), so they hedged their bets and did *more* logical leapfrogging and set it up so that it ended with Steve Austin v. HHH v. Mankind for the title, which would essentially let Mick Foley do all the hard work and HHH get all the benefit. Unfortunately, it didn't work all that well as the match was okay, but nothing special. Foley scored an upset win over Austin to capture his third (and final) WWF title.

SCENE EIGHT
True Love (Even Badly Acted) Conquers All

And speaking of okay, but nothing special, many people (especially those who are around me a lot) started noticing that with the year more than half over, there was absolutely no contenders for the Match of the Year for 1999. Frankly, the in-ring aspect of the WWF (and WCW for that matter) was screwing the pooch, to put it delicately. HHH being on top didn't seem to provide much hope in that direction, either. In fact, it got so bad that the leading candidate up to then happened at *Summerslam*, when rookie Test took on Shane McMahon in a street fight for the hand of Stephanie McMahon. Had we known the way that this match would indirectly change the direction of the WWF for years to come, we probably would have voted it higher. It ended up in second place for the year as it was.

Back story: The Union (remember them?) was trying to annoy Shane McMahon at every opportunity, and they were given one such opportunity in June when Commissioner Michaels offered them each one match of their choosing, whatever they wanted. Test, ever the romantic, decided to go for the gusto and really egg on the old man by asking for a date with the innocent and lovely Stephanie McMahon. Well, it did indeed suitably piss off Vince, but amazingly they actually followed through with the story and one date led to another, and another, and soon Test and Steph were a regular item on WWF TV. In fact, by August, Test asked Stephanie to marry him, and she accepted, with an October wedding date set. *Awww*. Shane McMahon, ever the protective big brother, demanded *REVENGE!* (You have to say it like that or else it doesn't work) in the name of Steph's honor. And so the "love her or leave her" match was set for *Summerslam*, and it was actually a doozy. Here's my review:

"Love Her or Leave Her":
Test v. Shane McMahon

The Mean Street Posse (with various casts and bandages) make their way to ringside, where a couch and champagne are awaiting them. Test totally destroys Shane to start, then tosses him into the arms of the Posse. Test gets laid out by them as a result while the crowd is chanting "Posse Sucks!" They start handing Shane a variety of weapons, the funniest of which is a framed portrait of themselves. It gets shattered over Test's head, of course.

Back in the ring and Shane actually goes for a corkscrew senton off the top! It misses, and Test powerbombs Shane, but the ref is distracted by Rodney. Ref bump follows, which makes no sense in a no-DQ match. The Posse lays out Test on the Spanish announcer table . . . and Shane hits a flying elbow off the top rope, through the table! WHOA! Shane is the McMAN!

Back in the ring, but it only gets two for Shane. Pete

accidentally nails Shane with a sign, giving Test a two-count. Crowd is going NUTS. Rodney hits Test with the cast, which I thought was the end, but it gets two. Finally, after all that interference, the Stooges make their return, taking out the punks (BIG pop for that), leaving Shane and Test mano-a-mano. And from there, it's Meltdown and flying elbow for the Test pin, which was TOTALLY the right booking and got a HUGE pop from the crowd, and the group of people watching the show at our gathering tonight, including a few non-fans. When you can make people who haven't been following wrestling pop for the finish, it's something good. Stephanie and Test have a celebration as Test makes his first big PPV shot COUNT. ★★★½

Shane was even gracious enough to step aside the next night on *RAW* and declare Test the better man, and in fact they have been best buds in story line terms ever since. Gets you right there. Of course, being the cynical bastards that most of us wrestling fans are, our only thought was "Who's gonna break up the marriage at the altar?" In news unrelated at that point, on that same show, HHH got a rematch against new WWF champion Mankind, and with copious amounts of help from Shane McMahon, finally got the belt after months of being pushed down our throats.

SCENE NINE
This Is Your Life, Rocky!

Going from good to awful for a moment, I just want to hit on the fascinatingly bad hardcore title feud between Al Snow and Big Bossman. Actually, I don't want to, but one must suffer for one's art. Snow was an interesting case, as he was last seen in the WWF in 1996 as goofy faux rock star Leif Cassidy, who then morphed into psychotic mat wrestler Leif Cassidy in 1997, who then became a jobber and was basically sold to ECW in hopes of him finding a

voice down there. His solution? After jobbing out some more in his initial run, he did a bizarre promo in which he talked about everyone in the WWF's telling him that the only way to get a push was to "give a little head." So he produced just that—a little mannequin head, which was apparently named Head. And he began carrying it to the ring with him and talking to it. And wouldn't you know, pretty soon the ECW faithful picked up on it, and Snow became their biggest star, and suddenly Vince wanted him back after all.

After floundering for much of '98, Snow found his calling with the hardcore division, and developed a truly bizarre persona in which he would become emotionally involved with the mannequin head and take in-ring advice from it. Midway through 1999, he had a lover's spat with it, and took up with a moosehead named Pierre instead. And, finally, he settled on a small dog named Pepper, who could also talk, and he seemed happy. But Big Bossman, perhaps jealous of Snow's strange but fulfilling relationship with the dog, took it personally and a feud was a brewin'!

In a tragic occurrence, Bossman kidnapped the helpless dog one week, and then offered peace talks with Snow soon after, during which he served him a suspicious-looking chow mein. Yes, Pepper was dinner. Yes, people were actually paid to write this stuff with a straight face. And yes, it all led up to Kennel in a Cell, the unanimous choice for Worst Match of the Year within the entire wrestling community at *Unforgiven '99*. Here's my review:

Kennel from Hell Match:
Al Snow v. Big Bossman

I'm kinda dreading this one, but we'll see what happens. Okay, so you've got the big blue cage around the ring, and over that the Hell in a Cell. Between them, rottweilers. Yeah.

Other contenders for Worst Match of the Year in 1999: Jake Roberts & Yokozuna v. King Kong Bundy & Jim Neidhart from the *Heroes of Wrestling* PPV, which featured Jake showing up obviously drunk, and Kevin Nash v. Hulk Hogan from *Nitro*, which lasted two seconds and featured Nash lying down for a fingerpoke.

Snow locks Bossman out of the inner cage, and they fight on the cage with the dogs below. It's supposed to be dramatic, but just looks stupid. JR notes that the match has "bowling shoe tendencies," making reference to his description of how the main event could either be a classic or "bowling shoe ugly" in the "Ross Report" this week.

*Al Snow has brought a bag of goodies with him, and he gets hit with a few of them by Bossman. Bossman has thought far enough ahead to pack a pair of wire cutters in his pants, and uses them to cut open a hole in the ceiling to climb out of. Powder and a stick get involved, and now Bossman is bleeding. Snow loosens the bottom rope, but nothing comes of it. Bossman gets some shots with the shovel in, then handcuffs Snow to the top rope. Bossman tries to climb out over the dogs through the roof (wow, psychology), but Snow actually snaps the handcuffs (to quote Bill Cosby: "Yeah. Right.") to make the save. Snow reaches into the bag, pulls out Head (oh, Lord, not this again), nails Bossman, and escapes at 11:37. Chalk that one up to experience, and let's not talk about it again, shall we? Give 'em * for effort.*

Okay, I admit, I was a little more forgiving than most, but *man* it was bad nonetheless. The important thing was that Snow and Head were reunited again, friends forever.

And speaking of friendship, there was another rather unusual one about to form at this time. In real life, Mick Foley was looking for an easier schedule and a less-demanding role in the company, leading to his retirement at Sur-

vivor Series '99, according to the plan. So after Undertaker (becoming increasingly cartoonish by the day) and Big Show (already having turned four or five times since his debut a few months earlier) won the tag-team titles at *Summerslam* from X-Pac and Kane, a scenario was set up whereby Rock would be coerced into a handicap match against the champions as a result of threats thrown back and forth.

However, kindhearted soul that he was, Mick Foley couldn't just stand by and see someone whom he respected as much as Rocky face that situation alone. And so, one night in September on *RAW*, while tennis preempted it for a few hours, The Rock and Mankind teamed up to face the tag-team champions, and ended up using a first-ever Double People's Elbow to finish Big Show and capture the tag-team titles. The Rock 'N' Sock Connection was born.

This was infinitely preferable to the WWF's last master plan for The Rock—feuding with Mr. Ass in "Kiss My Ass" matches. There was, however, an ulterior motive here as Mick Foley wanted desperately to turn heel for one last run as psychopath Cactus Jack, where he could put The Rock over huge. So a subtle story line began backstage with the team, as Mankind would shower affection and gifts on Rock, and would find his attentions completely unwanted and often ignored entirely. This story line arc led to the peak moment of the "sports entertainment" genre as artform, with the infamous "This Is Your Life, Rocky!" sketch on *RAW*. Essentially constructed as an opportunity for Rock and Foley to go out and improvise a twenty-five-minute comedy routine, it had Foley throwing a birthday party for The Rock and giving him presents—a "Rock 'N' Sock" jacket and a "Mr. Rocko" hand puppet.

Foley then began bringing out various people from Rock's past, including an "old girl-friend" who instantly became the biggest heel in the WWF when Rock announced that she had "cut the Rock off at second base!" in high school. This also spawned another Rock catch-phrase, as he talked about wanting a slice of "poontang pie" from her. The segment began to falter rapidly and limped to an end as Foley brought out Yurple the Clown and a birthday cake, only to have Rock walk away from the whole thing. It was essentially pointless and silly and lacked an ending, but it sent shockwaves through smart fans when it scored an unheard-of 8.4 rating for that quarter hour. Vince Russo was truly at his high point in the WWF in terms of power and leverage.

SCENE TEN
And Don't Let the Doorknob Hit You on the Ass on the Way Out

But no one has ever been higher on the totem pole than Vince McMahon himself, and nowhere was that more evident than in September of 1999. Lacking confidence in HHH's drawing power as champion and needing a whiz-bang surprise for the then-burgeoning *Smackdown* show on UPN, Vince came up with a doozy of a solution to both problems. Vince challenged HHH to a title match, and with the help of Steve Austin, captured the WWF title in a fluke upset. This is generally considered the low point in the history of the WWF title.

The title was put up for grabs at the *Unforgiven* PPV in a "six-pack challenge" match after Vince had forfeited it, and HHH regained it. Here's my review:

WWF Title Match: HHH v. Bulldog v. Rock v. Mankind v. Big Show v. Kane

Bulldog has a better mix for his music, it should be noted. And Kane has the SWANK road uniform on. Austin does color commentary while "enforcing." Rock and Bulldog start. It's the retarded four-corners rule, where anyone tags anyone and only two people are legal at one time. First pin wins.

Rock gets some of HHH until Kane tags himself in. He destroys HHH, but pisses off The Big Slow and gets knocked off the top. Mick tags in against Kane, and doesn't get very far, so Big Show tags in. Kane pulls out the enzuigiri and dropkicks and Bulldog tags in. He tags out quickly, leaving Mick and Big Slow. It quickly becomes Rock and Bulldog with a well-timed low blow turning the tide for Bulldog. Mick gets the tag, but won't fight his buddy so he tags Kane. Tombstone gets reversed to a legsweep for two. Mick in with a piledriver for two as fans chant for Rocky.

HHH and Mick brawl on the floor, and everyone fights down the aisle to join in. HHH gets a nasty piledriver on the steps from Mick, and Mick and Bulldog end up back in the ring. Mick stops to allow Rock to get his shots in. Rock does his Big Slow impression, drawing the big guy in. Meanwhile, the striking refs are out to jaw at Jim Corderas, the scab.

Meanwhile Part II, Big Slow pounds on Mick for a two-count. Rock tags in and takes Slow's head off with a clothesline for two. Rock and HHH brawl again. Back in the ring for Kane and Mick. DDT, but Big Slow tags himself in. Kane with the tombstone, but the Show is the legal man now. And away we go: chokeslam to Mick, but Kane clotheslines Show off the top to block. Bulldog powerslams Kane, HHH Pedigrees Bulldog, Rock nails HHH, and Mick finishes the sequence by applying Mr. Socko to Rock! So much for friendship.

Rock reverses to Rock Bottom for two. HHH makes the save. Big Show headbutts everyone and chokeslams Mick. It's all over . . . but the refs pull Corderas out at two and BEAT HIM DOWN! This is wild. Austin decides enough is enough and goes over to clean house on the rebelling refs. No wonder they're on strike. In the ring, Rock DDTs HHH for two, with Austin reffing now. Rock Bottom and the People's Elbow, but Big Show pulls Austin out at two. Bulldog nails Rock with a chair, Austin nails Bulldog with the same chair, but HHH gets the Pedigree in the meantime and Austin is forced to count it and HHH regains the WWF title at

20:25. I assume this sets up HHH v. Austin at No Mercy. HHH gets in Austin's face, so it's Stunner and beers all around. I think we may have our Match of the Year, finally. ★★★★½

As it turned out, the Match of the Year would come at the *next* PPV.

But bigger changes were afoot in the meantime. And it all started when Vince Russo did an interview for a Web site. Up until that point, Russo was not a well-known name. In fact, for the most part, he was hardly known at all. He was best known by smart fans as Vic Venom, his own trash-talking alter-ego who edited the WWF magazines and wrote "insider" columns. But for most of 1999, rumors persisted that Russo actually had a part in writing the shows. And then rumors got stronger that Russo was actually writing the shows. And then, in an interview with Ben Miller of WrestleLine.com, Russo shocked everyone by taking complete credit for all the writing since 1998, along with partner Ed Ferrera, and claimed that the shows were essentially being booked show-to-show, much of the time on a napkin three hours before they were to begin.

He also noted that he was working without a contract. It took awhile for most people to get their heads around Russo as the main writer of the WWF when we had all been conditioned to thinking of Vince McMahon as the prime force in his own promotion, but another shock was to come. In retrospect, it appears that the interview where he "came out" as the head creative guy in the WWF was merely a power play to boost his name value because, soon after, one day before everyone flew to England for a UK-only PPV in fact, Russo and Ferrera shocked the world by signing a long-term, big-money contract with WCW, without even giving McMahon notice or a chance to match the offer. Here's Russo's take, from an interview conducted by Wade Keller of

the *Pro Wrestling Torch* shortly after Russo had signed:

Let me put it this way and I'll be as honest with you as I can. Up until *Smackdown,* Vince was paying me very fairly. And I didn't have a beef, I didn't have an argument, he was taking care of me. But the reality was, once *Smackdown* started, my life had changed. And I've got to be honest with you and if I sound cocky, I apologize, as far as what I thought I should be making—I felt personally that I was far more responsible to the success of the World Wrestling Federation than any vice president he was paying whatever.

And you've got to understand, the whole company and how the company functioned and their success started from my brain. That's where everything began. So I looked at all these vice presidents and I knew they were making a good piece of change, but I never compared myself to anybody because as far as I'm concerned, without me, I don't know where you start. So what happened was, I gave him that dollar figure and he said to me, "Give me some time to think about it." What happened was maybe about a week passed. As each day was passing and as I was still in my routine of the grind, I just came to my conclusion, I said to myself, "You know what, even if Vince McMahon does come back with the money, realistically, I can't do this." That's what I said to myself. It got to the point that it wasn't a matter of the money. It got to the point that I was sacrificing my entire life and I couldn't do it. I knew in my head that realistically, I would be able to perform for Vince and give him results until the end of the year. Under those circumstances, I knew that by January, I would be done. So what happened was, having that sink in and realizing that, it was just a matter of time before I couldn't do this anymore. I took it upon myself to contact WCW.

The shockwaves throughout the industry and in the WWF in particular were immediate. McMahon asked all nonperforming employees to sign a one-year, no-compete clause in their contracts stating that if they quit or were fired from the WWF for any reason, they could not seek employment with WCW for one year. Almost everyone capitulated, except for Terry Taylor, who immediately jumped to WCW for the sake of his own family. It was supposedly on good terms, but after WCW folded Taylor wasn't one of the people brought into the WWF again, so draw your own conclusions.

WCW fans and spin doctors alike crowed over the Russo signing, although the general consensus among the online world was that after signing the WWF's talent, executives, producers, music guys, ring announcers, referees, color commentators, directors, and probably even the guy who catered the shows, one more acquisition wasn't going to turn the tide. There's a whole other book to be written on what the long-term effects of Russo coming to WCW actually were, but suffice it to say that the WWF is still around and WCW isn't, which is the argument I generally use to anyone who tries to tell me that *anything* WCW did in the last few years of its existence was useful and/or good.

Before we leave the topic of Vince Russo and never mention him again, I just want to clear the air on a couple of things. History has shown that Russo did tons of damage to the WWF's in-ring product because he lacked a fundamental understanding of what wrestling was. He also had a predilection for cheesy, soap-opera story lines. However, Russo did a few good things that

changed wrestling for the better, like the introduction of the backstage sketch, and a great concentration on developing characters for *everyone*, not just the main eventers. It's just Russo's own fault that he let his ego and wild ideas overwhelm the good ideas that he did have until he was turfed out of wrestling in late 2000 and made into the punchline of everyone's jokes about WCW.

SCENE ELEVEN
The Ladder Match Returns

Back in the fake world, there were a few immediate problems because of Russo's departure. The main one was that he had planned out the Test-Stephanie wedding, to be held in October, and no one else knew where he'd been going with it. So they did what all great soap-opera writers do in that situation—gave Stephanie amnesia as a result of getting hit in the head with a garbage can and delayed the wedding until late November.

A less-major problem was that Russo was in the ear of Jeff Jarrett, then the intercontinental champion, and a champion whose contract expired at the end of the month, a fact that astonishingly managed to elude management until the day before it was to expire . . . which happened to be the day he was scheduled to drop the title to Chyna at the *No Mercy* PPV. Whoops. Jarrett was unhappy in his role at that point, feeling (like a couple of other people) that Steve Austin was unwilling to work with him as a "tippy top guy" (to quote HHH) and that he would never advance past his current level in that environment. We never found out if that would have been true or not because the day of the *No Mercy* show, he asked Vince McMahon for an extra six-figure buyout, in cash, and told him he was joining Russo in WCW, where he could be a big star. And as promised, he did the job and left.

September to November was kind of a pointless dead zone as far as story lines were concerned. HHH was champion in name only and used lame, heel mannerisms while the WWF desperately cycled through a new persona for him each week trying to find a number-one killer heel in what they had. He defended against Austin in a pretty good match at *No Mercy*, but the match that everyone ended up paying attention to from that show seemed less important at the time. It was called the Terri Invitational Tournament (or T.I.T., nyuk nyuk) and the idea was that Goldust-less Terri Runnells was looking for a new team to manage, and had her eye on both hearthrobs-turned-goth The Hardy Boyz and goth-turned-hearthrobs Edge and Christian. So they did a series of matches on *RAW* and *Smackdown* and ended up tied in wins going into the PPV for a decisive ladder match for Terri's services.

Up until then, The Hardy Boyz had been given a fluke win over the Acolytes for the tag titles, but not much else, while Edge and Christian were used as flunkies for Undertaker and occasional enhancement talent. This match changed everything. Here's my review:

Ladder Match:
Edge and Christian v. The Hardy Boyz

Ref tosses Gangrel right off the bat. LET THE SPOTS BEGIN! Christian gets the first try for the money, and they take turns tossing one another off of the ladder. Christian impales Jeff with the ladder in the corner, then runs up the ladder and dropkicks him in the face. Nasty. Edge misses the dive to the corner and hits the ladder. Jeff goes for the money and Christian hits an inverted DDT off the ladder. Yow! Christian gets suplexed off that ladder, Matt gets powerbombed off, and Edge gets dropkicked off. Jeff puts Edge on the ladder and hits the senton bomb. More insanity as Jeff

goes to the top, leapfrogs the ladder, and legdrops Christian. Big round of applause for that one.

Edge finds another ladder (it's a tag-team match, why not two ladders?) and takes a swing, knocking Jeff off the other ladder. Matt returns the favor. Edge ducks a ladder clothesline and Christian cross-bodies the ladder off the top, nailing both Hardyz in the process. The Blonds baseball slide the ladder into Matt's crotch, drawing more standing ovations from the crowd. They put Jeff inside the ladder and slam it on him ten times, with the crowd counting along. May I just say all four of these guys are SUICIDAL?

Both ladders get set up, and Jeff and Edge race up. Edge gets the Downward Spiral on Jeff from the ladder. Matt gives Edge a neckbreaker from the ladder. Now it's Christian and Jeff, with a hiptoss to Jeff being the move in question this time. Then an unbelievably cool spot as the Blonds set up the ladders with one folded, sitting on top of the other, which is open. They try the assisted superplex onto that, but Jeff escapes, then dives onto the folded ladder, sending it into the air like a seesaw and nailing the Blonds in the face. Amazing. You just have to see that one to believe it. Another standing ovation for that one.

All the ladders get set up again, and now all four head to the top, and then all go crashing to the mat in a spectacular trainwreck. Another ovation for that one.

Now Matt and Edge race up a ladder, triggering a complex domino series that ends up with Jeff standing on the primary ladder and everyone else on the mat. That allows Jeff to grab the money at 16:22 for the win. An amazing, brutal, suicidal, instant classic. Note to ECW: If you're gonna do a spotfest, do a SPOTFEST. They all get a standing ovation, and after all that I feel like doing the same. ★★★★½

And *that* was your Match of the Year, unanimously voted as such by fans everywhere. It took awhile for both teams to really become the stars they eventually became, but it was a huge start in getting there.

Your other contenders for Best Match of the Year in 1999: Bret Hart v. Chris Benoit from *Nitro* (my personal pick) and Test v. Shane McMahon (covered earlier in the section).

SCENE TWELVE
Can the Belt Actually Fit Him?

By November, it was becoming obvious to the fans that the WWF wanted to run with Rock v. Austin II at *Wrestlemania 2000* and was building to it with HHH as the middleman. Undertaker was suffering from a severe groin injury and was going to be out for months, if not longer, and Mick Foley was busy putting over guys like Val Venis and Al Snow in the mid-card. So it seemed that Rock-Austin was the only logical choice left unless by some miracle they could get HHH over.

Survivor Series '99 was scheduled to be a three-way between Rock, Austin, and HHH for the WWF title (which HHH would win to advance the Rock-Austin mini-feud), but fate intervened in the worst way possible for the WWF. Steve Austin could no longer wrestle in his current condition. He needed neck surgery immediately. Of course, being the class acts they were, the WWF continued promoting Austin as being part of the main event all the way up until the show started despite knowing about his condition. Early in the show, an angle was shot in which Austin was run over by a mysterious hit-and-run driver and taken out of the match. It was obviously a stunt double, but I guess Austin had sympathetic back pains or something. The end result of all this silliness was that the WWF needed someone else in the main event because they were saving Rock v. HHH for later on as a backup plan. Test was pitched as a last-minute replacement up until, well, the last minute, but in the end sanity won out and we got . . . The Big Show.

The Show-Bossman feud gave Bossman one of the few great lines of his career ("You're a nasty bastard and your mama said so!"), but alas the blowoff match at Armageddon only lasted one minute and featured Bossman getting squashed like a bug.

See, Big Bossman, who was beginning to make cartoon supervillains look subtle by comparison, had hatched an insidious plot against Big Show by telling him that his father was dead (when he wasn't, although in real life had died years before) and then stealing the coffin when he actually did "die," and then topping it off by coercing Show's supposed mother into admitting that Show was conceived out of wedlock. So things were pretty bad all around for Big Show, leading up to:

WWF World Title:
HHH v. The Rock v. ????

We're betting on Test as the obvious replacement for Austin, but everyone is shocked when it turns out to be . . . The Big Show! Whoa. Show takes on both guys and does pretty well at it. Rock hits a legsweep on Show, but HHH breaks up the People's Elbow. They brawl to the entrance, and stay there for a while. Geez, another one of THOSE matches.

Back to ringside, more brawling. Nice spot as HHH and Rock suplex Big Show through the Spanish table. MORE brawling into the stands. Back in the ring (what a concept) where HHH and Rock bump the ref. Rock Bottom, no ref. Shane-o-Mac slides in and counts two. Another Rock Bottom, but Show pulls Shane out at two. Show and Rock fight on the floor as HHH grabs his belt. Shane wrests it away from him, and gets Pedigreed. D-X runs in, and Vince storms in after them. Vince takes a swing at HHH and misses, but takes another swing and connects, chokeslam, new champion.

Holy mother of God, who could've seen THAT coming? The match was the usual, overbooked junk, but the swerve was neat. * Big Show does the Shawn-esque celebration, essentially dedicating the win to his "just buried" father, which is a really good way to pay off the story line for the marks and give the big guy the credibility he's been sorely lacking.

So Big Show was the champion, who no one was waiting for, and HHH was back to square one again. The last three months were basically a write-off thanks to Russo's departure and all the injuries, so there was one positive out of it in that they were able to just try something new with the characters and start from scratch. So they did.

SCENE THIRTEEN
Stephanie Sets Rape Victim Rights Back Twenty Years

Rock was now the undisputed number-one baby-face, Show was put into a program with Big Bossman for the WWF title, and there was still the matter of that wedding to attend to. Plus, ex-Olympian Kurt Angle finally debuted at *Survivor Series* after a year of dark matches, and everyone immediately booed him out of the building for his boring technical style and smarmy "holier than thou" promos. For HHH, they were still desperate to get him over as a heel by any means necessary, so they ditched the entire Billy Gunn singles push and reunited the New Age Outlaws, then turned everyone heel and reformed D-X to act as HHH's cronies. When that *still* didn't work, the WWF had one more ace up its sleeve.

On the November 29 *RAW*, dubbed "RAW Is Love" before the show, Test was all set to marry his sweetheart, Stephanie McMahon. They spent the show doing vignettes of Steph's bachelorette party, plus other wrestlers congratulating Test, all leading up to the wedding at the end of the show. It seemed to be going smoothly, even with everyone in the WWF present, until the minister asked if anyone objected . . . and HHH's music hit.

It seems they had forgotten to play one vignette from the night before. Specifically, one shot by HHH's private cameraman, wherein the bartender at Steph's party had slipped a drug into her drink and helped HHH load her into a car. From there, they headed to Vegas, where a drive-thru wedding ceremony (and some impromptu acting from HHH as Stephanie) made them Mr. and Mrs. Hunter Hearst Helmsley.

The whole angle was later revealed to be a setup from the start, with Stephanie in on it all along, but that wasn't until months after we actually had to sit through HHH drugging his bride and then bragging about raping her. The really sad indictment of wrestling fans is that once it was revealed that Stephanie was no longer a virgin, despite it being not her choice, they began to chant "slut" at her.

Steph was in tears, and HHH made sure everyone knew that the marriage had been consummated several times that night. But the WWF doesn't do rape, according to their PR men. Just wanted to remind you. Vince was so enraged that the next week, he wanted a match against HHH at the next PPV, *Armageddon*, for the honor of his daughter. If he won, the marriage would be annulled. If he lost, HHH got another shot at the WWF title. And after nearly a year of trying new personalities and nicknames and tactics and styles, a good old-fashioned double-cross ended up being that one thing missing. Here's my review:

Vince McMahon v. HHH

Vince tosses powder into HHH's face to get the early advantage. Brawl outside the ring and to the back right away. Back through the crowd, then Mankind helpfully brings out a shopping cart full of goodies. More brawling on the floor, and now we go out to the military set. SANDBAG! SANDBAG! SANDBAG! Man, I wonder if JR was sitting there trying to resist calling the match that way. Why is there no juice yet?

Vince takes a Gatling gun to the head. Ouch. They fight to the back and Hunter escapes to the parking lot. Hunter has become the hunted, you might say. Or not. Vince wanders around looking for him, and almost gets run over as Hunter seems to have stolen Mankind's car and has taken a run at Vince.

HHH with a slam and an elbowdrop on top of a limo, and we do the "I have your hair, so let's walk, bee-yotch!" bit all the way back to the arena. HHH climbs up a conveniently placed scaffolding, and Vince follows. Oh, geez, this is gonna be bad for one of them. Vince takes the monster bump to a pile of mattresses below, and you can just TELL the crowd is waiting for HHH to follow with an elbow or something, but he just wusses out and climbs down. Vince finally blades after that fall.

HHH wanders down to ringside and trash talks Stephanie. Hey, wait a sec, isn't she wearing his leather jacket? Vince drags his carcass back to ringside and generally bleeds all over the place. Back in the ring and HHH goes for his trusty sledgehammer. Vince blocks with a low blow and grabs it. Stephanie runs in, but SHE wants the honors. Oh, like we don't all know what's going on here. Sure enough, she "changes her mind," allowing HHH to "steal" it from her, nail Vince, and get the pin at 29:44 (!). Yeah, they gave it thirty minutes, it blows my mind, too. And then, as everyone had figured out by last week's Smackdown,

HHH and Steph do the HUG OF DOOM, thus revealing that they were playing Test and Vince for suckers all along. Whether it was "predictable" or not, it was the correct ending to do even if the match could have stood to lose ten minutes or so. * * *

And now, finally, HHH was the badass, number-one heel in the promotion that they had wanted him to be since *Wrestlemania XV*. In fact, he was quickly becoming so hot as a heel that they couldn't justify keeping the WWF title off him any longer, especially with the fans' anemic response to Big Show as the number-one guy in the promotion. Unfortunately for Test, his involvement in the biggest angle of HHH's career was quickly buried when he did the job in a tag match and got sent into the mid-card doldrums for the next year.

> Some conspiracy-minded people have suggested that Test was buried because his hair was too similar to HHH's and thus threatened him.

As the year closed, HHH was poised for great things, the New Age Outlaws were once again the WWF tag-team champions (albeit not very deserving ones judging by the general boredom with their stale act) and Mick Foley was still strangely nonretired. In fact, there was a strange rumor floating around that for *Royal Rumble*, the WWF wanted him to main-event against HHH.

Within two weeks, that wouldn't seem strange at all.

Act Five

The McMahon-Helmsley Era (2000)

"Your Highness is also like a stream of bat's piss."
"What!?"
"I merely meant, your Majesty, that you shine out like a band of gold when all around is dark."

—Monty Python

"I want it all, and I want it now!"

—Queen

Champions as the year began:

WWF World Champion: The Big Show

Intercontinental Champion: Chris Jericho

WWF Tag-Team Champions: The New Age Outlaws

European Champion: Val Venis

Mutiny is never pretty, and never was that more clear than in the opening weeks of 2000 when WCW's situation went from worse to even worse. Whereas Vince Russo had jumped ship in October 1999, only two months later the power structure in the promotion was reeling and new, Turner suit Bill Busch took it upon himself to quell the uprising by offering releases for anyone who didn't like how they were being used in the company. Dozens of wrestlers made public overtures about leaving after the job was given to Kevin Sullivan, long noted for his failures as booker and for personal grudges.

With a week before the first WCW PPV of the year, *Souled Out*, it was down to a dozen. By the day of the show, it was down to four: Chris Benoit, Eddy Guerrero, Perry Saturn, and Dean Malenko. Benoit and interim booker Kevin Sullivan hated each other in real life due to a complex feud over Kevin's ex-wife Nancy (which then became a real-life soap opera), and Benoit realized that if Sullivan took over the booking from Russo, he'd never get a fair shake in the company. To prove him wrong, Busch told the beleaguered bookers to put the WCW world title on him at the PPV and said that after the show, if he still wanted his release, he could have it. The day after the show, Benoit tossed the WCW world title into Busch's trash can and was suddenly the hottest free agent in the wrestling business. Shortly thereafter, he and the other dissidents were WWF employees. This seemingly small talent exchange jumpstarted the WWF to their most successful year in history—creatively, financially, and qualitativey.

SCENE ONE
The Rock Wrestling Federation

HHH, the hottest heel for the WWF in years, was quickly reinstated as WWF champion, winning the title on the January 3 *RAW* by beating

The Benoit v. Sullivan story line from the WCW, in which Benoit stole Nancy Sullivan on TV and then in real life, became the template by which all wrestling break-up story lines have been measured by, and has also become one of the funniest running gags (at Sullivan's expense) in wrestling history. The joke (although it's mostly true, too) is that no one wants to have a real-life relationship extend to the TV world because, according to the Sullivan Precendent, when it ends on TV, it ends in real life.

Big Show cleanly with the Pedigree. And his standing in the company, story line–wise, was further increased using the WWF's own brand of twisted logic, because Vince McMahon was taking a leave of absence to recover from the match with HHH, Shane was nowhere to be found, and Linda was busy running the company. Thus, Stephanie was left with all the power in the WWF, and she and her new hubbie began using it to the best of their abilities, calling themselves the McMahon-Helmsley Era (remember, they were evil, not necessarily honor students in English class). This was just the latest in a long line of "Eras," "Factions," "Regimes," "Alliances," and other lame team names dealing with scheming heels, but for whatever reason this one actually clicked and HHH began acting like a jerk and as surrogate boss for Vince McMahon.

First order of business: annoy your enemies. In this case, the Rock 'N' Sock Connection, a constant thorn in the side of D-X. HHH set up a special "pink slip on a pole match" between Rock and Mankind, with the loser getting fired. This would seem to contradict logic, which would say that the person who grabbed the pink slip should get fired. But that didn't matter because Rock won the match and, alas, poor Mick Foley was kicked to the curb yet again by the world.

It didn't last long, though—early in January, Rock and the entire WWF roster set up camp in the ring and threatened to do a mass walkout if HHH didn't rehire Foley immediately *and* put him in a match against D-Generation X in that very ring. So HHH, always about fairness above all, granted the Rock's request and made an eight-man match between D-X and the team of Rock, Foley, and the Acolytes. Kind of a shame because I, personally, would have paid to see the "Rock Wrestling Federation" instead of Vince's nonsense much of the time.

By the end of the match, everyone had bugged off to the dressing room in a big brawl, leaving Foley and HHH one-on-one. And, to no one's shock, Foley got bloodied, battered, and pinned by the Game. That would seem to be the proverbial "that," but Foley had one last ace up his sleeve before he conceded defeat: On *Smackdown*, the arrogant champion boasted of defeating Foley, until Mick (still wearing the same, bloodstained shirt from *RAW*) came out to issue a challenge to HHH for a street fight at the *Royal Rumble* to determine once and for all who the tougher guy was. HHH pointed out that Foley was in no condition to do that match. Foley agreed, but amended that by noting he knew someone who *was*—and suddenly pulled off the bloody shirt and morphed back into his evil alter ego, Cactus Jack. HHH sold it as though Beelzebub himself were coming down that aisle after him. This was what we call the good stuff, folks. And can you believe—the match actually lived up to the hype and then some. Here's my review:

WWF Title Match: HHH v. Cactus Jack

Cactus gets a quick start, so HHH bails and grabs a chair. Jack gets it and legdrops it on his face. Out to the floor, where HHH gets suplexed onto a pair of pallets. And a garbage can. And onto the stairs. Note to self: don't piss off Mick Foley.

Cactus searches under the ring and finds a barbed-wire covered two-by-four. The ref gets in his way, so HHH steals it and delivers some shots with it. Ouch. It ends up at ringside with the Spanish announcers. Jack hits a double-arm DDT and then retrieves his two-by-four, which has been miraculously rewrapped with suspiciously rubberized-looking barbed wire. Well, I don't expect anyone to rip themselves apart with real barbed wire, but it looks silly to have different-looking weapons like that.

He drops an elbow with it and then bludgeons HHH with it, drawing some good juice. It's a MANLY blade job, turning HHH's blond hair red. Must have eaten his aspirin before the match. Jack tries the piledriver on the table, but HHH reverses. Back in the ring, and Jack then reverses the Pedigree, slingshots HHH into the post, then rams him face-first into the barbed wire. It gets two. Back out, and Jack pulls an older spot out of mothballs, taking a hiptoss into the stairs, right on his knee.

Back in and HHH works on that knee, then finds a pair of handcuffs at the announcing table. Oh, Lord, it's '99 all over again. HHH charges with the stairs, but Jack drop toeholds him and HHH goes face-first into the stairs. HHH finds a chair and starts doing a Rocky job on Jack, so he retreats outside as HHH closes in for the kill. Then, ironically, The Rock himself emerges with his own chair and bashes HHH's brains in. A cop unlocks the cuffs for Jack and now the crowd is just going BERSERK.

Jack stalks him back to ringside and delivers the piledriver on the Spanish table, successfully this time, but the table doesn't break. Man, that looked VICIOUS. Jack then finds a jumbo bag of thumbtacks and scatters them in the ring. Stephanie joins us at ringside. Cactus takes a backdrop in the tacks, and HHH gets the Pedigree for . . . TWO? Crowd starts chanting "Foley," but Jack walks into another Pedigree, ON THE TACKS, and that's enough to finish

it at 26:48. Oh. My. God. What an AWESOME brawl. I have new respect for HHH's brawling abilities after this brutal war. ***** I know I'm probably opening a huge can of worms with that rating, but after that, they deserve it.

> **T**he original ending to this match had HHH winning after the first Pedigree, but Foley kicked out on his own. This momentarily annoyed HHH until Foley asked him to do it AGAIN, this time on the tacks.

This was the match that *made* HHH. Before he was just a hot heel with a McMahon by his side—now he was a badass machine who just beat the shit out of the hardcore legend in his own match. What else can you say? Feuds like that are why I still watch wrestling after all these years of disappointments and toilet jokes masquerading as wit. Meanwhile, Rocky won the *Royal Rumble*, ousting Big Show in controversial fashion, and suddenly the buzz was on for *Wrestlemania*, big time: Rock v. HHH for the WWF title. But the twist du jour to that story line was Big Show's beef about Rock eliminating him under dubious circumstances (Show claimed that Rock's feet hit the floor first), and so a match was signed for *No Way Out* to determine who actually would go to *Wrestlemania* and face HHH for the title.

SCENE TWO
Goodbye, Mick. See You in Six Weeks

In the meantime, Cactus Jack wanted another shot at HHH's title, this time in the deadly Hell in a Cell environment. But, HHH noted, Jack already got a title shot in his own match, and lost. So more incentive was needed—in this case, Mick Foley's very career.

No one was terribly worried because much of the advertising for *Wrestlemania 2000* was already being built around Foley living out his lifelong dream of main-eventing a *Wrestlemania*, but the logic didn't really seem to click with that. I mean, if Foley wins the title, it's Foley v. Rock, and what the people really want to see is Rock v. HHH. So how could they book themselves out of that corner when the match had to have a winner and it was title v. career?

Well, unfortunately for Mick Foley and his fans, they didn't. Here's my review:

WWF World Title v. Career Match, Hell in a Cell: HHH v. Cactus Jack

The door is pretty clearly chained shut here, preventing Jack from reaching the top of the cage. Jack hammers HHH to start, then futilely tries to open the door. They fight on the floor, then back in where HHH gets the upper hand. Facebuster, but Jack backdrops him to the floor and grabs a chair. HHH uses the knee and sends Jack crashing into the cell. He tosses Jack into the stairs and into the ringpost. Jack gets up, so HHH tosses the stairs and beans him right in the head. Ouch.

HHH pounds the stairs with a chair for good measure. Back in, HHH batters Jack with a chair for two. DDT gets two, as do two more attempts. Cactus gets a low blow and a DDT on the chair for two. Russian legsweep onto the chair gets two. Jack seats HHH in the chair, but charges and takes a drop toehold into the chair for two. Back outside, HHH rams Jack into the cage a couple of times. Jack responds by slingshotting him into the cage, drawing blood. HHH does his Ric Flair impersonation as Jack rubs his face on the mesh to draw more blood.

Jack drops a chair-assisted elbow onto HHH on the floor. He tosses the stairs at HHH, who then ducks, and the stairs break through the cage. BINGO! Jack sees his chance and sends HHH crashing out of the cage, and piledrives him on the announcer table. He climbs the cage, but Steph pulls him down. Mick shoves the timekeeper aside and finds his favorite toy: the barbed-wire two-by-four. And this one ain't fake. HHH takes it in the face and climbs to the top to escape, and BOY does the crowd start to buzz.

By this time, the WWF crew was smartening up to how crazy their own guys were, and so precut handholds in the side of the cage in case someone wanted to climb up to the top. If you're gonna throw yourself fifteen feet to the ground and through a table below, you might as well be safe on the way up, I guess.

Mick follows, and gets shoved off onto the Spanish table. Crowd rewards HHH with the "asshole" chant. Jack blades. He tries, and fails, to toss a chair onto the roof. He climbs up, and HHH goes to town with the two-by-four on him. They slug it out on top, with HHH teasing a fall through the cage. Foley suplexes him and DDTs him. So what could be worse than a two-by-four wrapped in barbed wire? Lawler asked earlier in the match. Answer: A FLAMING two-by-four wrapped in barbed wire. Well, if you gotta do it, do it with style. HHH takes one of those to the head, and Mick tries to piledrive him on it, and that proves to be his undoing. HHH backdrops him off, and the cage gives way, sending Cactus plummeting to the mat below, which then BREAKS. Crowd chants "holy shit" for that one. Thank God they gimmicked the ring to break his fall.

HHH drops down and is horrified to see Mick crawling out of the wreckage like Frankenstein. It would prove to be an empty comeback, however, as a Pedigree is enough to finish him at 23:55 and rip the hearts out of everyone watching. That's the first retirement match where I can honestly say that I had absolutely no idea who was winning until the moment the ref counted three. And at least it was clean, without any of the shenanigans theorized by sheet writers so they can "un-retire" Mick on RAW due to a technicality. Well, if this is the end, it was a hell of a match to go out on. * * * * *

And if you think *that* was a weird bit of booking, people were really blown away when Rock *lost* the big match to Big Show when Shane McMahon interfered, thus making the main event of *Wrestlemania 2000* . . . HHH v. Big Show?

On a happier note, Chris Benoit and his merry band of malcontents made their official debut early in February, along with ECW import Tazz, adding some much-needed depth to the mid-card. Tazz beat Kurt Angle at the *Royal Rumble* in easy fashion, but soon got buried due to backstage politics and perceived "attitude problems." Benoit, Malenko, Saturn, and Guerrero (quickly dubbed "The Radicalz" by the WWF brain trust) fared little better, losing a three-match series to D-Generation X on *Smackdown* in their first official in-ring appearance.

The reasoning behind Chris Benoit losing his first match in the WWF to HHH on national TV boggles my mind: because he hadn't "paid his dues" yet. Benoit started wrestling in 1987, HHH started TRAINING in 1994. Think about that one.

Unfortunately, Eddy Guerrero suffered a broken arm in his match against the New Age Outlaws, immediately putting him on the shelf. Benoit was clearly the guy they wanted to push out of the bunch, however, and when The Radicalz turned heel the next week, Benoit was kept separated while in a leadership role for the group. A feud with fellow WCW escapee Chris Jericho seemed imminent and had hardcore workrate fanatics salivating.

Jericho, for his part, was stuck in a dead-end feud with Chyna, who insisted on staying in the male portion of the heavyweight division while having facial surgery done to make her look more feminine. Follow that logic if you can. Even after Jericho won the feud he couldn't escape her be-

cause she was booked to be his partner (not valet, because Chyna was "above" that sort of role) and equal. But he was still stuck in the mid-card, with no end in sight.

However, the fastest-rising star at that point had to be Kurt Angle. Initially met with boredom from the jaded fans, Angle soon played into that by becoming even more annoying and obnoxious than ever, and his rise became downright meteoric once that happened. He beat Val Venis to win the dead European title and bring it back to life, and then at *No Way Out*, upset Chris Jericho to capture the intercontinental title as well. Angle's post-match "celebration" with the fans by the concession stands was truly hilarious, and he started hitting his peak as a heel at this point, going to college campuses and campaigning for abstinence, among other things.

Oh, and Stephanie McMahon-Helmsley had a crush on him. Just a little one, though. Nothing that could possibly *mean* anything.

SCENE THREE
The Dudley Boyz Get the Tables . . . and the Titles

But with the McMahon-Helmsley Era running roughshod over the WWF and Big Show having cheated his way into the main event of the biggest show of the year, you just knew something had to give sooner or later. And finally, at the end of February, something did when Shane and Show gave Rock one last chance to earn a place in the *Wrestlemania* main event with a one-on-one match on *RAW* against Show . . . and Shane as the referee. Well, that was going about as well as you'd imagine for Rock . . . until Vince McMahon came out of seclusion (via a limo ride, of course) and stormed to the ring, punching out his own flesh and blood and making the final three-count himself to put The Rock into the main event.

Well, now it was a three-way match at *WM2000*, but there's *four* McMahons, and Vince was never one to let a perfectly good marketing gimmick get by him. Obviously he needed a way to work Linda "Couldn't Act Like She Was Burning if Her Pants Were on Fire" McMahon in there somewhere, too. And that way was Mick Foley, retired for all of two weeks and already getting right into the spirit of getting out of shape again. The match was announced as being Foley's "one night only" return, but the message again came through loud and clear: stipulations mean nothing. People who lose "retirement" matches are back again in two weeks. In fact, Foley already had lost one such match to set up the *Royal Rumble* match, and now was two for two in returning prematurely from his own retirement. He even joked about it on *RAW*, noting that most people return from "retirement" in six weeks, whereas he did it in two.

There is a theory within the WWF that they can keep trotting Linda out there whenever they need a ratings boost, because whenever she appears it's only to make an earth-shattering announcement, and thus her incredibly bad on-screen presence shouldn't matter. One could argue that they should just get someone else to play the role of Earth-Shattering Announcement Maker, but that wouldn't get another McMahon on TV, so you can see where the circular logic used by the WWF would immediately rule that one out.

In the real world, Vince McMahon called a press conference to announce the formation of his own football league, the XFL, which would begin play in February 2001. To this day, the meaning of the X has never actually been explained. More on Vince's pet project later.

Mainstream publicity proved to be a double-edged sword for McMahon, however—while the XFL was the laughingstock of the sporting world twelve months before ever playing a game, The Rock scored big points as the host of *Saturday Night Live* on March 18, bringing Big Show, HHH, and Mick Foley along for the ride. In fact, it was one of the highest-rated *SNLs* of the season, and Big Show proved so charismatic that the WWF actually found another excuse to push him—this time as a fun-loving guy who liked to imitate other wrestlers. Too bad he didn't learn how to imitate actual wrestling, too. That gimmick lasted about a month before getting as tired as the rest.

Meanwhile, in the tag-team ranks, things were getting all shook up in a dramatic way. Reigning champions, the New Age Outlaws, were as stale as a two-week old loaf of bread and could no longer be counted as "over" in any real sense of the word. In fact, breathing down their necks were three main teams: Edge and Christian, The Hardy Boyz, and the new and red-hot Dudley Boyz.

Well, to call the Dudley Boyz "new" isn't exactly accurate, as they had been honing their act in ECW since 1996, albeit with major differences from their WWF run. The gimmick was pretty high-concept stuff for wrestling: Bubba Ray Dudley was a big fat white guy, D-Von Dudley was a big black guy. They were brothers due to having for a father (Willie Love 'em Dudley) a traveling salesman who made sure to leave his business card in every town, wink, wink, nudge, nudge. There was also Little Spike Dudley, who was a 130-pound former English major and stockbroker turned wrestler-cum-punching bag. He was also related to the Dudleyz. Sadly, the WWF failed to import the rest of the Dudley clan to really beat the joke into the crowd, so we were denied the honor of having Big Dick Dudley, Dances with Dudley, Sign Guy Dudley, Chubby Dudley, and of course Dudley Dudley, lifting the intellectual bar for us all. On the bright side, the door is still open in the future.

> **S**adly, Alex "Big Dick Dudley" Rizzo passed away in 2002, robbing me forever of my jokes about people "beating on Big Dick" during the course of a match.

In ECW, their main thing was getting on the microphone and calling young girls in the front row bad names and nearly inciting riots due to bad blood from the fans. By September of 1999, with ECW about to get a slot on nationally available TNN, owner Paul Heyman wisely decided to get them off of TV and into the WWF lest they incite a riot on national TV. As it turned out, it might have helped his ratings enough for the company to survive—sometimes you need a good riot to stir things up.

The Dudleyz (remember—to be truly cool, you can't pluralize with an s, you have to use a z. This could come in handy if you need to impress a teenager one day, so write it down somewhere) came in with their tie-dye outfits and were given no mike time, and thus didn't get over in the least. However, their killer finisher, the Dudley Death Drop (aka 3D) kept them on TV long enough to find their voice. The first thing needed was a change in appearance, so the tie-dye was out and military fatigues were in. This immediately freshened the look and feel of the team, and soon one other element was added: tables. Long known for putting people through tables in ECW, that part of their personality hadn't been exploited in the WWF because the opportunity was just never there. Yes, I know, only in wrestling could one "freshen up" a character by having them throw someone through a table, but there it is. However, by January 2000, the Dudleyz were gaining a cult following and an issue was needed to set up a match with The Hardy Boyz at the *Royal Rumble*

(possibly over which team got to keep the z in their name, I'm not sure), so on the January 17 edition of *RAW*, Buh Buh powerbombed Jeff Hardy through a table and got a weird, trance-like look on his face.

Quick word of explanation: Although the current spelling of the name is "Bubba Ray Dudley," originally it was "Buh Buh Ray Dudley" because in ECW, when he was a babyface, he used to stutter and thus tuh-tuh-talk like this. Indeed, it wasn't what you'd call politically correct, but on the bright side at least he hadn't moved on to asking young girls whether they'd learned fellatio techniques from their mothers or not.

Speaking of which, the next week, the victim was the Hardyz' manager, Terri, which not only put more heat on the Dudley Boyz but got her away from The Hardy Boyz. The Dudleyz got a taste of their own medicine at *Royal Rumble*, losing in a table match to The Hardyz, but the table gimmick got accelerated soon after when they put woman after woman through the tables, most notably ninety-something Mae Young on an episode of *RAW* . . . off of the stage near the entrance, no less!

Suddenly, the Dudley Boyz had an over gimmick, an over finisher, and an over catchphrase ("D-Von . . . GET THE TABLES!") all without the swearing and violence inherent in their ECW days. By *No Way Out 2000* in February, it was time to put the tag titles on them as they manhandled the New Age Outlaws and won the belts while hardly breaking a sweat. The natural opponents seemed to be The Hardy Boyz, but the WWF wanted something a little more special for the big blowoff at *Wrestlemania 2000*, so they added underutilized Edge and Christian into the mix and made the first-ever triangle tag-team ladder match for the belts. From that point on, the tag-team division in the WWF was headlined by combinations of those three teams. Here's my review:

WWF World Tag-Title Match:
Dudley Boyz v. Edge and Christian v.
The Hardy Boyz

There's three ladders to start, with more to come presumably. ON WITH THE SPOTS! Three-way brawl to start. Buh Buh nails Jeff with a backdrop and full-nelson drop. Ladder comes into the ring and Buh Buh gets splatted with it. Matt elbowdrops D-Von on a ladder. Jeff misses a 450 on a ladder and looks to kill his leg. Buh Buh sentons him under a ladder. He then does the Terry Funk spinning ladder bit to knock everyone down. He gets dropkicked, however, and the Blonds pancake D-Von onto the ladder. Christian puts the ladder near the apron and dives off it onto Buh Buh and Matt, drawing the first "holy shit" chant of the night.

Jeff climbs for the belts, but Edge spears him off of it from the second rope. Edge goes up and gets powerbombed off by Matt. D-Von slams Matt off. Christian knocks D-Von off with a ladder. Three ladders get set up, and Buh Buh hits his half of 3D off of the top on Christian. Another "holy shit" chant for that. Hardyz go up one ladder each and hit Rolling thunder off of them. Jeff takes a crazy bump to the floor then, and back in the ring, the Blonds double-suplex D-Von off of the top of the ladder. Hardyz and Blonds each go up and knock one another off. Crowd chants for tables.

All six climb ladders, and Christian and Jeff go flying to the floor in a suicidal bump, while Edge and Matt get crotched on the top rope. This leaves the Dudleys alone. Christian crawls back in and gets smashed. Edge gets 3D. Tables are introduced to a HUGE pop. Dudleys put a table on top of two ladders, making a scaffold of sorts. Oh man, that's kinda insane. Much like the rest of this match. Two more are set up below in the ring. Buh Buh takes Matt outside and powerbombs him through a table as D-Von misses a dive and goes through one in the ring. Jeff's rail run is blocked with a VICIOUS ladder shot to the face. Holy shit!

Buh Buh finds a HUGE twenty-foot ladder down the

aisle and sets it up, plus a table, but gets nailed with the ringbell and put on the table by Jeff, who proceeds to deliver the SENTON BOMB FROM THE LADDER, THROUGH THE TABLE! Buh Buh is dead. Back in, D-Von gets taken out by Matt and Christian, who proceed to climb onto the scaffold. Edge joins them, knocks Matt off, and Edge and Christian grab the titles to become the new WWF tag-team champions. I need a vacation after just WATCHING that. * * * * * I'm starting to fear for Jeff Hardy's life, however.

The main highlight for *Wrestlemania 2000*, however (well, besides the eight-hour pregame show) proved to be the main event. As a match, it wasn't that great (especially with out-of-shape Mick Foley and Big Show weighing things down), but it proved historic if nothing else because HHH shocked everyone by retaining the WWF title with a pinfall victory over The Rock at the end. Indeed, it required yet another heel turn by Vince McMahon to accomplish the deed, but no heel had ever walked out of *Wrestlemania* with a successful title defense until that match. The show made millions, scoring a monster 2.0 buy rate and grossing over 13 million dollars, and the rationale quickly became: "If people will pay that much money to see a potential HHH v. Rock match once, they'll pay that much to see a *guaranteed* one."

SCENE FOUR
The Good Guys Finally Win

And so, after the obligatory McMahon family reunion the next night on *RAW*, a rematch was signed for *Backlash*, between HHH and The Rock, with a twist: Steve Austin would be the special ringside enforcer. Oooh, aaaah. In the meantime, however, Chris Jericho was busy calling Stephanie a whore on a regular basis, so HHH decided to get revenge. Well, really, what husband *wouldn't?* The more important question:

Would *you* walk up to someone who looked like HHH and call his wife names? And since this is wrestling, revenge happens in the ring, in this case a title match against Jericho on the April 17 *RAW*. And since HHH had been particularly abusive to referees lately, when Jericho got a rollup on HHH late in the match, he also got a fast three-count and the WWF title!

HHH was none too happy about that situation, so he made referee Earl Hebner a deal: reverse the decision and give him back the WWF title, or he'd kick his ass. Hebner made a counter-proposal: Promise never to touch him again while he's a WWF referee, and he'd reverse the decision. HHH went for that deal, and then (because it was the evil thing to do), fired Hebner and kicked the crap out of him. Why Jericho went along with giving the title back, we'll never know, but he did.

Sidenote: There have been many cases of "too much too soon" in wrestling, but Chris Jericho is not one of them. By April 2000, he was already perceived as a main-event guy by the fanbase at large, and was nearly as over as most of those already at that level. But those with the most to lose from a new face entering the main-event scene started finding things wrong with Jericho: He was too short, he worked too stiffly, he worked too loosely, he hadn't paid his dues, he couldn't work "WWF-style" matches (whatever that meant), his tights were the wrong color, whatever. The bottom line was that Jericho was excluded from the main event and put back into the mid-card, despite mammoth crowd reactions. This wasn't a sign of the end of the WWF main-event scene or anything—what with the WWF drawing in the vicinity of 50 million dollars total for their first four PPVs they had to be doing *something* the fans liked—but it was one of the little things that started to contribute to the problems they would face later on. No upward mobility—keep that one in mind for later.

Coming back to HHH for a moment, he was

on fire in the ring for the first half of the year, selflessly giving amazing amounts of himself in every match. Most notably, he was put into a meaningless squash against Taka Michinoku on *RAW*, and not only worked a nearly ✱✱✱✱ match against the hopelessly overmatched light heavyweight, but even put himself in several near falls until the audience actually believed that the 170-pound Taka might actually have a chance. Of course, he didn't, but that's part of the magic of wrestling—if the audience *thinks* he does, then he does.

A word on light heavyweights, if I may.

In the great debates, argued about in lecture halls and libraries the world over, one question keeps coming up more than any other: Which title is more worthless . . . the hardcore title, the European title, or the light heavyweight title? Now, gut instinct is usually to say the "hardcore title" because it once changed hands ten times in a single *match*, but at least it's still on TV now and then. Some might even say that the European title is the grand stinkeroo because it once changed hands when Owen Hart pinned a guy dressed like the champion.

> **I**n 1998, Owen Hart pinned Goldust, dressed as HHH, to win the European title. Almost one year to the day later, HHH dressed as Goldust to ambush Kane. I have no idea what significance this has.

However, I feel those interpretations don't look deeply enough at the issue, which is this: which of the titles does the WWF themselves often forget even exists? Yes, the light heavyweight title. In fact, as of January 2002, X-Pac held the title and he'd been injured for the better part of two months, with no return in sight. The title was established in December 1997, but in fact dates back to the early '80s, when it was the WWF junior heavyweight title. How prestigious a title was it? It was taken on a tour of Japan shortly after its creation and stayed there until 1996 because the WWF forgot to ask for it back. Once Taka won the first title, he became involved in such epic feuds as teaming with Val Venis to take on his fellow Japanese brethren in Kaientai until he learned that Val was making time with his sister. At that point, thanks to the established code of conduct for Japanese stereotypes, Kaientai's manager threatened to "choppy-choppy [Val's] pee-pee" and hacked up a salami with a samurai sword in order to stress that point.

Update: X-Pac never lost the title, as it was retired for good upon his return in March 2002.

Things got worse for the title late in 1998 when comedy jobber Duane Gill won the title from Christian, and then underwent a personality makeover to become Gillberg, a spoof on WCW's Goldberg. After that fizzled, Gill was allowed to leave and continue working indy shows with the gimmick. Nearly a *year* later, they remembered that Gill still had the belt and brought it back for Essa Rios to get over with. Of course, Rios was quickly overshadowed by his own valet, Lita, and the title ended up with Dean Malenko, where people finally thought it might gain some measure of respect at *Backlash* against Scotty 2 Hotty. But I digress.

Backlash was quite awesome overall, as The Radicalz started working their magic on the midcard—Dean Malenko got a Match of the Year Candidate out of comedy wrestler Scotty 2 Hotty, Chris Benoit finally started that feud with Chris Jericho over the IC title, and it was fabulous, and Eddy Guerrero did his part to get the European title up from the quagmire, despite a ludicrous, stereotyped Cheech and Chong gim-

mick. But even with all that great wrestling going on, the best moment of the show proved to be the last, as Rock finally beat the Game to end the reign of terror and send the fans home happy. Here's my review:

WWF Title Match:
HHH v. The Rock

Vince comes out and notes that Steve Austin will NOT be here tonight, no sirree. Big staredown to start. Slugfest goes HHH's way, but Rock gets a quick elbow. Pedigree reversed and Rock stomps a mudhole. Shane pulls him off. HHH hits a neckbreaker during the interference. Brawl outside and Rock eats table. Vince sends him to the ringpost and tosses him back in for two. High knee gets a fast two. High suplex and kneedrop gets two, three times. Into the chinlock. Shane ignores the feet in the ropes, thus giving it a purpose. Rock fights out and gets clotheslined down for two. HHH pummels him in the corner, but Rock drops him on the top turnbuckle. Vince KO's him with the title for two. Rock comes back and tosses HHH. Brawl outside, where HHH hurts his shoulder.

Back in, Rock gets a DDT, but Shane won't count, so Rock decks him. Back outside, Rock hits the stairs, and HHH goes for the Pedigree on the Spanish table. Rock reverses, however, and grabs BOTH HHH and Shane and delivers a double Rock Bottom through the table! That had to be seen to be believed. Back in, Vince attacks Rock, and Rock goes after him, only to get a low blow from behind by HHH and Pedigreed. Shane is still dead, however, so no ref.

Brisco and Patterson run out in ref gear and a big beatdown follows. Vince hits a wicked chairshot on Rock, and HHH goes for the final Pedigree . . . and THE GLASS BREAKS. The crowd goes INSANE as Austin (beer gut and all) uses a chair to destroy anything that moves. Everyone is out cold except for Rock, and Linda leads Earl Hebner in, shoving Stephanie aside on her way.

Back in, and Rock hits the spinebuster and academic People's Elbow on HHH as Hebner comes in to *count the pin at 19:22, and FINALLY it's game over as The Rock is the four-time WWF champion. ****½ Austin celebrates by towing the D-X Express remains to the ring and sharing some cold ones with The Rock.*

SCENE FIVE
Dance, Fatass, Dance

But while HHH and The Rock waged war in the main event over the WWF title, the *real* war was being waged in the boardroom. After signing a long-term contract with CBS/Viacom to put *Smackdown* on the UPN network, the WWF and Viacom began serious talks to end the nine-year relationship that the WWF had had with the USA network and move all WWF programming to Viacom-owned stations: *RAW* was to be moved to the Nashville Network (TNN), while *Sunday Night Heat* would go to MTV. USA made what it felt was a matching offer, and months of legal wrangling and bad blood followed. The end result? The WWF was legally in bed with Viacom because USA wouldn't promise never to preempt *RAW*, whereas TNN would. On that small bit of negotiation, the deal went Viacom's way and *Monday Night RAW* left for TNN in September 2000.

The move to TNN was particularly ironic as Vince had spent the better part of his last three years of commentating duties calling TNN "The Hee-Haw Network" in a dismissive tone of voice whenever he needed something to compare his hillbilly teams to.

Back in the tag-team scene, more happenings kept on a happenin'. For instance, Edge and Christian, formerly the nice (and *quiet*) Canadian lads who'd won the belts at *Wrestlemania* in an upset, suddenly started talking. A lot. In fact, they wouldn't shut up much of the time, insulting both The Hardyz and Dudleyz, and letting the fans know about a special five-second pose that they would do at the beginning of matches for the benefit of those with flash photography. Suddenly the term "reeking of awesomeness" was on the lips of everyone. Well, not everyone, but they were pretty cool. In fact, their heel turn was so effective that they turned the Dudley Boyz babyface by proxy, since no one in the tag scene could possibly be more obnoxious than Edge and Christian. And God bless 'em for it. The Dudleyz started developing babyface mannerisms of their own, like the "Wazzup" drop where Bubba Dudley would yell the famous beer slogan before diving face-first into his opponent's groin. Well, it doesn't *sound* all that cool, but it worked, trust me. And speaking of cool, there was Too Cool.

An unlikely success story if there ever was one, Too Cool came about in 1998 after the failed singles push of Brian Lawler, who wrestled as "Too Sexy" Brian Christopher. Still looking for a gimmick to get him over, he was paired with fellow light heavyweight/jobber Scott "Too Hot" Taylor and given the team name of Too Much. They proceeded to do nothing more interesting than hang around the dregs of the tag-team world and spent much of their time on syndicated shows like *Shotgun* and later *Metal*, generally losing matches to more established teams. Finally, by late 1998, the WWF was so ready to give up on them that they came up with a story line for Valentine's Day 1999, where the already vaguely homoerotic team would admit their love for each other and get married!

Luckily, Brian Christopher had the most well-timed injury in the history of wrestling right about

The gay tag-team gimmick would eventually land in the laps of Billy Gunn and Chuck Palumbo, showing that the truly shitty ideas will always survive.

then, leaving Taylor temporarily partnered with jobber Kevin Quinn while Christopher healed and the story was retooled. By the time Christopher returned a few months later, ECW rejects The Public Enemy had come and gone. Enemy's big thing was acting like bad-boy white rappers and street toughs, so as a kind of spoof of them, Too Much came out as Too Cool one week with Christopher now sporting goggles and huge pants and calling himself Grandmaster Sexay. Taylor became Scotty 2 Hotty, complete with fright-wig hairstyle and a goofy breakdancing spot in which he would do the "Worm" before dropping a chop on someone.

They would both dance after the match. It was all very stupid—and as 1999 progressed, it was getting over. What no one could have predicted was the element that put them over the top—Solofa Fatu. Picked up as a meaningless addition to the under-card in late 1999, Fatu (who had been part of the Headshrinkers and also the ill-fated Sultan character in 1997) was looking quite portly by that time and was given a sumo-wrestler gimmick as a sort of tribute to his cousin Rodney Anoia (aka Yokozuna). His original name under Vince Russo was Sammy Sumo, but once Russo left it was changed to the more sumo-sounding Rikishi Fatu. He was vaguely involved in a couple of mid-card feuds until one week, Too Cool was wrestling Val Venis and British Bulldog, only to get attacked by the Mean Street Posse. Rikishi made the save for no adequately explained reason, and for even less of a reason, danced with Too Cool after they had cleared the ring. The reasons proved not to matter, however, and by the beginning of 2000, Rikishi was coming out with Too Cool for every match, dancing after every victory, and all three were becoming the most over thing in the entire mid-card.

I personally never got the "fat guy dancing with the silly white guys" appeal of it all, but the crowds seemed to dig it, so good for them. But

Rikishi was still mid-card comedy relief . . . until HHH. In February 2000, HHH faced Rikishi on *Smackdown* for the WWF title, and gave him one of the first great singles matches of his career, making him look like a serious contender for the first time *ever*. The match ended in a DQ nonfinish, but Rikishi had arrived.

By May 2000, Too Cool had defeated Edge and Christian to win their first WWF tag-team titles and Rikishi was the intercontinental champion. Not bad for a team they wanted to marry to each other to get some heat, eh?

Elsewhere in the mid-card, the poor Radicalz were already falling apart at the seams as Eddy Guerrero's torrid love affair with the manlike Chyna tore the group asunder and drove Perry Saturn into the arms of Terri Runnells. The women in the WWF tend to get around. Chris Benoit was faring somewhat better, feuding with Chris Jericho and trading the intercontinental title back and forth in great matches. It's a dirty job, but someone's gotta do it. Benoit was supposedly being primed for a run at the top.

SCENE SIX
Morality Sucks

Back at the top, HHH wanted a rematch for the WWF title after losing it to The Rock under dubious circumstances, and furthermore he wanted a sixty-minute Iron Man match to settle things once and for all. Well, all of us cynical types were instantly suspicious of their ability to do a full hour given their limited movesets and inexperience at that sort of thing (hell, just look at what a mess their thirty-minute draw in 1998 was for evidence of that). Furthermore, Shawn Michaels (at that point in the "on" portion of his "off and on" relationship with the WWF) was named as special guest referee, making people think even more shenanigans would be in order.

Shawn had disappeared from his on-screen

role midway through 1999 after casually commenting that the WWF had screwed his buddy HHH over by not putting the WWF title on him at *Summerslam* and instead waiting for *RAW* the next night. Well, Shawn suddenly disappeared from the face of the wrestling world until he said 200 "Hail Vinces" or whatever the proper etiquette for sucking up to management was at the time, and in fact disappeared again shortly after that match. But such is life for retired wrestlers with big mouths.

But, once again, the power of awesome workrate made wrestling fans the world over stand up and say "Dang, Jethro!" in unison upon seeing the match. Oh, and that Undertaker guy finally came back, too, to top things off. Here's my review:

Iron Man Match, WWF title: The Rock v. HHH

Make or break time, kids. HHH sends the Regime back to the dressing room because he wants to do this himself.

First fall: Staredown to start. Rock hits the headlock and they fight over that for a while. Rock gets a pair of two-counts on rollups and HHH bails. Back to the headlock. HHH breaks and works the arm. Single-arm DDT gets two. Back to the arm. Rock gets a Rock Bottom out of nowhere at eleven minutes for the pin. 1–0 Rock.

Second fall: They brawl outside. HHH drops Rock onto the railing, but charges and hits his knee on the railing. Rock works the knee on the floor, dropping it onto the stairs. Back in, Rock kicks at the knee and applies a figure four, one which is thankfully 1,000 percent better than the one he'd busted out on Smackdown. It gets a few two-counts. HHH reverses and they brawl into the crowd. Back in with twenty minutes gone, HHH drops a pair of elbows for two. He keeps trying for the pin. I love that spot, especially in the context of a long match. HHH dumps Rock to the floor, then back in for a Pedigree and the pin to even it up. 1–1 tie.

Third fall: The Rock is still groggy, so HHH small packages him for the pin. 2–1 HHH. Great spot.

Fourth fall: Rock bails to recover and they brawl at the entrance. Back in, Rock tries a spinebuster, but that's reversed to a facebuster and a piledriver for ANOTHER HHH pin. 3–1 HHH.

Fifth fall: HHH goes up top and gets slammed off, and Rock busts out La Magistral for two. Whoa! Moveset, baby! HHH hits a high knee for two. Sleeper follows. Rock fights out and hits a belly-to-belly, then a botched floatover DDT for the pin. 3–2 HHH.

Sixth fall: Back to the floor for more brawling. HHH grabs a chair and wallops Rock in the ring, drawing a DQ. 3–3 tie.

Seventh fall: Rock is out cold, so HHH calmly pins him. 4–3 HHH, and another great bit of booking there.

Eighth fall: Fifteen minutes left, so HHH goes to the sleeper again. And it WORKS! 5–3 HHH. Man, what a well-booked match this is, with all sorts of finishes that you don't see every day.

Ninth fall: HHH and Shawn get into a fight, allowing Rock to come back. HHH takes a wicked bump over the top onto the cameraman, and they fight on the floor. Back in, HHH gets two. Rock superplexes him for a double-KO spot. He rolls over for two. Back to the floor, Rock slingshots HHH into the ringpost, but gets whipped into the stairs. Over to the announcer table, where HHH tries a Rock Bottom of his own, but Rock reverses and Pedigrees HHH! And the table doesn't break . . . OUCH! HHH gets counted out. 5–4 Rock.

Tenth fall: Four minutes to go, the McMahons make their return en masse. Rock takes them all out as they come, People's Elbow, good-bye. 5–5 tie.

Deciding fall: Two minutes left, and all of D-X charges the ring and attacks, but the nursery rhyme video plays on the Titantron, and The Undertaker returns! The crowd goes apeshit as he chokeslams everything in sight (with Shawn having been bumped onto the floor) as time expires . . . but Shawn recovers, calls for one last DQ at the bell, and HHH wins the match 6–5 to win the WWF title for a fourth time. Could've *lived without the finish, but the match was the best old-school WRESTLING MATCH I've seen since the '80s. HHH is God. ★★★★¾*

Yes, life was good in the ring, but outside the pressure was on. Eric Bischoff once gave a prophetic interview in which he warned Vince (three years earlier, mind you) that if the raunch and smut weren't toned down and out of the product soon, advertisers would begin deserting the WWF. And with a lot of pressure from the PTC (Parents' Television Council), that's exactly what started happening. And since this is the WWF we're talking about, it ended up turning into a complicated game of semantics and back-and-forth accusations between them and the PTC as to who was a sponsor to begin with and who actually had left and who would have left anyway and who was thinking of leaving but decided to stay until a tornado destroyed their offices and forced them to cancel the contract, whatever lame excuse came to mind for either side, they took it.

However, the WWF had crossed the line several times, including Kat going topless at the *Armageddon '99* PPV (that's one *g*, two *d*s for you fourteen-year-old boys who want to rush to the video store right about now and need the proper spelling), and with their future riding on the success of a network TV show, they couldn't afford the kind of pressure that the PTC was putting on them each and every week, no matter how unfounded it may or may not have been. Finally, the WWF devised a strategy to back-pedal on their bad-boy image without actually coming out and saying "We were wrong to market to children with this philosophy of wrestling"—the RTC (Right to Censor).

The RTC began when jobber Stevie Richards interrupted a nonsensical match between Dean Malenko and Jerry Lawler, where their respective seconds (Terri and The Kat) would have to remove clothing every time either guy got

RTC stands for "Right To Censor," which is a completely misleading twisting of the truth from Vince and company since it was the WWF themselves who pulled the plug on the raunch, not the PTC. It's certainly not as bad as the original idea for the RTC gimmick, which had an L. Brent Bozell lookalike wandering the audience with a picket sign glorifying censorship.

thrown over the top rope. When Terri went to remove her top, Stevie Richards blocked the view with a giant "censored" sign, while sporting a newly conservative shirt-and-tie look. He quickly changed his preferred name to Steven Richards (because, in the wrestling world, formal names are a good sign of evil intentions, along with sudden growths of beard. For example, Steve Austin is a good-old-boy redneck, Steven Regal was a stuffy British fop until they changed his name to William to counter the "Steve" glut in the WWF), and started recruiting members—namely Bull Buchanan, The Godfather (who became the more conservative Goodfather), and Val Venis (who was no longer a porn star, although he did cut the sleeves off his shirt and wear a white tie instead of a black one. Rebel to the end, he was). Ivory was later added as the prudish voice of reason from the female side, playing a shrill bitch with faint undertones of homosexuality, thus putting forth that old chestnut about how those conservative elements against the persecuted WWF would loosen up if they just got laid once in a while.

Presumably negotiations were ongoing to get Rodney Dangerfield to throw a kegger to destroy the RTC once and for all, but that's just speculation on my part. Keep in mind that this was a billion-dollar, publicly traded company shooting angles that were solely intended to take shots at their critics. Even worse, these goofs were actually pushed. Buchanan and

Goodfather won the tag titles from The Hardy Boyz later in the year and stunk up the entire tag-team division in the process. I mean, Charles "Godfather" Wright is a hideous enough wrestler when he's having fun—you can imagine how boring the guy got once he was reduced to playing the voice of reason and wearing a tie everywhere. It took almost an entire year for the writers to come to their senses and scrap the idea, but the damage had been done and the PTC started fighting even harder to get *Smackdown* taken off the air.

SCENE SEVEN
This Is Elevation?

As we get back into the fake world again, *King of the Ring* was approaching and to say that the writers were having trouble finding another combination of Rock-HHH without having it look completely stupid is an understatement, to be sure. So instead they chose to focus on the tournament itself that year. (Even though common sense said that either Angle or Jericho almost had to win it, and with those two meeting each other in the first round . . . can you say "forgone conclusion"?)

With a strong field and many booking possibilities, it seemed to be a can't-miss year. But it did. Rikishi was inexplicably pushed to the finals against Kurt Angle, who won easily to become King Kurt Angle. The main event of the show proved to be equally forgettable. Rock teamed up with the returning Undertaker and his brother Kane to face HHH and the McMahon family—Vince and Shane. For those keeping score, Undertaker returned as a babyface and Kane happened to be one himself at that point, so they were aligned and remained that way almost one whole PPV before splitting up and violently feuding again. Next time on Jerry Springer: "My Brother Is a Former Undead Devil-

Worshipper Turned Redneck Biker, and I'm a Fire-Throwing Masked Freak Who Couldn't Talk but Now Can!"

The stipulation to sell the match was that whoever scored the winning pinfall would become the WWF champion. Rock pinned Vince McMahon to win the match and the title, his fifth one. Only in wrestling can titles change hands without the champion actually losing. Imagine the Colorado Avalanche playing six games of the Stanley Cup Finals against the New Jersey Devils, only to have Gary Bettman declare that the Chicago Blackhawks would play the seventh game on behalf of one of the teams and the winner would be the champion. That sort of thing happens all the time in our so-called sport and we as fans hardly even blink an eye anymore. Of course, we hardly even blink an eye if Rob Van Dam does a frog splash from the top of the arena and lands headfirst in a medium soda from a burger joint. So perhaps we're not the best people to ask about it. Anyway, this show is generally considered a "cutoff point" in the story lines because things went in new directions immediately after.

Direction number one: Chris Benoit was suddenly established as the big challenger to Rock's WWF title, and paired with Shane McMahon in order to give him main-event credibility. Of course, the only main eventer who would ever put him over was The Rock, but that was the *idea* behind it, at any rate. A pretty cool little stable called "The Conspiracy" (yeah, I know, $100K a year for writing this stuff and that's the best they can come up with . . .) was formed with Benoit, Edge, Christian, and Kurt Angle, but it was forgotten after the *Fully Loaded* PPV in July and never mentioned again. Such was life in the WWF.

Direction number two: HHH was darn sick and darn tired of hearing Chris Jericho calling his blushing bride, Stephanie, a whore, so he challenged him to a Last Man Standing match at the PPV to settle things man-to-man. And since it's HHH, the interview took twenty minutes and was very boring. Standard logic pegged this as a perfectly good opportunity to give Jericho the big win and make him into a main eventer.

Direction number three: King Kurt Angle, excited over his winning of the tournament, has an impromptu celebration at the catering table backstage during *RAW* and accidentally spills refreshments all over Undertaker's motorcycle. Undertaker is miffed at the blunder, so Angle offers a perfectly good (and economical) scooter to replace the gas-guzzling bike as a show of good faith. Undertaker refuses and wants instead to beat up Angle, which struck me as a bit extreme for an honest mistake. In order to stress his point, Undertaker tosses the scooter off the stage and destroys it. Of course, Angle gave the scooter to Undertaker as a gift, so really he was destroying his own property, but the rubes ate it up, so what can ya do? The inevitable match is signed for the PPV.

Direction number four: Given Shawn Michaels's hasty exit from the WWF (again), a new figurehead was needed, and Mick Foley was just the man for the job. He assumed the commissioner position on the *RAW* following *King of the Ring* and immediately promised no more boring twenty-minute interviews. HHH immediately launched into a boring twenty-minute interview to protest the decision. Foley was soon seen backstage in every other segment, annoying Edge and Christian at every turn, and banging his gavel. As a pleasant side effect, Foley gave Edge a soda as a friendship offering, prompting Edge to declare that "Sodas rule!" and giving them a new catchphrase. Their run as heel tag champions launched into the stratosphere soon after. Soda companies rejoiced at the free PR.

Direction number five: Stephanie still had the hots for Kurt Angle, but HHH wasn't clued in

yet. But it was still hanging in the background, mentioned now and then in passing.

The booking of the matches leading up to the PPV seemed really strange, however, as the "new blood" never really got any kind of advantage on the old guard, and in particular Angle was getting the beats put on him by Undertaker week after week with no retribution seen. This seemed somewhat counterproductive in regard to people they were trying to elevate, but most assumed the payoff would come at the PPV. Well, the matches were certainly great, but the outcomes weren't quite what we had wanted. From my review:

Kurt Angle v. Undertaker

Brawl outside to start. Into the ring, Nash . . . er . . . Undertaker drops an elbow, but picks him up at two. Suplex gets two, but again he picks him up. Whew, good thing, because I don't think Angle could survive that devastating vertical suplex. Angle tries a sleeper, which goes nowhere. Emerald City Slam gets two for Diesel III, and Angle gets tossed to the floor. He finds his cartoonishly huge wrench and clips the American Fatass with it.

Back in, Angle works the knee as the great and powerful Oz gets to show off his range of selling by lying on the mat and going "ouch" occasionally. Wow, way to put over the new talent, Mark. Poochietaker comes back and they slug it out, won by Taker. What a shock. Chokeslam and the Poochiebomb finish at 7:36. Retire now, you crippled, has-been, slow-moving, fried-food eating, motorcycle-riding, no-selling, tobacco-chewing, no-money-drawing, talentless piece of selfish SHIT. Kurt Angle is the future, you are NOTHING. Deal with it. And take Kane with you when you go. I'm sure the idiot rubes will cry and Ask the Rick where you went again for six months the next time you leave, but I'll be happy to see you gone for good, where you can't drag down any more PPVs. ½*

Last Man Standing:
HHH v. Chris Jericho

Jericho pounds away to start, and HHH bails. Jericho follows with a springboard dropkick and we brawl. Back in, HHH USES THE KNEE, and puts Jericho onto the floor. Hotshot on the barricade furthers the damage. Into the ring, HHH works the ribs and chokes Jericho down with his own bandages. Onto the floor—HHH suplexes him onto the concrete. Jericho is up at five. Into the ring, HHH goes to the abdominal stretch, a move which makes sense within the context of the match. Jericho hiptosses out and comes back. Lionsault hits the knees, and HHH DDTs Y2J for a seven-count.

HHH tries the sleeper, hooking a body-scissors, at which point the dorky UFC-supporting contingent smugly points out that such a move would be counter-productive due to the placement of the legs. You see what I have to put up with? It gets a nine-count. HHH slugs him down, Jericho keeps asking for more. HHH adds a Pedigree and relaxes on the top rope. Jericho gets up at nine. HHH grabs a chair and BRINGS THE PAIN. He gets stopped from Pedigreeing Jericho on the chair by a low blow, and Jericho DESTROYS him with a chairshot, triggering a MANLY, primo bladejob that immediately pours all over the ring and hits 0.65 Muta with no effort at all. Have I mentioned HHH is God?

Jericho fires back with a flying forearm and a missile dropkick. Bulldog to the chair, HHH is up at four. HHH goes over the top, but whips Jericho into the stairs. He tries a Pedigree on the stairs, but Jericho reverses. They each ram a monitor into each other's heads, and both are up at nine. Back in, Jericho gets the Liontamer, and for a moment we think they might do the Austin-Bret ending. No such luck as Stephanie breaks it up and takes one herself. HHH knocks Jericho to the floor and finds the sledgehammer. He misses and Jericho slingshots him into the post, then nails him in the gut with the hammer. He tries a Moonsault off of the railing, but HHH blocks, suplexes him through the table, and BARELY beats the count at 9.99999 to win the match at 23:13. That was quite the little emotional roller coaster and a Match of the Year Candidate to boot. ****¾ Can Rock-Benoit top that?

WWF Title Match:
The Rock v. Chris Benoit

As is the norm tonight, brawl to start. Rock chases Shane, then stops to slingshot Benoit into him, which gets two. Rock goes for a crossface, and Benoit bails. Back in, Benoit hits a gutbuster and gets a running knee for two. Benoit goes to the apron, but gets superplexed. Benoit blasts Rock with the belt for two. Rock's powerslam gets two, but Benoit hits a backdrop suplex and a Sharpshooter. Rock escapes, but Benoit dumps him onto the floor. They fight outside and Benoit gets posted.

Back in, Rock pulls out a dragon-screw legwhip and figure four (!). Benoit makes the ropes. Rock hits the floor, where Shane smokes him. Benoit and Rock hit the crowd, and Benoit suplexes Rock back in. Into the ring, Rock gets a DDT for two. Benoit lariat gets two. Benoit backbreaker gets two. Standing neckbreaker gets two. Slugfest, and Rock powerbombs Benoit backward onto the top rope, which was either an ugly mess up by Rock or an awesome sell job by Benoit. Pick 'em.

Benoit gets a running elbow for two. Diving headbutt cues the double-KO. Rock rolls over for two. Slugfest, and Rock hits the spinebuster and People's Elbow . . . but Shane is distracting the ref. Rock only gets two as a result. Benoit comes back with a superplex for two. Benoit stomps Rock into the corner. Rock blasts out with a lariat, Benoit responds in kind. WICKED! Benoit grabs a chair, and Rock takes it, but Shane finds another one, blasts the ref with it, and leaves the smoking gun (chair?) in Rock's hands. Rock slaps his crossface onto Benoit as the ref revives, and DQs the Rock . . . and BENOIT WINS THE TITLE! WHOO-HOO!

But wait, there's more . . . as Benoit celebrates, that bastard Foley comes out and orders the match to continue. DAMMIT! Benoit hits the triple suplex for two. Crossface, and Rock makes the ropes. Again, and Rock makes them again, but more slowly. Rock Bottom finishes quickly after, at 22:08. I hope Benoit beats the holy hell out of Mick Foley tomorrow night because it would not only advance his badass persona and elevate him, but I'd feel much better. The match rocked my world, but the ending was a little too Dusty Rhodes for my liking. Still, another MOTYC, minus ¼* for disrespecting Canada's finest with a three-minute teased title reign. ****½

The supposed elevation failed to come as Angle survived unscathed, but Benoit and Jericho were back fighting each other at the very next show. People began commenting that HHH may have been the smartest man in professional wrestling by getting out of doing the job to Jericho in that match. He would continue to prove that as the year proceeded. In fact, he was thrust back into the WWF title scene again with a number-one contender's match involving HHH v. Angle v. Jericho ending up in a bizarre double-pinfall between HHH and Angle, making the main event of *Summerslam* into a three-way featuring Rock defending against both Angle and HHH.

SCENE EIGHT
Idiots of All Sorts

But that wasn't the story line that everyone was waiting on—the really good stuff was coming via the happenings backstage. Stephanie was hanging around Kurt Angle much more frequently than should have been healthy, a situation that HHH would normally have been quick to deal with by whatever means necessary. However, he had suddenly developed a crippling brain injury, which had rendered him a total idiot, and as a result he found himself being seduced by Trish Stratus while Stephanie walked in at the worst possible time. Good thing no one in the WWF watches TV.

A word on TV for a moment, if I may.

One of the main differences between the WWF and normal sitcoms (besides the steroids, injuries, incoherent story lines, and megalomaniacal owners) is that the WWF destroyed the "fourth wall" separating the program from the viewer long ago. Ever since the Russofiction of the WWF and the proliferation of the mindless, backstage segments that came with it, cameramen have become like invisible men in the WWF, hanging out in the most private and intimate moments of discussion and even bodily emissions without a second thought from the performers. You'd think, for instance, that a cameraman standing there shooting video in the bathroom while someone was on the toilet might arouse suspicion from the pooper in question, but you'd think wrong because it's been seen several times in the WWF since 1999, many of them involving Big Show.

However, in the irony to end all ironies, while cameras in every nook and cranny don't faze anyone in the least, at the same time no one in the WWF ever watches their own TV show. Because, logically, a couple of hours a week of watching *RAW* on the monitors backstage would sure clear up a lot of the dumb misunderstandings that fuel the business in a hurry. Film critic Roger Ebert defined this phenomenon as the "idiot plot," because the characters have to be idiots not to ask the one or two simple questions that would clear the whole situation up in two minutes or less. "Hey, Rock, did you hit me with that belt?"

"No, look, it was that other guy, see it's right there on screen."

"Cool, let's go get a beer."

That would make for a much shorter show, of course.

Mick Foley, ever a caring and concerned family man, noticed the tension inherent in the whole Kurt-Stephanie-HHH-Trish mess, and did his part to stir shit up by forcing HHH to team with Trish on a regular basis, thus annoying Stephanie more and more, and driving her further toward Kurt Angle. This led to situations like HHH showing Trish a few basic wrestling moves before a match, only to have Stephanie walk in while he had her bent over in a hammerlock. Obviously the training worked, however, as late in 2001 Trish went on to win the very prestigious women's title using her vast array of wrestling knowledge, and she had HHH to thank for the training. I think that once, while she was wrestling Stacy Keibler in a giant plastic pool filled with gravy, she actually used that very hammerlock reversal that got HHH into trouble in the first place.

> **U**pdate: Trish Stratus, in all seriousness, has actually turned into a very good woman's wrestler.

A quick word on the women's title, if I may.

This period also marked the glory days for that belt because Stephanie McMahon won the title in classic screwjob manner just before *Wrestlemania*, and proceeded to hold it for months afterward. Why is this a good thing? Because she never defended it and thus we were spared the agony of watching poorly wrestled women's matches for the entirety of her reign. Truly I long for those days. But I digress.

As trouble brewed and *Summerslam* approached, Angle took advantage of the situation, waiting until Stephanie was accidentally knocked out cold by her own husband after a match, and then helping her recover backstage with a well-timed kiss on the lips. This was, without a doubt, the most engaging soap opera wrestling had ever seen, and most people thought

it would be impossible to blow the angle. They were wrong.

Summerslam was, for the most part, a fairly innocuous show that year, but again there was some good wrestling on top. Benoit and Jericho put on another show-stealing performance, and in a case of "don't tinker with perfection," chairs were added to the mix for another match between Edge and Christian, The Hardy Boyz, and the Dudley Boyz. Here's the crux of the wrestling mindset summarized for you in one sentence, right here: If in doubt, throw a chair into the ring. The result? Tables, Ladders, and Chairs, aka TLC. Here's my review:

TLC Match:
Edge and Christian v. The Hardy Boyz v. Dudley Boyz

Chair-throwing exhibition to start. The ladders come in early and Buh Buh makes the first run at it. Edge legsweeps both him and Matt off of the ladders. Christian climbs, but Buh Buh takes him off with the full-nelson bomb from the ladder! OUCH! Jeff climbs and Edge pushes him off, onto another ladder that snaps up and smashes the prone Matt in the face. DOUBLE OUCH! Dudleyz hit the Wazzup Drop from the ladder, and D-Von brings the tables. Christian takes 3D through one. They stack the tables outside two-on-two, but Edge foils that spot with a chairshot. Matt hits the Twist of Fate on Edge and a legdrop off of the ladder, and Jeff follows with the leapfrog legdrop OVER the ladder. Edge gets sandwiched in a ladder and Matt tosses Christian off of the top rope, onto that ladder, killing Edge. Oh man, these guys are INSANE.

Outside, Jeff tries the swanton bomb spot from WM2000, but Buh Buh is onto him this time and moves. Continuity! Big ladder gets set up, and four guys climb. All four fall off. Buh Buh's still alive so he tries, but the champs push the ladder over and he takes a dive through that table stack outside. Awesome spot. Matt tries it, but D-Von is okay now, so HE pushes the ladder over, and Matt goes through AN-

OTHER table stack on the OTHER side of the ring. I fear for these guys' lives, I really do.

Edge and Christian climb, but now Lita comes out and pushes THEM off. She takes a spear from Edge moments later and rams her head into the mat. Man, even the people running in are bumping like freaks. D-Von and Jeff, the last survivors, race up the ladder and each one grabs a belt . . . and the ladder falls over, leaving them swinging in the air! Wild! D-Von falls off and the crowd explodes . . . but Jeff can't loosen the belts, and Edge and Christian smash a ladder into him to knock him off, then climb up and grab the belts to retain. Canadians SO rule. Gotta go the full monty here again. * * * * * No thirty-seven-second pose from the champs, though.

Of course, the thing with these sorts of matches is that the spots look increasingly less cool every time you see them, but initially as a spectacle first and match second it was incredible. And speaking of making spectacles of themselves, things weren't going very well for HHH and Stephanie's marriage, as Stephanie again got nailed by HHH (in the wrestling sense, not the less-than-proper sense) during the main event of the show, and again Kurt Angle was there to rescue her. The Rock pinning HHH to retain the WWF title was largely incidental next to the grand soap opera that was unfolding before our eyes. And since this is wrestling we're talking about, there was only one way for that soap opera to end: in the ring.

A word on the writing for a moment, if I may.

The WWF has had an internal personality conflict in the past few years, but this was the point where it really began to take its toll on the booking and on-screen product. The problem was that Vince McMahon, in his infinite wisdom, didn't visualize his product as "wrestling," because that has a negative stigma in the legitimate media, so when you talk to him about shows like *RAW* and *Smackdown*, it's a "live action-adventure series." However, the people on the writing committee he uses to script the shows generally come from one of three different backgrounds:

a) Wrestling (Bruce Pritchard, Michael Hayes, Paul Heyman)
b) Soap Opera (Vince Russo, Stephanie McMahon)
c) Comedy (Ed Ferrera, Brian Gewirtz)

So what you have is a combination of soap opera and comedy writers with a wrestling background trying to write an "action-adventure" series. So you'll get some backstage comedy skits, some love triangles (actually, a lot of them in the case of Stephanie's writing), and some in-ring action tacked on as an afterthought. In fact, one WWF producer was once heard to comment during the heyday of Vince Russo that once they get rid of the ring, then things would get a lot more fun. But the thing that the WWF never seemed to understand was the thing that promoters have known for decades: The backstage stuff (or "ga-ga," as it's usually called) is just there to build to the matches. It's not an attraction on its own. People don't go to arenas to listen to HHH bickering with Stephanie or see Mick Foley do a comedy routine with Edge and Christian. If the story line doesn't eventually lead to an in-ring payoff, or if the payoff in the ring isn't built to by a good story line, then business falls. It's a balance, and by mid-2000, the WWF was getting fooled into thinking that the matches were just an afterthought and the long-term effects of that would soon show themselves. But not yet.

Because Steve Austin was getting ready to return.

SCENE NINE
Kurt Strikes Out

See, someone had run Austin over with a car at *Survivor Series '99*, and boy was he pissed about it. The WWF was smart enough to keep him off TV until he was ready to be there again, but they announced that he was starting an "investigation" into whoever did the evil deed, at which point presumably the person would be reported to the police for attempted murder like any normal person would. Ha ha, just kidding, I wanted to see if you were paying attention. No, see, because the WWF doesn't do murder, they say so all the time—what the car incident became in WWF-speak was "attempted vehicular homicide." Well, that's *much* better for all the kids watching. And since the story lines take place in a bizarro amoral fantasyland, the only way to settle things was for a match once the culprit was revealed. If only the real world were so easy to deal with.

Chris Benoit was getting screwed over, again, as the plan for *Unforgiven* originally had Rock v. Undertaker v. Kane in a triple-threat match for the WWF title (Undertaker and Kane were fighting again, for those like myself who have trouble keeping track), until they came to their senses and realized how much that match would suck. So Benoit got inserted into it as both the guy to carry the match and do the job at the end. Lucky him. Here's my review:

WWF World Title Match:
The Rock v. Chris Benoit v. Undertaker v. Kane

Big brawl to start. Rock and Benoit head into the crowd. Kane hits a flying lariat on UT for two. UT hits a clothesline for two. Big boot gets two. Rock comes in, Samoan drop on Kane gets two. Rock and Kane slug it out, then UT joins in and they double-team Kane. UT

and Rock go, and Taker gets a side slam for two. Rock reverses the ropewalk and UNDERTAKER TAKES A BUMP! Whoa! Kane in, and the ref is bumped. At 7:00?

Taker chairs Rock, and Benoit chairs Taker . . . and gets the pin and the WWF title at 7:11! No, wait, Mick Foley comes out and takes the title away because Undertaker's feet were on the ropes. I have never understood the logic behind booking matches where any manner of weapons were completely legal and pinfalls count anywhere in the state, but pinfalls are stopped for having a foot on the ropes. So it's a Dusty Finish in the main event as the match continues.

All three lay the beats on Benoit. UT elbowdrop gets two. Benoit lays in some Canadian Violence on Rock, and the rolling Germans get two. Diving headbutt gets two, but Rock reverses to a crossface on him. Undertaker breaks it up. Kane chokeslams him for one. Rock catches Kane with the spinebuster coming off the ropes, and Benoit DESTROYS Rocky with a clothesline to break up the People's Elbow. BENOIT IS YOUR SAVIOR!

Undertaker wedgiebombs Rock for two, Kane saves. Taker and Kane fight outside, and Benoit blasts both with a chair and slaps the crossface on The Rock. We're all cheering for a pass-out finish, but Undertaker breaks it up after about two minutes in the hold. Chokeslam to Benoit for two, and Kane and Taker fight again. Rock Bottom for Benoit finishes at 16:07 and Rock retains. I figured either Rock or Benoit would walk with the title, and we'll probably see a rematch on the first TNN RAW. Hot ending, match was totally carried by his holiness, Mr. Benoit. * * *

Even though this was the match to end the show, it wasn't the one that people had spent money for, nor was it promoted as the main event. That honor went to the Angle-HHH showdown, which by now was getting so heated that Commissioner Foley inserted himself into the match as special referee. The fans, casual and hardcore alike, were prepped for the big angle at the end when Stephanie dumps HHH to turn him babyface, and sides with Kurt Angle to begin a big heel run at the top for him. Instead:

Kurt Angle v. HHH

Angle sings "Happy Birthday" to Stephanie. HHH's ribs are heavily taped from the sledgehammer attack on Smackdown. Angle works them to start, but Hunter backdrops him out. Brawl on the floor, and HHH spears him as they head back in. Angle suplexes him on the ribs, and we go kicky-punchy for a bit. Angle gets a German suplex for two and shoves Foley, who shoves back. SMELL THE CONFLICT!

Angle backdrop suplex gets two. More punching. HHH messes up a neckbreaker and they slug it out. Knee-Fu from HHH gets two. They do some weak brawling outside and HHH tries that Pedigree on the table again, but Angle reverses and suplexes him onto the Spanish table. Cool spot. Back in, Angle goes to the ribs and works them like a pro. Belly-to-belly superplex gets two. The lack of heat for this match is pretty astonishing, and yet at the same time not astonishing considering the pace of the match. Angle hooks the ABDOMINAL STRETCH OF DOOM. Well, might as well ring the bell right now.

Moonsault misses, and HHH comes back. A sort-of Pedigree (his one arm is dead so it's only a half-Pedigree) puts Angle down, and then HHH calls Stephanie in and tells her to choose. She reluctantly nutshots Angle, and HHH finishes him with the Pedigree at 17:24. Pretty disappointing. **¾ HHH gives Steph a weird, bloody kiss after the win to rub it into Angle. So this basically resolved nothing after six months of buildup, and didn't advance anything, either. Great use of my thirty dollars, guys. And what was the point of Foley refereeing? What an oddly booked match.

And that was that. The angle was never followed up on again as HHH remained a heel, remained married to Stephanie, and remained a tippy-top guy in the WWF. Probably not coincidentally, RAW never again reached the heights

What we DIDN'T know at the time, but do now, is that HHH had actually dumped Chyna in real life for Stephanie, at the same time that Stephanie was gaining more and more power as part of the writing team. Funny how that worked out for poor Kurt, isn't it?

of ratings it had been doing throughout 1999–2000. The political forces backstage had spoken, and Angle had been deemed unworthy of getting the blowoff win that would have catapulted HHH into a babyface slot on top.

SCENE TEN
Kurt Makes His Comeback

Another big thing happened the night after *Unforgiven*, however, as *RAW* moved from the USA network to The National Network (formerly The Nashville Network) as part of the new deal with Viacom. The WWF immediately began blaming the ratings decline on people not being able to find the new home for the show, but that seemed a little weak and forced, even for their usual spin doctors. I mean, how hard was it to check a *TV Guide*, anyway? But they certainly went all out with the initial show with Steve Austin making his first appearance on *RAW* in ages after punking out Shane McMahon the night before and getting into a verbal confrontation with Mick Foley over who exactly should be investigating.

With the plans being for Austin to meet his attacker in the ring at the next PPV, *No Mercy*, most people figured (correctly) that things would get wrapped up within the next four weeks. And, well, *Columbo* it wasn't, but it was enough to keep the fans guessing while Foley revealed little snippets of information (like "the driver had blond hair," which was roughly half of the dressing room at the time) and tension between Foley and Austin grew.

However, the more people with blond hair that Foley asked, the more things pointed to one man: The Rock. Who of course doesn't have blond hair. But then if they stopped to think about stuff like that, people might change the channel. So on the October 9 RAW, after Rock and Rikishi won a tag-team match, Foley came out to confront Rocky on the matter once and for all. He laid out all the evidence, and then declared him . . . not guilty. And since it wasn't him, it had to have been Rikishi. The reasoning? First, Rikishi had no reason to be there that night (since he hadn't been hired yet, even though he was, but I guess we were all just supposed to not know that) and second, the car was somehow built for someone bigger.

Well, Mick should have been a lawyer in another life, because Rikishi immediately broke down and admitted everything, then brought a racial argument into things about the WWF holding down Samoans. Amazingly, and I'm as shocked as anyone about this, Rikishi didn't immediately get over as the monster main-event heel that they wanted. In fact, without his little dancing buddies Too Cool, he really had no gimmick left at all.

I know what you're thinking: "Scott, a big fat Samoan guy who enjoys shoving his ass in people's faces reveals that he's really a hit-and-run driver avenging the cruel treatment to Samoan people the world over . . . and it doesn't draw millions?" Yes. It is indeed true.

Austin met Rikishi at No Mercy in October, and to the shock of no one, the match sucked because Austin was still recovering from the neck injury and Rikishi was, well, Rikishi. But fear not! HHH, the smartest man in professional wrestling, was waiting on the sidelines (after beating Chris Benoit in the semi—main event to quash his upward mobility) to save the angle and propel the WWF into the heavens of ratings

bliss and gold-paved roads. He was also taking an interesting character turn, as he was being turned into a de facto babyface by his wife's decision to become Kurt Angle's permanent manager, and by his hard work and cool entrance, which involved spitting out a bottle of water with precision timing and giving a primal scream (which looked a lot like a yawn) in time with the music.

Astonishingly, in the main event of that show, Kurt Angle won the WWF title from The Rock—actually, not *that* astonishing, really, because Stephanie doesn't align herself with losers. Here's my review:

WWF Title:
The Rock v. Kurt Angle

Slugfest, and Angle gets a chairshot on the floor. Back in for some choking. Rock hits a Samoan drop and Angle bails. They fight to the back and Angle gets tossed through the backdrop. Angle whips him into the tech area and back to the ring we go. Rock goes punchy-kicky, and works on the knee. Dragon-screw into the Sharpshooter, but Steph distracts the ref so he can't see the tapout. Angle hits a belly-to-belly off Rock's chase of Stephanie (Run, Steph, run! Free them melons!) and gets a flying forearm for two. We HIT THE CHINLOCK, and Rock comes back and dumps Angle for more brawling outside.

The EVIAN SPEW OF DOOM cues the comeback, but Angle grabs the title belt as Steph distracts the ref. It's a no-DQ match, just hit him! Angle KOs Rock for two. Angle goes upstairs and gets crotched and superplexed for two. A sweet, German suplex by Angle sets up the ARM-BREAKING MOONSAULT OF DEATH, which misses. Lucky for Rock. Rocky comes back with the Hurricane DDT for two. Belly-to-belly sets up the spinebuster, and Stephanie tries to interfere, but gets Rock Bottomed for her troubles.

Angle sneaks off and HHH runs in to beat on him, then stops to Pedigree The Rock for hitting his woman. Kurt crawls back in and covers for two. Crowd thought that was it. Another DDT gets two for The Rock. Angle bails, and now Rikishi waddles in for some more interference. Angle low blow, but Rock gets the Rock Bottom. Rikishi comes in, but avalanches Rocky by mistake, then superkicks him by mistake. Angle gives both guys the Olympic Slam, and we have a NEW WWF champion at 21:33! Nice to see someone at least get the title off a pinfall for once. **** *Great drama and pacing, despite the interference.*

This was something of a revelation with multiple ref bumps, people running in, managerial interference, and foreign objects being practically scientific classics compared to some of the more stupid ways that titles had changed hands that year alone, such as cochampions, tag matches for singles titles, three-way matches where the champion never got pinned, and the hardcore title in general.

Not surprisingly, Stephanie's "permanent" run as Angle's manager didn't even last until the next PPV, as anyone with any knowledge could tell you of what the "permanent" in wrestling actually means most of the time. The HHH-Angle angle was kinda still boiling under the surface, with HHH getting bigger face pops and Angle moving in on HHH's woman in a more subtle fashion, but once Steve Austin killed Rikishi in a cage match a couple of weeks after the *No Mercy* PPV, that issue was dead and buried and it was suddenly revealed that Rikishi was working for someone else when he'd made the hit on Austin. And, after burying Angle in a nontitle match once and for all, HHH then turned on Austin and revealed himself as the mastermind behind the whole thing. Note to future wrestlers: do the wild thing with the boss's daughter to increase your chances of getting a push.

It should also be noted that HHH finished his master plan by . . . you guessed it . . . hitting Austin with a sledgehammer.

SCENE ELEVEN
HHH No-Sells Death

I would be remiss if I didn't mention the Conquistadors story line at this point, a plot so horribly complex that it would have made Einstein go cross-eyed. Basically (and I hesitate to use the word "basic" to describe anything involved with this feud), The Hardy Boyz won the WWF tag titles from Edge and Christian at *Unforgiven* in a cage match. But . . . the former champions couldn't get a rematch, so a mysterious Mexican team called Los Conquistadors (a reference to a famous jobber team from the '80s) made their debut and started racking up cheap wins. They looked suspiciously like Edge and Christian under masks.

The original Conquistadors were played by Miguel Perez (father of the Boriquas member of the same name) and Jose Luis Rivera. In case you care.

At *No Mercy*, they actually won the tag titles from The Hardy Boyz, but the next night on *RAW* Edge and Christian were scheduled to face the Conquistadors for the titles! Edge and Christian thought that it would be two jobbers playing the role, but after Christian was injured and Edge was forced to face the new champions alone (and lost), they unmasked to reveal The Hardy Boyz. So, in effect, The Hardy Boyz had won the titles from themselves the night before! And you thought *Pulp Fiction* was hard to follow. . . .

Speaking of stupid story lines, the one that took the cake had to be Chris Jericho v. Kane, which was started over Jericho accidentally spilling coffee on Kane, triggering their feud. Sadly, there were no classic one-liners like "You want cream and sugar with that, *bitch*?" The really sad thing is that the WWF saw Kane as a "top guy" and figured that pairing him with Jericho would actually help Jericho, instead of doing what it did: force Jericho to wrestle a big, slow goof and thus hinder his own style to the point of unwatchability. Oh, well, live and learn.

> **A**mazingly, the shitty quality of the matches was blamed on Jericho, who apparently couldn't work "WWF style" like Kane could.

Poor Kurt Angle got stuck facing Undertaker again at *Survivor Series* while everything treaded water with Stephanie McMahon's transition to head writer in real life. Meanwhile, Steve Austin faced HHH in the main event. Here's my review:

Steve Austin v. HHH

Austin whoops Hunter to start, and they punch each other. Thesz press and elbow from Austin, and they brawl outside. Not much happens; crowd's dead. Back to the ring, Austin nails him with a monitor and he does his traditional bladejob. Austin sits and grabs a couple of beers. Finally, we head back into the ring. Kick and punch, and HHH reverses the KICK WHAM STUNNER with a neckbreaker, but can't capitalize. More kicking and punching gets two for HHH. Austin spinebuster, but the second-rope elbow misses.

Back outside, more weak brawling. HHH gets backdropped through a table. Back in, it's KICK WHAM STUNNER, but Austin doesn't want the pin. He grabs a chair and tries to Pillmanize HHH, but he escapes and they fight to the back. The Radicalz attack and beat Austin down, but since none of them are tippity-top guys, they just provide a distraction while HHH warms up the car.

Austin counters with a forklift, however, and drops HHH, car and all, fifteen feet through the air onto the concrete, which in all likelihood should have killed him in real life. I don't quite see how that's not worse than HHH running Austin down last year, but maybe that's

just me. Besides, I'm sure that with a second opinion from Dr. James Andrews, HHH's death will be downgraded to a 6–8 weeks' recuperation period and some rehabilitation before returning from the afterlife to do a run-in at Royal Rumble. Ah, the Sportz Entertainment finish, God bless the legacy of Vince Russo. No contest at 25:00 or so. *½

Luckily HHH had a really good doctor because that case of death was downgraded to "alive" the next night on *RAW* and he returned a week later to screw Austin out of the WWF title in a match against Kurt Angle. I guess his conditioner had given him mutant healing powers like Wolverine or something. Unfortunately, those healing powers wouldn't last forever, as we'll discover in 2001.

In the sporting world, the rest of the year would be classified as the "rebuilding phase" while Vinnie Mac was preoccupied with recruiting cheerleaders for the XFL or whatever he actually did to prepare for the start-up of his league. He was also busy trying to buy the free-falling WCW at this point, but the deal fell through at the last minute. He'd keep trying, however.

SCENE TWELVE
Some Other Stuff Happens

The year closed out with *Armageddon*, a good but ultimately meaningless show that saw a Hell in a Cell match for the WWF title, with Angle defending against all the top guys: Rock, HHH, Austin, Undertaker, and Rikishi. Okay, four top guys and Rikishi. Everyone knew that eventually the road would lead to Rock-Austin at *Wrestlemania* anyway, the only question was "Which one would get the title before then?" That wasn't answered here as Angle barely got a win to retain.

As 2000 came to a close, Vince McMahon

was going through a mid-life crisis and was tiring of his marriage to Linda. Mick Foley wanted time off to write another book, so an angle was shot whereby Edge and Christian would finally get their revenge on him, destroying Mick to earn points with Mr. McMahon, who then fired Foley from his position as commissioner as a Christmas gift to himself. Linda had a nervous breakdown as a result of all the chaos, and Trish Stratus started to move up the pecking order, seducing Vince McMahon instead of HHH, now.

But 2001 would bring the biggest stories in the history of the WWF, both good and bad. Very, very bad.

Act Six

There Goes the Neighborhood (2001)

"He who fights with monsters might take care lest he thereby become a monster. And if you gaze for long into an abyss, the abyss gazes also into you."

—Friedrich Nietzsche

Champions as the year began:

WWF World Champion: Kurt Angle

Intercontinental Champion: Chris Benoit

WWF Tag-Team Champions: Edge and Christian

European Champion: William Regal

It's funny—it's always said that wrestling is a cyclical business, and as we get into the home-stretch of our little story, things start to collapse back in on themselves again. We began with Hulk Hogan leaving the sinking ship called the WWF in 1993 and going to Eric Bischoff's WCW, which was on the verge of self-destruction and needing a last-minute boost to survive much longer. And as we reach the beginning of the end, we again find WCW self-destructing and in need of a last-minute boost to survive.

Only this time, there would be no knight in yellow-and-red armor to save them because he was smart enough to know when to desert the ship before the rats could even start jumping overboard. Hogan's exit from the wrestling business came in July 2000, when an increasingly insane Vince Russo wrote an interview for him-self wherein he went off on Hogan for a good ten minutes, calling him every name in the book and blaming the entire downfall of the promo-tion on him. This may or may not have been 100 percent real. Of course, Hogan still has a job and Russo doesn't, so it once again proves where the brains in *that* relationship were.

By January 2001, World Championship Wrest-ling, once a force in the industry and for two years the recognized number-one promotion in the world, was like a dying, cancer-ridden pa-tient waiting for someone to pull the plug. The talent pool had dried up, the deep pockets of Ted Turner had been replaced by the brutally hardline economics of AOL Time Warner, and the company was losing upward of $100,000,000 for 2000–2001 alone.

SCENE ONE
Monopoly Isn't Just a Game Anymore

Vince McMahon had not only won the war, but he had shot the body after death, stomped on it, cremated it, and then pissed on the ashes. Pie-in-the-sky dreams of start-up Fusient buying out

WCW with former wunderkind Eric Bischoff at the helm soon went by the wayside as ratings and pay-per-view revenues dropped to levels embarrassing even for Time Warner, the company that puts the WB network on the air. By March, it was decided that *Greed* would be the final WCW PPV under the current ownership, and whatever happened past then was someone else's problem. We just couldn't believe in our hearts whose problem it would actually end up being.

Things were even worse for debt-ridden, badboy, last-of-the-indy-giants Paul Heyman as his wanna-be national company ECW was millions of dollars in debt with no possible way of paying it back. Of course, since it was a private rather than public company, he simply lied about the lack of money to anyone who asked, got months behind in paying the talent, and finally filed for bankruptcy before crawling to Vince McMahon yet again—not for money to support his promotion this time, but simply for a job so he could continue surviving. ECW's brainwashed fanbase continued denying the inevitable from the day the TNN show was unceremoniously cancelled, right through to the date of the fictitious February PPV, which came and went with no sign of any further signs of life from Extreme Championship Wrestling.

And through it all, there was Vince, alive and kicking, actually trying to peddle the XFL as serious competition to the National Football League. His own marketing people couldn't even decide what the *X* stood for and this was supposed to revolutionize the industry? Thankfully, Vince did come up with one interesting idea at this time—*Tough Enough*. Pitched to MTV as a mix of the *Real World* and the WWF, it would be a wrestling-based reality show where the goal would be to train thirteen people to be "WWF superstars" (even with most of the show focused on in-ring training, the vile word "wrestler" is still taboo), with two eventual winners—one male, one female—who would get guaranteed WWF contracts as a result.

The funny thing (funny-ironic, not so much funny–ha ha) is that all the WWF's spin doctoring and PR brainwashing is generally dedicated to stressing how this isn't "rasslin'" and how the WWF superstars are in fact action-adventure stars who rely more on their charisma and backstage skit skills than banging and crashing like in the old days. And yet for thirteen episodes, these poor kids were learning to run the ropes and take bodyslams and work psychology into the matches just like in those bad ol' "rasslin'" matches. Unintentional irony aside, the show was a much-needed ratings hit for both the WWF and MTV, but nearly half the contestants left the show with permanent and serious injuries before it was won by male winner Maven and female winner Nidia. Maven got a few in-ring shots on *RAW* and *Smackdown*, while Nidia made a cameo and then disappeared into the minor leagues. The show, for all intents and purposes, was a success, and MTV committed to at least another year of programming after the first season.

Nidia eventually reappeared playing the psychotic ex-girlfriend of delusional wanna-be superhero The Hurricane, while acting as manager for Jamie Knoble, best known in the WCW for playing one-third of a Japanese team despite having a Southern accent. So really she ended up no worse off than anyone else in wrestling.

Thankfully, Vince's seeming insanity (both on- and off-screen) didn't generally extend to the in-ring product as Steve Austin was becoming downright resurgent in the ring against fresh opponents like Kurt Angle and Chris Benoit. Many people still felt that the true money in having a *Wrestlemania* rematch against The Rock lay in heel Austin v. face Rock, but Austin's popularity was once again making that hard to do. Both Rock and Austin were entered in the *Royal Rumble* to try to earn a shot at the champion at *Wrestlemania*, while the actual champion (who was becoming more of a nonfactor by the minute), Kurt Angle, defended the belt against HHH in a match that was hopefully going to settle their feud once and for all. It didn't quite work out that way. Here's my review:

WWF Title Match:
Kurt Angle v. HHH

Wristlock sequence to start, and Angle gets a hiptoss. HHH bails. Back in, HHH pounds him down in the corner, but Angle backdrops him and goes back to the arm. Three suplexes get two. Brawl outside, which HHH gets the best of. Back in, HHH drop toeholds Angle into a Native American deathlock. This political correctness stuff is going too far. And where are these same, tree-hugging morons to stand up for truth, justice, and the American Way when someone lumps all the wrestling fans together as knuckle-dragging Neanderthals on a national broadcast and laughs about it? Ah well, the world is going to hell, what can ya do? Oh yeah, the match.

Hunter gets a legwhip, but Angle gives him an enzuigiri on a second try and gets two. HHH goes back to the knee as the announcers' conversation veers to Andy Kaufman and how little money Man on the Moon made. HHH bails, but an attempt to post Angle from the outside backfires. Brawl outside, HHH meets the stairs. Back in, Angle misses a blind charge and gets posted, and HHH adds a chairshot to the knee for good measure. He drops Angle kneefirst onto the stairs, then back for a clip. He pounds the knee à la Ric Flair.

I apologize in advance to any HHH advocates out there for comparing him to an aging, semi-retired ex-star currently wrestling in the WCW. I further apologize in advance to any Flair advocates out there for comparing him to a gassed up, egomaniacal manipulator with a limited moveset and bad music. If, in the body of the previous two apologies I have offended either HHH or Flair advocates while apologizing to the opposite number, I apologize in advance also. Man, this political correctness stuff is complicated. Is there some kind of "Spiritual Enlightenment for Dummies" book out there I can brush up on so I, too, can find my inner child, move to Florida, and vote Democrat? I hear Chyna's book is a good start. On second thought, I think I'd rather just poke my own eyes out.

HHH goes into a weird deathlock variation, and Angle fights out, but walks into a facebuster. HHH slaps a figure four on him and uses the ropes, but Trish gets involved and suddenly a HUGE catfight with Stephanie erupts, drawing about one hundred times more heat than the match. They're impressively banging each other around outside the ring and seem ready to move on to clawing each other's eyes out, but Vince struts out to stop them. They continue fighting right around him, drawing a big pop from the crowd. Vince finally resorts to putting Trish over his shoulder and carrying her out, but Steph knocks them over and goes to town again before everyone eventually makes it back to the dressing room.

Everyone suddenly remembers the ongoing match, and Angle gets a small package for two. He shoves HHH to the post on a figure four attempt, and they slug it out. DDT gets two. Atomic drop and German suplex get two. Russian legsweep sets up a trip to the top, which HHH prevents via a Razor's Edge (!!!) for two. The conspiracist in me would go "hmm" right about now.

Pedigree attempt is blocked with a slingshot, which is in turn blocked by HHH, which is in turn accidentally countered by Angle with a low blow. Moonsault gets two for Angle. Hunter dumps him and the ref is bumped. Hunter posts Angle . . . and goes to the top? Angle armdrags him off, no ref. Angle goes to help him up, but the poor sap gets bumped AGAIN. HHH grabs the belt, but Angle meets him with a belly-to-belly. HHH comes back with the Pedigree, no ref. Steve Austin runs in, tosses the ref back in, KICK WHAM STUNNER and Angle gets the pin to retain at 24:12.

See, now that's the finish that Austin-Angle from RAW should have had. Although a clean finish on a PPV is infinitely preferable, especially when Angle is turning into Honky Tonk Man 2000 with all the cheap wins and frequent nontitle jobs. Overbooking stupidity and crowd apathy aside, this was much better worked than the Unforgiven match. ***¾

Meanwhile, Steve Austin won the *Royal Rumble*, outlasting such luminaries as Drew Carey, Haku, the Honky Tonk Man, and the returning Big Show.

Funny story about Haku's involvement: Up until the day before the show, he was the WCW hardcore champion known as THE MONSTER MENG (you have to spell it like that for the full effect), but was (incredibly) working without a contract. The WWF simply signed him away, and the next day the WCW hardcore title was completely forgotten and its entire history erased from the WCW Web site. Oh, and of course they aired a match on their syndicated *worldwide* show featuring Meng a week later. That's when everyone pretty much knew that they were ready to pack it in and give up completely. There wasn't even any fanfare surrounding what even a year earlier would have been a pretty big deal—he just showed up as Haku again (his former WWF character) and was never mentioned by WCW again.

SCENE TWO
The Glass Ceiling

Jericho and Benoit, seemingly with nothing else to do but wrestle each other on every PPV, had another ****¾ classic (this time a ladder match), but clearly neither guy was going anywhere. Some people, myself included, felt that this was becoming indicative of a so-called glass ceiling effect, where only a select few people were on top of the promotion and everyone else was on the bottom looking up, so to speak. Combi-

nations of Rock, HHH, Austin, and Undertaker always seemed to get the main-event slots, while everyone else was deemed "not ready" or "not over enough" or "too short" or "wrestles like a cruiserweight" . . . kind of like what had been happening over in WCW for the past few years. Ah, the other side argued, but Vince can't possibly be stupid enough to make the exact same mistakes . . . could he?

Speaking of the same combinations on top, the mix-and-match special for February featured HHH and Steve Austin renewing their rivalry again for the *No Way Out* show in Las Vegas. They even pulled out the old "post-contract-signing attack" angle just to make sure we knew in no uncertain terms that Hunter was a bad person.

This contract-signing business falls under the "Birthday Cake Rule" of wrestling, which states that if you see a birthday cake or trophy being presented by one person to another on a wrestling show, a heel will smash it or steal it or both by the end of the show.

Meanwhile, Rock won a four-way (over Big Show and, surprise, surprise, Benoit and Jericho—one guess as to who got to do the job there) in order to earn a title shot at Kurt Angle at the PPV. Of course, then you get into the internal logic of why Austin needed to win the *Rumble* to earn a title shot when Rock got one simply by pinning Benoit, but then you're opening up a whole can of worms that requires more thought than the WWF was typically putting into the product at the time.

Thankfully, even though Stephanie's booking left a lot to be desired, everyone in the main-event circle could still bring the goods. In fact, Kurt Angle, who until then had been playing a clueless buffoon, was even given something of a heel edge leading up to the show when he started using an anklelock as a submission finisher. Not that it mattered so much since Rock's victory in that match was so assured that you could set your watch by it. And indeed, that's what happened. Here's my review:

WWF Title Match:
Kurt Angle v. The Rock

Ticktock, ticktock. Rock lays the smackdown with a lariat and a Russian legsweep for two. Angle gets the upper hand and chokes away. Rock comes out of the corner and into the Angle-Lock. Rock makes the ropes. Angle gets a belly-to-belly, but Rock hits his own. Double-KO and slugfest follows. Rock hits an insane lariat and hooks the Sharpshooter. Angle makes the ropes. Samoan drop gets two. Angle comes back with a backdrop suplex and goes upstairs, but gets crotched. Superplex gets two for Rock. Angle dumps Rock, who hurts his knee on the landing.

Back in, Rock gets a DDT . . . and the sound of that giant toilet flushing is The Big Show making his walk-on to chokeslam both guys. Thrilling. Well, that helped nothing. A couple of refs help the first one as Angle covers Rock for two. Rock blasts him with the title for two while Earl Hebner drops the first ref to valiantly take over as referee. Funny stuff. Rock hobbles over, but gets caught again in the Angle-Lock. Angle WRENCHES it in, and yells, and I quote, "Give it up before I break your fucking ankle, Rock!" I love this match.

Rock finally makes the ropes again and fights back, but Angle pounds him down. Rock gets a spinebuster out of nowhere, followed by the People's Elbow . . . for two??? Crowd is shocked. Angle retreats to the corner, but gets stomped. Angle low blows him and removes the turnbuckle pad. Rock Bottom is countered by a shove into the STEEL bolt and Olympic Slam, which ninetynine times out of one hundred finishes . . . but this ain't one of them. Rock kicks out at two, and Angle is hysterical.

*Rock beatdown in the corner is stopped with a kick to the ankle. Angle is my HERO. Angle charges and gets thrown into his own exposed turnbuckle (IRONY!), Rock Bottom gets a dubious two, and another Rock Bottom gets a decisive three for his SIXTH WWF title at 16:53. And the world is right again. ****½*

The Austin-HHH match was equally great in its essential awesomeness as they beat the hell out of each other for forty minutes before HHH fell on top for the win. Everyone thought that this was done in order to build up HHH as a strong challenger to Austin after he'd won the title from Rock at *Wrestlemania*. Everyone was wrong. Apparently it was just so that HHH could get a win over Steve Austin. Which is funny because HHH masterminded a plot to have Austin killed, then was "killed" in a fifteen-foot drop in a car, only to come back and cost Austin the world title a week later, and in the end who got the big blowoff win to end the feud? HHH. So really, Austin never got his revenge for HHH's trying to kill him.

> It's stuff like this that earned HHH the moniker "The Smartest Man in Pro Wrestling" by online fans.

The other big feud going on was pretty much a 180-degree turn from the physical intensity of the Austin-HHH wars. Stephanie squabbled with Trish Stratus over which of them really was "daddy's little girl." Now, as a relatively normal and healthy person without an Oedipus or Electra complex, I've gotta nominate this whole thing for entrance in the Creepiest Story Line of the Year competition. It's not like it wasn't bad enough to have to watch senior citizen Vince McMahon fondling twenty-something Trish Stratus at every opportunity, on live TV no less, but for his own daughter to then get jealous? Trust me, you haven't experienced pain and suffering until you've sat through a backstage skit with Stephanie looking longingly into Vince's eyes while she tells him how much she wants to be daddy's little girl and have him all to herself. Pardon me, I have to go vomit just thinking of this again.

SCENE THREE
Monday Nitraw

Okay, we're back. And from the unbearable we move to the unthinkable as the deal to sell WCW to Fusient fell through in March 2001, and the TNT network cancelled the flagship show, *Nitro*, as a result. With no other options for survival left, WCW was sold to Vince McMahon and the WWF, along with the entire Turner tape library covering more than thirty years, for a figure so low ball that it might as well have been free—a little under $4 million. The WWF immediately announced plans to revive WCW with a show on TNN focusing on WCW stars, and they signed up much of the under-million set, leaving the high-dollar contracts to twist in the wind.

This led to one of the most surreal things ever seen in wrestling. The final broadcast of *Nitro* on March 26 was a simulcast with *RAW*, featuring Vince McMahon watching WCW clips on *RAW* and then coming out for an interview that aired on both *RAW* and *Nitro* at the same time. Most notably, Vince fired (on-air, mind you) Jeff Jarrett, Lex Luger, and Dustin Rhodes in retaliation for their perceived betrayal of him years earlier. Note to any aspiring wrestlers: do *not* piss off Vince McMahon because he will remember you.

The bizarre *Nitro* ended with Flair putting Sting over one last time (which actually ended up being Sting's retirement match) before Vince went into another bizarre monologue during which he asked fans in attendance for *RAW*

Dustin Rhodes somehow managed to get hired AGAIN in 2002, once again reprising the Goldust character. So throw out that theory about Vince ALWAYS holding a grudge.

which WCW stars he should keep and which he should jettison. In fact, fan reaction to Buff Bagwell was so positive that he actually got a job out of it. Scott Steiner was another favorite, but he was too injured to even carry on as a full-time wrestler at that point. The overwhelming crowd favorite was Goldberg, but with a contract that paid him $6 million a year, he was just as well-off sitting at home and collecting the remainder of his money from Time Warner.

The final *Nitro* ended with an angle: Vince and Shane McMahon did a story line whereby Vince was going to sign the final papers at *Wrestlemania*, but Shane (in attendance at *Nitro*) interrupted and revealed that he, in fact, had already bought the company out from under Vince. This was the first sign that the WWF Era of WCW was going to be a disaster because WCW fans wanted to hear about what would happen to their favorite promotion next, not listen to the Vince and Shane show. And in fact, nothing was announced for WCW and the entire promotion was put on the backburner immediately. Some laughingly suggested that the WCW curse was in full effect from that moment on—it wouldn't be funny later.

But forget all that because the biggest show of the year was here—*Wrestlemania X-7*. No, I don't get what's up with the *X*, either. But regardless, they sold out the Houston Astrodome with it as over 60,000 people packed the stadium to watch The Rock defend the title against Steve Austin. Unfortunately, as was rapidly becoming a regular thing, the rest of the undercard didn't even finish coming about until the week before the show, when patented WWF Insta-Feuds™ between HHH and Undertaker, and Kurt Angle and Chris Benoit, filled up the mid- to upper-card with little time to spare. You'd think that would have handicapped the show, but au contraire: *Wrestlemania X-7* was quite simply the best PPV that the WWF had ever put on and may or may not have been as good as my own personal favorite for the last thirteen years: WCW *Great American Bash '89.*

Insta-Feuds™ refer to the WWF tendancy to bypass regular conventions of storytelling, like motivation and logic, by having one guy get really pissed off at another for no adequately explained reason and challenge him to a match.

First up, Benoit and Angle put on a technical marvel early in the show, to a surprisingly great reaction from the Sportz Entertainment fanbase. Here's my review:

Kurt Angle v. Chris Benoit

Angle takes him down and they go into a mat sequence. Another amateur sequence gets a good response. Angle with another takedown and into a facelock. They fight for a cradle, more applause. Benoit works for the crossface, and Angle makes the ropes. Again, Angle escapes again. Again and again Angle escapes. He then clobbers Benoit, having been frustrated on the mat, and tosses him. Brawl to the Spanish table, and Benoit meets the steps.

Back in, suplex gets two. Backdrop suplex gets two. Angle pounds him into the corner, but Benoit comes back with some CANADIAN VIOLENCE. Angle hits his own and a belly-to-belly. Another one follows. Benoit comes back with a short-arm clothesline and more Canadian Violence. They slug it out, but Benoit kneelifts him and comes back. Snap suplex gets two. Superplex gets two. Rolling Germans are reversed to the Angle-Lock, reversed again by Benoit to his own! Oh, yeah. Crossface, Angle reverses to HIS own! This is SO awesome.

Benoit makes the ropes, and the ref is bumped (groan). Crossface for real, no ref. Benoit revives the ref, Olympic Slam . . . gets two. Moonsault hits knee. Benoit gets the headbutt for two. Angle goes low and rolls him up for the cheap pin at 14:03. ★★★★¼ *Oh man, minus that dumb finish, this was AWESOME.*

But wait, there's more! For lack of anything better to do with the tag division, they held yet another TLC match between the usual suspects (Hardyz/Dudleyz/Edge and Christian), which was yet another spectacular ★★★★★ spotfest, but completely exposed the lack of depth in the tag-team division, a lack that would be multiplied tenfold in the coming weeks.

"Spotfests" refer to my shorthand for matches where much of the action is comprised of doing a series of breathtaking stunts, but not having anything in-between them to act as transition moves. They're generally either really really good (like the TLC matches) or staggeringly bad (like the ECW matches near the end).

The McMahon soap opera also continued dragging along as dirty-old-man Vince dumped Trish in favor of his daughter, Stephanie (no, honestly, that was the payoff), and this led to Shane standing up for his poor mother, Linda, who had been put into a mental institution and kept sedated twenty-four hours a day. One positive was that putting Linda in a wheelchair and having her stare at the wall for all her appearances at least played to her dramatic range. Sadly, the ideal role for her would not continue past *Wrestlemania* because she made a miraculous recovery with the help of the wronged Trish and helped Shane beat Vince in a street fight. The match was quite good for the usual overbooked garbagey nonsense that the McMahons tended to limit themselves to. I wouldn't take it home to meet my parents or anything, but they hit each other with enough large objects and Shane took enough crazy bumps to make it a worthwhile outing.

By contrast, the main event of the show was both a wild brawl and an in-ring classic that not only rocked your world but didn't even bother to call you back in the morning . . . and you liked it. Sure, everyone knew that Rock was going to lose because he had to go film *Scorpion King* and that Austin was going to be turned heel for reasons that were increasingly inexplicable, but then everyone knows that Santa Claus comes every Christmas Eve, and it doesn't make him any less welcome, either. Here's my review:

WWF Title Match:
The Rock v. Stone Cold Steve Austin

The pop Austin gets is insane. Austin attacks to start, and they slug it out. Thesz press and FU Elbow. Rock neckbreaker sets up Rock Bottom, which is blocked, Stunner is blocked, Rock's Stunner is blocked and they head outside. Into the crowd and back to ringside, where Austin gets a short-arm clothesline. Into the ring, Austin hits the rope straddle for two. Superplex gets two. Rock fights back with a flying lariat and belly-to-belly for two. Brawl to ringside, where Austin nails him with the bell . . . and Rocky drops his blade. Oh geez, very professional, guys. Rock finally does a wussy blade, and back in we go.

Austin methodically pounds him. Neckbreaker and mudhole stomping follow. Rock blasts out with a lariat (Crowd: "Boooo!"), then rams him into the STEEL turnbuckle bolt. He nails him with the bell for good measure as Austin shows him how a REAL man blades. Rock pounds him and works on the neck. Back outside, Austin drops Rock onto the barricade. Catapult drives Rock headfirst into the post. And I mean HEADFIRST. Awesome. Rock staggers back . . . into a monitor to the head.

Back in, it gets two. Stunner is reversed by Rock into the Sharpshooter. Austin makes the ropes after

two tries. Back to it, Austin breaks and hooks his own version! Rock powers out and Austin works on the knee. Back to the Sharpshooter, Rock makes the ropes. Million Dollar Dream is tried next, and Rock is fading. He climbs the ropes à la Bret Hart '96 and gets two, but Austin now knows the counter and escapes. This match is just so great on so many levels.

Rock's Roody Poo Stunner . . . gets two. Vince wanders out. Austin gets a spinebuster on Rock for two. Rock gets his own and follows with the Elbow for two . . . but Vince saves, getting a huge face pop. Rock chases Vince, but walks into a Rock Bottom from Austin (The Bottom Line?) for two. Stunner is blocked, ref bump. Enough with that already! It's a friggin' NO-DQ match.

Vince comes in and chairs Rock. It gets two. Rock blocks another chairshot with Rock Bottom and goes after Vince, but turns around and it's KICK WHAM STUNNER . . . for two. Austin chairs Rock for two. He gets sick of Rock altogether, beats him like the proverbial redheaded stepchild for about two minutes with that chair until Rock is a quivering mass of Jell-O, and pins him to win the WWF title at 28:07 to a THUNDEROUS babyface pop.

Vince and Austin shake hands as JR declares that Austin has "sold his soul to the devil himself." Wasn't that exactly the sort of thing that the WWF was blasting "The Media" for when they said that about Vince and the XFL? And I guess all the rhetoric about listening to the fans goes out the window once you're determined to turn your number-one babyface heel. Retarded ending aside, the match kicked 900 types of ass and still had a lineup around the corner of asses to be kicked at leisure. ★★★★¾

SCENE FOUR
The "X" Is for "Excellent"

Well, of course, everyone was expecting Austin to explain his shocking heel turn the next night on *RAW*, and everyone of course was wrong because that would have required foresight and thought by the "creative" team, something that seemingly had become in short supply since Vince had gone off to play football with the XFL. Vince was seemingly going more insane by the day thanks to his so-called football league, which was increasingly becoming the punchline to every late-night talk show host's monologue jokes. So naturally Vince responded the only way he knew how—blaming the Media Bogeyman who was somehow skewing the numbers against him and poisoning the minds of America's youth with evil statistics. It has been said that a test pattern in prime-time network TV could draw a 1.0—the XFL was doing 0.5–0.9 by the end. And what were Vince's solutions to this problem?

1) Have Jim Ross go on *RAW* and ask fans to write in and demand more XFL coverage in their local papers.
2) Shortly thereafter, fire Jim Ross from announcing the games because the announcers might actually matter to ratings or something.
3) Promise footage of the cheerleaders' dressing room and then fail to deliver.
4) Pay attention to the very valid criticisms levied by the fans and media and adjust the product accordingly. Ha ha, just wanted to see if you were paying attention.

It was bad for Vince in other areas, too, which were not as blatantly obvious as the XFL debacle—the WWF went public in 2000, becoming WWFE Inc. and raising $250 million through an IPO for the purposes of diversifying the WWF name into other, nonwrestling, areas. Those areas?

1) The XFL. No explanation needed here, although to really rub salt into the wounds I have to point out that the league on its own lost more than $100 million and is still losing money to this day through unpaid contracts and advertising deals, and may hit $250 million by itself.
2) WWF New York, a chain of WWF-themed nightclub/restaurants. The first one was set to be in New York, with more to follow. Despite constant pimping on WWF TV at every possible opportunity with every shameless bit of hucksterism possible, the reportedly lousy service, lousy food, and lousy prices have relegated it to also-ran status on Times Square and turned it into something of a money pit. No further franchising appears to be in the works.
3) WWF.com and the associated Web sites. Once a big revenue stream for the WWF, they (like everyone else) fell victim to the complete collapse of the online ad market in 2001, causing them to take a bath in maintaining the Web site and slash almost all of the corollary Web sites in order to save money. The Web site is almost a loss-leader at this point, useful only for advertising the TV shows and leading people to ShopZone, the WWF's online store, and not much else. Add to that the legal spanking that the WWF took in the battle with the World Wildlife Fund, which will probably result in the surrender of the WWF.com name entirely by the end of 2002, and the Web business doesn't appear long for the world.

> The WWF.com legal spanking got even uglier when the final decision left the WWF without their very name—by the middle of the year, they had changed to "World Wrestling Entertainment," or WWE.

4) Books. Well, they had Mick Foley and his hundreds of thousands of copies sold (al-

though his picture book didn't do quite as well) until he got so fed up with his treatment and direction of the product that he quit completely, thus robbing Vince of his ridiculously high cut of the proceeds. Rock's did well (at about 600,000 copies sold), but everything in his life was covered in 200 pages so a sequel doesn't seem likely. And then there's Chyna and her Big Book of Bullshit, which did amazingly well on *The New York Times* best-seller list (although not as well as Foley's), presumably for the same reason that people go to dwarf-tossing exhibitions and watch Tom Green. She also was gone from the WWF by year's end. Kurt Angle's autobiography was a bomb, and a biography on The Hardy Boyz should be out and burning up the charts by the time you read this. Another attempt at WWF literature, a cookbook, is generally not spoken of due to disappointing sales. The original deal with Regan Books was quite a low ball against the WWF (since the standard line is that wrestling fans don't read, which is easily disproven by you reading about this), so much of the money to be made from it was in royalties, not in up-front cash. The WWF recently inked a deal with Simon & Schuster to produce WWF books, including fiction and nonfiction, but one wonders how readers will tell the difference.

5) Television shows. They tried one—*Manhunter*—and did about half a season worth of this "reality" show in the "World's Most Dangerous Game" vein (contestants are "hunted" by a WWF developmental wrestler) before a scandal broke about the show being fixed. The WWF quickly disassociated themselves from it, and I'll leave any obvious punchlines as an exercise for the reader.

6) Expanded or split WWF product. We'll get to this one a little later.

So, basically, $250 million down the drain-ola thanks to poor business decisions. And this from a guy who proclaims himself at every opportunity to be a genius. On the bright side (for us, not him) Vince's reputation has been so completely destroyed outside the realms of his "rasslin'" that we'll likely never have to endure another outside project again—or at least no more of them on NBC.

But I digress.

Getting back to my main point here, Vince's biggest mistake within the wrestling business (well, for that year) came at *Wrestlemania*, where he was determined to take his number-one babyface and turn him heel. This is not to say that Austin is a bad heel, because he's not. He's an awesome heel. But he's not the number-one-drawing heel of all time, which is what he is on the babyface side of things. That's the fatal flaw in the logic behind the heel turn—which would have worked to freshen up the character had it been done in December 2000, when the character actually was getting stale again. No matter how big the turn would have worked out to be, it wasn't going to be as big as Stone Cold Steve Austin was for most of '98–'99, and thus was doomed to failure from the start.

SCENE FIVE
The "X" Is for "Excrutiating"

Then there's the matter of HHH, who wasn't helping things any while Vince was off running his "football" league into the ground 24/7. The original idea from months earlier was for Austin to turn heel on Rock at *Wrestlemania* while winning the WWF title with Vince's help (check), Rock to take a few months off to shoot the *Scorpion King* (check), and HHH to step up to the number-one babyface role with a well-timed turn that would lead into a successful summer run between HHH and Austin (wait a second). . . .

Ah, that third part proved to be a bit of a sticking point because Hunter balked at turning babyface, possibly feeling that Rock's eventual return would just overshadow him. So after Austin had now done a totally unwanted (by the fans) heel turn with an explanation no more in-depth than "I wanted an insurance policy," he was being forced to play comedy sidekick to HHH, who can out-intense Charles Manson when it comes to being a badass heel. Rather than playing a straightforward monster heel like HHH was doing (and getting the respect of the crowd with it like HHH was), Austin took an entirely different tack with his new character. He instead chose to play a man on the verge of insanity, literally clinging to Vince McMahon for support and love. It was an interesting character choice for someone doing Shakespeare in the park, but for a multi-billion dollar industry, fuhgeddaboudit. Less is more in wrestling, and Austin constantly hugging Vince McMahon in a weird, Freudian psychodrama proved to be way over the heads of the average viewer, who just didn't understand why the character had taken this turn.

Even worse, Austin played the character as though he were hearing voices in his head, constantly interrupting people by asking them "What?" in the middle of their sentences. It was weird and quite different and the smarter fans loved it, but ratings started dropping at an alarming rate due to the sudden lack of strong babyfaces to counteract Austin's bizarre heel act. If ever there was the time for a rash move, like turning him back to babyface again, this was it, but they decided to see if they could salvage the character. That proved to be an even bigger mistake.

Undertaker and Kane (who, for those like myself have trouble keeping track, were friends

> **The same people were fooled by the same crowd reactions in 2002, when Hogan returned to a hero's welcome, only to send the company into the toilet, financially speaking.**

again) were chosen as the first sacrificial lambs to the newly dubbed Two Man Powertrip. Again, the creative team showed their incompetence without Vince McMahon hovering over them at all times, as Undertaker and Kane received huge pops upon entering the arena, but were no longer a positive factor toward ratings and buy rates. However, the pop factor has fooled many bookers in the past, and this was no different. Undertaker and Kane won the tag titles from Edge and Christian (which was the Canadian duo's final title reign, a run that ended at seven reigns) and were pushed all over WWF TV during April to prepare for *Backlash*, which featured a main event of Undertaker and Kane v. Steve Austin and HHH for the tag titles. The result seemed to be not very much in doubt, and you can probably guess it right now. Here's my review:

WWF World Title, Intercontinental Title, Tag-team Title Match: Undertaker and Kane v. Steve Austin and HHH

Heels bail right away and the Long Stall begins. UT beats on Austin in the ring, then Kane beats on HHH. Austin gets the same. HHH uses the knee on Kane and goes after the arm, but gets clotheslined. Austin comes in and runs from UT like a chickenshit. The Austin character gets weaker by the week. Taker stomps him and whips him hither and thither for a bit, and Kane comes in to continue. Austin nails the arm and tags HHH, who walks into a big UT right. Ropewalk on both heels and both bail.

Back in, a HHH cheapshot puts UT down and they double-team. They beat on him on the floor and Austin hits a kneedrop back in the ring. More beating in the corner. DDT on HHH turns the tide, and Kane almost gets a tag, but not quite. Thesz press for UT and FU elbow, but he no-sells and hits a double-clothesline on the heels. Hot tag Kane. Sideslam for Austin and Kane goes up with a lariat and slams HHH off the top. They nail the arm, but Kane fights them off. Austin finally gets the arm and they work on it . . . for TEN MINUTES. Seriously, that's all it is.

Austin comes off the top of what feels like a year later and hits boot, and Kane breaks a sleeper with a suplex. HHH gets the Pedigree, but Austin wants the cover and gets one. Taker chokeslams him, and Kane gets two. Kanezuigiri for HHH, hot tag UT, but the ref misses it. UT cleans house and wedgiebombs HHH, but HE'S NOT LEGAL. Of course, it'll go uncalled the other ninety-nine out of one hundred times it happens, but such is life. Stunner for Kane, and Austin goes brawling with UT and is basically forgotten. Vince runs in, gives HHH his trusty sledgehammer, and that finishes Kane at 25:02 to give HHH and Austin the tag titles. Like anyone cares. **½ I know it's a main event and all, but thirty minutes (with stalling at the beginning) is just INSANELY long for what these guys are limited to right now. Notice how HHH gets the winning pin on Kane, a finish that pretty much everyone called, once again proving HHH is indeed the most intelligent person in our so-called sport. The match would have been higher on the spectrum of the good end if they hadn't had that immensely boring middle portion and if Austin wasn't Budro to HHH's Bill.

Indeed, the HHH situation was getting so out of hand that people began wondering if HHH and Stephanie (who was the head writer and HHH's real-life love interest) were trying to usurp things for themselves with Vince gone all the time. The evidence was piling up, like the week of April 3–10. It began on *Smackdown*, with Hunter winning the intercontinental title from Chris Jericho in a finish so horribly selfish and inexcusable that you just knew people were going to make excuses anyway. Sure, on the larger scale of the universe Jericho losing a title to HHH isn't

a big deal, but questions surrounding the win were immediately raised:

1) HHH was already the second-biggest star in the WWF at that point with Rock off shooting his movie, so how does it help him to beat a guy who is largely perceived as a mid-card choker?

2) Further on that point, how does it then help that mid-card choker shake that label when he loses to HHH every time he wrestles him? The answer to both questions is "It doesn't help," which made it all the more senseless and just made it seem like another step to keep Jericho "in his place." Several WWF apologists thought that Jericho would get his win back later, but he hadn't done so nearly a year later, with that match forgotten.

3) Why did HHH even need a secondary title like the intercontinental belt? Again, there was an immediate theory that this would somehow elevate the belt, but having the champion beat HHH would have elevated the title a lot more than HHH's beating the champion did, especially considering the eventual destinations for the title.

Then the conspiracy stuff got even weirder the next week on *Smackdown* when HHH dropped that title to Jeff Hardy of The Hardy Boyz (who were getting seriously over and were being prepped for singles pushes) in a fluke upset, only to come right back days later on *RAW* and squash him like a bug in a manner not seen since the days of Iron Mike Sharpe losing to bearhugs on syndicated programming. Jeff Hardy, regardless of whether or not he was "worthy" of a main-event push (which he wasn't—make no mistake, I'm not taking *that* side of things) was never given a chance to discover if he even might be. Consequently, The Hardy Boyz became complete nonfactors in record time, and even Jericho was hurt a lot in the short term. Karma would get HHH back shortly, much like it had with his best friend, Shawn Michaels.

A**fter HHH, the title went to Kane, then nonsensation Albert, then into mid-card hell via the invasion and bounced around from loser to loser before being mercifully unified with the WCW U.S. title at *Survivor Series* and stabilized a bit.**

The mid-card was becoming seriously neglected at this point as well as Benoit and Angle continued their feud with the clichéd but entertaining "Benoit steals Angle's gold medals" story line while everyone else under contract basically ran around like chickens with their collective heads cut off. Four or five people swapped in and out of a feud over the hardcore title, various low-level teams traded wins in the opening slot, guys like Test and William Regal went up and down on a show-by-show basis . . . it was becoming a huge mess.

SCENE SIX
Did I Mention the Glass Ceiling?

Paul Heyman, late of ECW ownership, was brought in to assist Stephanie and lend a fresh ear to booking, but everything the writers did had to go through Vince anyway so we still ended up with Austin v. Undertaker headlining another PPV, in this case the May show, *Judgment Day*. Even worse, this was Crazy Steve Austin v. Redneck Biker Undertaker in a dynamic that just didn't mesh well at all and an Austin character that simply was not lighting the world on fire. But, love it or hate it, Vince sticks with what has worked in the past until forced to

change, so everything was stuck in a holding pattern through May . . . until the night after the PPV on *RAW*.

Remember all my kvetching about the treatment of Jericho and Benoit and how the HHH loss hurt Jericho in the short term? And how karma would get HHH back? Well, here you go, everything resolved in a nice little package.

At the PPV, Chris Benoit lost the gold medals back to Kurt Angle in a finish that they absolutely had to do (I mean, they are *his* gold medals after all) and returned later in the night to team with Chris Jericho and win a sort-of tag-team tournament. Whereas Vince Russo's favorite cliché was the Wacky Tag-Team Partners Who Hate Each Other, new booker Paul Heyman's favorite cliché was the Serious Tag-Team Partners Who Used to Hate Each Other, and his first try at it in the WWF was Jericho and Benoit. See, after all those mid-card matches, they had decided that mutual respect was the most effective way to pool their talents and elevate themselves up the card. So after winning the number-one contender's tournament, they threw out a challenge to the champions on *RAW*, and this match resulted . . .

WWF Tag-Title Match:
Steve Austin and HHH v.
The Canadian Violence Connection

Does the WWF actually listen for once? Austin hammers Jericho and stomps a mudhole, but gets bodypressed. Canadian Violence and he go up with an elbow to the head off the top. Austin gets a cheapshot, to take over, and HHH comes in and gets double-teamed in the CVC corner. Benoit gets caught in the heel corner, however, and trades chops with Austin. He kneelifts Austin, and hits a snap suplex. Superplex gets two, and the Powertrip duo work Benoit over. Benoit gets the crossface, but HHH chairshots him to break for two.

Austin is all fists and fury. FU Elbow and choking follows. HHH sends Benoit to the stairs, and back in for a two-count. HHH pounds on him, and gets the facebuster for two. Austin goes low and chokes him out. HHH pounds him in the corner and they do an assisted abdominal stretch. Benoit escapes, but gets caught in a sleeper. He escapes with a German suplex, and it's a race for the tags. Enzuigiri, and . . . the ref doesn't see the tag. Austin punks out Benoit on the floor, triggering a brawl. Pedigree in the ring, no ref. Jericho goes up with a missile dropkick to put HHH down, and it's a tag race again. HOT TAG JERICHO, crowd explodes.

Forearm for Austin, and he dumps HHH. Austin gets the Walls of Jericho, but HHH saves, and the crowd HATES it. HHH preps the announcer table, but Jericho reverses a Pedigree into the Walls out there. In the ring, flying headbutt for Austin, no ref. KICK WHAM STUNNER . . . but Jericho pulls out the ref at two. Oh, man, this is giving me a heart attack. Bulldog for Austin, Lionsault misses, second one hits. HHH brings the sledgehammer in, in desperation, but hits Austin by "mistake," and JERICHO PINS AUSTIN! NEW CHAMPIONS! That match completely blew away anything the WWF had done since Wrestlemania, and a few of the matches AT Wrestlemania, too. ★★★★¾

However, all was not sunshine and roses because near the end of this match, HHH tore the quadriceps muscle clean off of his leg, and it was like a window shutter flapping open. Eight months on the shelf, see ya, wouldn't wanna be ya. Remember how I've been saying over and over how important elevating new stars is and how they hadn't done it? Well, at this point, The Rock was off filming and HHH was gone and Austin was flopping as a top-card heel, so this was exactly the kind of situation where it would have been nice to have some backup number-one babyfaces primed to carry the promotion. Whoops, guess they should have given Jericho and Benoit those big wins after all.

In a totally unrelated bit of trivia that has absolutely nothing to do with anyone mentioned in this book in any way, one of the main side effects of heavy steroid usage is the weakening of the tendons holding the muscles in place, often resulting in easy tearing or breaking of them with any sort of stress, say for example, a quad muscle that gets torn off during a wrestling match. Hypothetically speaking.

But fear not, for Shane McMahon was still around. Yes, amazingly, three months after buying the competition and letting their flagship program sink into cancellation without a fight, they suddenly decided to start talking about WCW again. Hey, an invasion angle, guaranteed money in every territory it's ever been tried, most notably WCW, where ex-WWF guys Hall and Nash invaded and springboarded the WWF's own fall into oblivion as a direct result. So no problem, right? Just shoot some top WCW stars out there and let's start a war! So they get some ex-WCW guys, and I'm talking huge, big-name, money-drawing stars like . . . um . . . Lance Storm and Hugh Morrus, and they did run-ins . . . once . . . and . . . um . . . well, okay, that's about it.

Stop and think about this for a second. Seriously. This is a company that spent millions of dollars (admittedly a pittance for Vince "I'm a Billionaire and I'll Tell You on Live TV" McMahon, but more than you or I will see in a lifetime) to purchase WCW, whose only (and I mean *only*) value was in an invasion story line. And they don't even do it until *three months* after the initial purchase, and even then they refuse to give any of the people involved significant airtime. This is like a Wall Street banking firm hiring a strung-out crack junkie because they happen to be able to pick the markets with 99 percent accuracy, and then using them to make coffee. *Dang, it makes no sense, Jethro.* But check this—the absolute masterstroke of stupidity on levels that even the WCW in its prime didn't tread into. Much.

SCENE SEVEN
No, Seriously, Glass Ceiling, Ever Heard of It?

Here's the setup: At a *RAW* in Calgary that I was actually in attendance for (on the WWF's nickel, no less—perks of being a journalist, even an Internet one), they showed a video vignette at Undertaker's house in which a mysterious voice talked about following Undertaker's new wife, Sara, around and being in love with her. Funny story: in the WWF canon, her name apparently is "Sara Undertaker," because there is no "Mark Callaway" in the WWF reality for her to be married to. My brain hurts thinking about that too hard.

Anyway, the mysterious voice was actually Vince McMahon's run through a simple sound editor on a computer with the pitch decreased to –2, but that was supposed to be a mystery, see. Funny story: One of my readers sent me a file containing the original stalker clip, with the pitch increased +2 from the standard, and the result was a normal-sounding Vince McMahon reading the lines. "Vince is the stalker!" quickly became the cheap headline du jour all over the Internet thanks to my Web site's "exposing" of the "big secret" that was supposed to last another four weeks. I got a note from the WWF legal team shortly after, and I don't expect to be getting any more passes to WWF events. I guess they didn't have quite the same self-deprecating sense of humor that Vince himself has been known to have. It wasn't actually supposed to be Vince doing the stalking anyway; he was just doing the voiceover work, but the WWF just hates being shown up like that.

Regardless, the story line went on like that for

a few weeks until the Stalker promised to reveal himself on *RAW* to much hoopla and foofaraw. And to no one's great shock, it was ex-WCW "main eventer" Diamond Dallas Page.

> **T**he really bizarre thing about this story line was that Kane, Sara's story line brother-in-law, was remarkably nonplussed about the abuse that DDP was heaping on her, and in fact never even commented on it in his interviews.

Here's the thing with good ol' DDP. Page Falkenberg is a hell of a guy and apparently a fan of my writing, so I try to avoid saying bad things about him because he doesn't deserve most of it. However, his introduction became symbolic of all the problems with the WCW invasion in general. Here we go:

1) DDP was never anything special in WCW to begin with. He'd made his bones by buying a house next to WCW president Eric Bischoff and sucking up to him 24/7 until DDP had ended up with multiple reigns as the WCW world champion and a sweetheart contract that lasted until WCW died. He could work solid, main-event style matches with a limited amount of workers who could adjust to his anal retentive, preplanned, and heavily choreographed match style, but when put in there with anyone outside of his MO, it was punch-punch-punch Diamond Cutter all the way as far as the moveset went. Most people know this. Most fans know him, kinda, and like him, sorta, but in an ugly-guy-and-gorgeous-gal-just-being-friends type of way rather than the electrifying-love-scene way that fans take to The Rock and Steve Austin. But this wasn't insurmountable—you can make anyone a

star given a fresh start in a new promotion, as long as the other guy is willing to sell and put him over. Which leads to problem number two . . .

2) The Undertaker. He wasn't selling ANYTHING for ANYONE at that point, let alone putting over some scruffy, Jersey, midcarder from WCW who was best known for jobbing the world title to David Arquette, thus making the whole thing a no-win situation for DDP no matter what. The fans didn't like him just because he was from a loser promotion, and Undertaker wouldn't take the necessary steps to make DDP something worthwhile in their eyes, so the "feud" was dead from square one. In fact, they never even made it to a blowoff match on PPV—they had a scheduled "confrontation" at the *King of the Ring* PPV that was supposed to tease a match, but Undertaker wouldn't even give him anything in the impromptu brawl and ended up beating the hell out of him so decisively that they pulled the plug on the entire story line the next week! That is truly a case of the inmates running the asylum.

3) Fan allegiances. The invading WCW forces were supposed to be babyface, but this was clearly a heel character. Do we boo him for stalking Sara or cheer him for being WCW?

4) Explanation. As in, no rational one given. Page is a well-known married man (his wife, Kimberly, who has done numerous spreads for *Penthouse*, had been all over WCW programming) and married to a *hottie* at that. Sara Undertaker is, shall we say, less so. So they went with "I just did it to play mindgames" as the explanation. Wow, what a money-drawing angle *that* is. A heel who didn't actually intend to follow through with his sleazy plan; gosh, that'll make millions. This is the kind of

stuff that the writers were coming up with even after being given weeks to think of a reason for his actions.

5) Payoff. DDP was pinned by Undertaker's *wife* in an actual match a couple of weeks into the "feud" to end it decisively. I don't think this one needs any further 'splaining, Lucy.

So that was the exciting Stalker angle, which had the dubious distinction of being voted as one of the worst of the year by numerous polls on the subject. And we haven't even gotten to the actual WCW invasion yet! In fact, let's skip *King of the Ring 2001* entirely because the WWF basically erased it from history anyway with Steve Austin's beating both Chris Jericho and Chris Benoit in a handicap match dressed up as a "three-way," and Benoit escaping the insanity by having major neck surgery done and taking twelve months off. Steve Austin and Chris Benoit had a couple of ****+ free-TV matches to help build up that three-way, but Vince McMahon lost all confidence in his would-be main eventers two weeks prior to the actual PPV (which did brisk business anyway, thank you very much) and basically pulled the plug on the push, choosing to concentrate on other things instead, like the impending WCW invasion.

So this, then, is the invasion:

The night after the May PPV, *Judgment Day*, Kurt Angle celebrated his Olympiclike triumph over Chris Benoit in regaining his medals by having his own medal ceremony on *RAW*. Shane McMahon interrupted for no adequately explored reason, made some vague threats regarding WCW in a promo so perversely bad that it was almost entertaining in a *Plan Nine from Outer Space* type of way, and got his butt handed to him as a result. After that promo, the highlight of which was Shane saying that the C in "WCW" stood for " 'cookie,' and that's good enough for me"; I was ready to kick his ass, too.

They had a match at *King of the Ring 2001*, where it was widely assumed that someone from WCW would interfere since it was a street fight and all. No one did, and the match was quite breathtakingly swank as a result of some really sick bumping from both guys. Just for the hell of it, here's my review:

Street Fight:
Shane-O-Mac v. Kurt Angle

Angle takes him down and suplexes him, but Shane works the mat. Angle tosses him, and reveals that Shane has apparently potatoed him and busted him open. Cool. Kurt gets pissed and offers Shane the down position, and Shane stupidly tries to wrestle him again. Kurt immediately reverses and pounds the hell out of him, then gutwrenches and belly-to-bellys him. Oklahoma roll and Angle rides him on the mat for humiliation purposes, then offers the down position again. This time, Shane uses his head and simply punts him in the ribs, then comes off the ropes with an elbow. Angle takes him again in vicious fashion, but Shane dumps him. They do a footrace and collide, then Shane comes off the apron, over the table, and nails Angle. He finds the kendo stick and adds some shots, then armdrags Kurt into the railing a couple of times.

Back in, Angle bridges out of a pinning attempt, which is just an awesome spot that you don't see enough of because the guys don't have the proper kind of training to do it. Shane loads up the plunder and unleashes the ROADSIGN OF DOOM for two. Shane pulls out a bad-looking anklelock and tornado DDT, then into a butt-ugly Sharpshooter. Man, that sequence was horrible. Angle makes the ropes and grabs the kendo stick to break. Shane slugs away for two. Double KO, and Shane uses the garbage can and goes up. The SHOOTING SHANE PRESS (!!!) misses. Man, this guy is gonna die one of these days.

Angle dumps him and they brawl on the floor and Shane suplexes him into the aisle. They head over to the entranceway, and Angle suplexes Shane into one of the Plexiglas "KOR" signs, and it doesn't break.

Shane lands SQUARE on his head and we're all sure he's done for. I mean, he landed on his goddamn HEAD on the CONCRETE. So Kurt picks him and DOES IT AGAIN, and this time the sign breaks, resulting in both guys becoming absolutely covered in their own blood from the pieces of glass.

So Angle then picks him up and suplexes him into ANOTHER sign, which again doesn't break. Oh my God, Shane is dead dead dead. Again, and this time Kurt is smart enough to prep for the lack of breakage by catching him on the way down. Finally, he gets fed up and tosses poor Shane through the sign, shattering it and adding more blood. That was one of the sickest and more brutal sequences I've ever seen in a wrestling match, including Foley's fall. The difference here being that it was in the context of the match and had some actual buildup instead of being a stuntman bump that was added to compensate for injuries. Shane is quite possibly legally deceased and pushing up the daisies as Angle loads him on an equipment cart and wheels him into the ring, where he gets two.

Realistically, that probably should have been the finish. Shane goes low and uses the can lid to come back, hitting an Angle Slam for two. Angle, however, catapults him into the ringpost, beats him with a piece of plywood, and then sets it on the top rope for an Angle Slam off of it that finishes at 26:00. Again, the final sequence was kinda overkill, but the wrestling stuff to start was really neat and the brawling stuff outside is probably un-toppable without serious injury, and the end result is an awesome match. ****¼ Addendum: Kurt Angle really was hurt in this match and was taken to the hospital. Just what they needed, more injuries.

Luckily, Angle was relatively fine because he rules and stuff. Shane couldn't even be bothered to wear a neck brace to pretend he was hurt from the match. He showed up on *RAW* the next night, fit as a fiddle. But maybe he was just energized by the momentous nature of that *RAW*, being live from the WWF stronghold of Madison Square Garden. A battered Angle did backstage skits all night with Steve Austin as they tried to out-dork each other (Austin playing the neurotic codependant, Angle playing the clueless putz) while competing for Vince's affections. This was actually a solid enough story line that they could have centered everything on it and ignored the invasion for a while if need be. But time and destiny wait for no man, or McMahon, and finally, after months of waiting, the invasion began—with Mike Awesome winning the hardcore title from Rhyno.

Don't shit your pants with excitement! I don't want any lawsuits for permanent bowel damage on my head after dropping such a huge bombshell on you. I know what you're thinking—"A midcard comedy wrestler from a dead promotion wins a joke title from a glorified job guy and people didn't start immediately lining up at the ticket windows? What's wrong with this country?" But hey, Booker T was at least there, calling out Steve Austin to throw down, sucka, and punking out Vince McMahon at the end of the night. And then came the two weeks of TV that simultaneously reenergized and destroyed the WWF product at the same time, truly an amazing feat: the Tacoma *RAW* and the Atlanta *RAW*.

This will require a teeny bit of back story, so hang tight.

> **S**peaking of Booker T, the WWF immediately picked up what the WCW couldn't: "Can you dig it, sucka?" as a catchphrase. WCW's brilliant attempt: "Don't hate the player, hate the game." I mean, that doesn't even make SENSE!

SCENE EIGHT
The WCW Invasion Begins!

Back story number one: Marcus "Buff" Bagwell is a useless lump of shit who has a million-dollar body thanks to genetics, but hasn't quite grasped

the English language well enough to speak anything but "Dumbass Georgia Hick" as a first language. He was brought into WCW early in his career (in 1992) and essentially peaked as a wrestler in his first match, and it was all downhill from there workrate-wise. He spent the better part of five years bouncing from increasingly homosexually tinged babyface gimmicks (like his suspiciously close partnership with Scotty Riggs as the "American Males") before finally butching up and joining the nWo in early 1997, transforming into the posing moron known as Buff Bagwell.

Ironically, he became best known as Scott Steiner's lapdog for much of his run with that group, carrying out the classic "prison bitch" dynamic with the larger and even-more-falsely-macho Steiner. But he had one secret weapon when the WWF bought out WCW in 2001: teenage girls, who were not only more airheaded than him as a general rule, but who also squealed with delight at the mention of his name. Never underestimate the power of a pretty boy. In fact, when Vince McMahon mentioned Bagwell's name on the *Nitro-RAW* simulcast, the Pavlovian girls in the audience squealed so loudly in unison that Vince actually gave Bagwell a job on the basis of that. But what Vince didn't know, and wouldn't know because WWF officials considered it "beneath" them to follow the competition, was that Bagwell had botched his end of a bulldog spot in 1998 and suffered a broken neck (live on TV, no less—as Roddy Piper once said, "If you're gonna die, do it on live TV because it'll make more money.") and was quite possibly one of the five or ten worst wrestlers in the business (for someone in his position) from that point onward. He was still in a few decent matches after that, but it took extraordinary opponents and very carefully structured booking to make him look good again.

Back story number two: Vince and the WWF

desperately wanted to spin WCW off into its own TV show to get rid of it, and in fact pitched such a show to TNN several times from the date of the initial purchase until that point. The new show would run in smaller arenas and give Shane McMahon a chance to make his bones as a promoter and would also allow them to dump their developmental guys into an atmosphere closer to that of the WWF itself while still training them. One problem: the XFL. Or, more accurately, the millions of dollars lost by the XFL and the egg on the face of Viacom after throwing their networks, UPN and TNN, behind it.

With Vince's crash and burn outside of wrestling, people weren't exactly ready to jump on the old "Vince is a genius!" bandwagon, even if it was within the confines that he supposedly knew best. So as Commissioner Foley might say, "The WCW TV show is DENIED." Instead, the dueling recap shows *LiveWire* and *Superstars* were cancelled and combined into the extra-special, two-hour crappy recap show that is *Excess*, hosted by the vacant Jonathan Coachman and the vapid Trish Stratus. Ratings only recently, as of this writing, broke the 1.0 barrier after more than eight months on the air.

As for the WCW show, the brain trust at Titan Towers went to Plan B: give either *RAW* or *Smackdown* to the WCW crew, while effectively splitting the remaining WWF guys 50/50 with a televised draft. But first, a trial run of the new "WWF Nitro" was needed, so they decided to go with a test match (but not a Test match—they were silly, not masochistic) on what would come to be known in hushed tones of scorn as the . . . Tacoma *RAW*.

On July 2, after running house show test-run matches to generally okay responses, someone in the booking committee decided it would be a grand idea to build an episode of their flagship TV show around presumed babyface WCW-owner Shane McMahon, who would set up a WCW title match between champion Booker T

and newly signed Buff Bagwell. To keep up that WCW flavor, Torrie Wilson would debut and spend the show seducing Vince McMahon. And finally, the APA and their merry band of mid-card, no-drawing, wanna-bes would seek to defend the honor of the WWF by discovering who was leaking info out of the WWF and into WCW. This little subplot was actually one of the most unintentionally funny (and yet telling) bits of the so-called invasion story line. Faarooq and Bradshaw rallied together a bunch of mid-card scrubs in the name of defending the WWF from the invaders. And yet Shane McMahon's invaders were supposed to be the heroes in this little war, which completely went against the speeches given by the WWF side as they portrayed themselves as under attack.

Even stranger, the resistance group was comprised of people who had never drawn a dime in the business, for the WWF or otherwise. Recent WCW rejects like Haku and Raven had to stand there with a straight face while Bradshaw talked about defending the history and honor of the WWF as if he were Bruno Sammartino or something. This coming from the guy who had spent the first five years of his career copying every mannerism from Stan Hansen in a desperate attempt to get over as a fighting cowboy. It just reeked of a company that wasn't in touch with what the fanbase was wanting—ratings trends clearly indicated, beyond any reasonable doubt, that the fans wanted to see WWF v. WCW and viewed WCW as the "bad guys" in the conflict. Further, they wanted to see the WWF big guns facing off against the WCW big guns, not Bradshaw giving pep talks to Crash Holly in preparation for facing Billy Kidman in cruiserweight matches!

It got worse as the night went on—Vince McMahon was apparently more concerned with getting himself over (I know, it's a shock) running a pointless, show-long story line whereby he would be seduced by incoming WCW bombshell Torrie Wilson, only to be swerved by her at the end. It all went nowhere fast. By the end of the show, fans were upset at the lack of direct interaction between WCW and the WWF (especially with a PPV called *InVasion* only a couple of weeks away) and were in no mood for the "main event" of the evening—a re-creation of WCW *Nitro* featuring Booker T defending the WCW title against Buff Bagwell. I don't think anyone quite expected what happened next. From my review:

WCW World Title Match: Booker T v. Buff Bagwell

JR and Paul departed when switched over to WCW TV. It was pretty wild as the watermark in the corner of the screen changed to "WCW" and the ring apron reads "WCW." Nick Patrick was the ref, and the upper seats were blacked out due to people's having left. No, seriously, they really blacked out the upper seats. Scott Hudson and Arn Anderson were commentators, and Stacy Keibler was the ring announcer. But first, William Regal had Shane escorted out. He agreed because, unlike his father, he would never build the promotion around himself. Yeah, right.

In perhaps the scariest sign I've ever heard, the crowd completely turned on the match right out of the gates. They booed both guys and sat on their hands before the match even got going.

Bagwell jumps Booker and gets a quick double-underhook DDT for two. Blind charge hits sidekick and Booker gets an elbow for two. Buff hotshots him and chokes him out. The crowd continues turning on the match, occupying themselves with other things. Buff gets a suplex for two and hits the chinlock. The crowd then gets downright hostile, openly chanting, "This match sucks," and basically saying, "We don't want WCW on our show." Booker kind of grazes Buff with a dropkick and they can't decide who should sell, so Buff keeps control. More choking, but Booker comes back with a sidekick and flying forearm for two. Axe kick, Spinaroonie, and Austin and Angle run in to a

big face pop and it's a Sportz Entertainment finish in WCW's very first match.

All three heels beat on Booker as Bagwell has apparently gone WWF. They beat Booker all the way up to the entranceway. That was NOT the start they wanted to get with WCW on WWF TV. –*

To say that the WWF panicked would be an understatement. Even before the ratings had come in (and they weren't much over "okay" in terms of success of that segment), Bagwell was on the verge of being fired for tanking the match (to add to his already long list of annoying behavior in a short span in the WWF), and suddenly they needed an entirely new creative direction for the company. This was all without so much as an announced match for the first-ever WWF v. WCW PPV. After a mere one month of direct interpromotional war between the oldest rival forces in wrestling, they pulled the plug on the entire thing and went in a whole new direction the following week, creating the show that is now remembered as the Atlanta *RAW*.

SCENE NINE
Did We Say WCW? We Meant WCW/ECW

For, you see, like a secretary pool on an extended coffee break, the whispers now were beginning in the back. After months of proudly trumpeting the happy backstage area that was totally under their thumb, the WWF front office started losing control of the inmates as increasingly catty comments began to slip out to the wrestling media.

"That Sean O'Haire . . . he never says hello to Droz backstage, he doesn't deserve his spot."

"That DDP, he doesn't know how to work WWF-style matches, he doesn't deserve his spot."

"Lance Storm misses too many spots and he's not big enough, he doesn't deserve his spot."

It was amazing that a group of people collectively paid into the millions to wrestle fake matches were suddenly growing so overprotective of their supposed harmonious locker room that they seemed to forget that it was an athletic exhibition, not a competition. It's money that matters. Soon, people like Sean O'Haire (a young monster with a frightening amount of charisma and power) were ostracized from the WWF environment completely for any little infraction of the "rules" that the locker-room goon squad could think of, and within two months he was down in the minors learning to work the "WWF style." By the time the failure of the "WCW experiment" had been fully registered, there was no need to pass the buck because the blame had already been apportioned and served up in WCW's collective lap on a silver platter. The rallying cry seemingly became, "You know, that WCW v. WWF angle would work great if we could just get rid of the WCW guys."

Sean O'Haire, one of the few bright spots of the last days of the WCW, was almost immediately sent down to the WWF's deprogramming facilities to make sure he wouldn't wrestle "WCW style" anymore. Most suspect this was as one final "fuck you" to Eric Bischoff, who had planned to build the "new WCW" around O'Haire had the financing gone through in time to save it.

So that's what they did.

On July 9, *RAW* began with a bang as Shane McMahon immediately turned heel, changing the WCW crew from sympathetic second-raters into Evil Invaders. This completely contradicted everything that had happened in the week leading up to this show, but they were on a roll so they didn't care. Booker T, now acting as a full-blown heel, cheated and connived his way to a win over Kurt Angle (now suddenly a babyface) to retain the WCW title. Later in the show (this was still the same show, mind you), Lance Storm and Mike Awesome of the WCW team challenged Chris Jericho and Kane of the WWF team to a tag match, which didn't look to be anything special. But then:

Kane and Chris Jericho v. Lance Storm and Mike Awesome

Fun fact: Arnie's part in End of Days *was "Jericho Kane."*

Awesome slugs it out with Kane, but gets clotheslined and sideslammed. Jericho uses MID-CARD VIOLENCE and a bodypress gets two. Elbow off the top, but Awesome nails him from behind and Storm comes in. Jericho makes with the chops and the bulldog, but Awesome hits him from behind with a chunk of the glass ceiling and Jericho is YOUR mid-carder-in-peril. Awesome plants him and drops an elbow for two. Team Canada pounds him, and may I just say that the loss of their WCW music is a travesty, and the loss of Mike Awesome's Canadian citizenship equally so.

Storm misses a dropkick, but Jericho misses the Lionsault. Awesome hits the chinlock, then gets a belly-to-belly for two. More double-teams, but Jericho gets an enzuigiri, hot tag Kane. Big boot Awesome, and powerslam sets up the flying lariat. Kane's hotter than a cup of coffee to the face! Storm saves at two, but Jericho dropkicks him. Storm and Awesome double-team Kane, but Jericho gets the Walls of Jericho on Storm . . . and all hell breaks loose.

Tommy Dreamer and Rob Van Dam proceed to run into the ring via the audience and team up with Storm and Awesome to beat on Kane and Jericho. And a bunch of WWF b-teamers run in to make the save . . . but wait a second, they seem to all have something in common . . . Tazz . . . the Dudley Boyz . . . Raven . . . Rhyno . . . Justin . . . it's a MONSTER ECW BEATDOWN! Storm and Awesome rejoin "Team

ECW," everyone kicks ass on Kane and Jericho, and Heyman tells off JR and joins them in the ring for a MONSTER PROMO. Markout city. He calls JR a fat pig, and says he's sick of being a corporate sellout whore who has to sit there week in and week out and shill the WCW-WWF "Invasion" nonsense. Basically, everyone can kiss his ass because ECW is BACK. The crowd eats it up with a spoon. Even Paul's creditors are chanting "E-C-Dub." Well, maybe not. ECW: We put the "fun" in "defunct." *¼

The smart fans of course realized how silly the underlying idea behind the angle really was since ECW was going through bankruptcy proceedings and the WWF shouldn't have been able to even use the name "ECW" to begin with. But the fans in attendance that night ate it up. But wait, there's more, because the show wasn't even over with. Later in the evening, an irate Vince McMahon decided to challenge this new "Team ECW" to a twenty-man tag match, basically featuring five of his scrubs and five WCW guys teaming up to face ECW. The WWF and WCW teams couldn't coexist and started to fight, at which point Team WCW turned on Team WWF and revealed their alliance with Team ECW. And then, to close out the show, Paul Heyman brought out Stephanie McMahon (with newly enlarged funbags) and sold his stock in ECW to her, at which point Shane and Stephanie merged their companies into the Alliance.

This was one show. *One show!* What you read above is enough material and story line twists to conceivably carry an entire promotion through nearly eight months of television and PPV, all blown in two hours with minimal direct effect on the ratings. There was another interesting side effect, too. Booker T was the only WCW import left in any kind of position of note. All the rest of the WCW crew were immediately shunted down to the under-card, with the remaining mid-card slots filled by Team ECW guys (who were in reality just more of the same, stale, WWF crew wearing ECW T-shirts). And woe be to anyone who actually managed to get over on their own, like Tajiri or, later, The Hurricane.

A word on Yoshihiro Tajiri, if I may.

Brought into the WWF as a favor to Paul Heyman, Tajiri was immediately given the very dignified role of playing houseboy to William Regal. Because, see, he's small and Japanese and can't speak very good English, so he's funny. Or something. The thing is, once Tajiri got into the ring and started his vicious kicks and blowing the dreaded (but cool) Green Asian Mist into opponents' faces to beat them, he was able to get over on his own merits without the need for an additional gimmick. So, the only theory I can possibly think of for Tajiri's low status was that he "threatened" too many people taller than 5'8" and Tajiri was thus turned into a job guy so as not to insinuate that you don't need to be (say it with me) tall, muscular, and have a full head of hair in order to get over. The WWF's own self-fulfilling prophecy said that Tajiri wouldn't get over, so he didn't. QED. Ah, politics.

SCENE TEN
Did We Say WCW/ECW? We Meant Shane & Stephanie

Amidst all the chaos backstage, a ten-man main event for the *InVasion* PPV was announced, pitting Team WWF (Austin, Angle, Jericho, Undertaker, and Kane) against Team WCW/ECW (Booker T, Diamond Dallas Page, Dudley Boyz, and Rhyno), and whatever the strife behind the scenes, the fans were majorly into it. To set up the match, Austin solidified his position as head babyface by returning to the beer-swilling, trashtalking, butt-kicking madman that the fans had loved for so many years. This, finally, seemed to indicate that the WWF had the winning formula for this angle down: Steve Austin fights off a succession of invading heels, one after another, leading up to the WWF bringing in a bigger name down the road (Steiner, Nash, Hogan, Goldberg?) for the big challenge at *Wrestlemania*. Fans who had desperately wanted to avoid booing their hero now could rest easy because the Rattlesnake was back and taking names and stuff.

Of course, that was, until the show, when he turned on Team WWF and joined the WCW/ECW alliance to yank the proverbial rug out from under all the fans. Hope you enjoyed the show, now go fuck yourselves. *InVasion* did an all-time high buy rate for a non–"Big Five" event (1.6), made millions, and ended up as the peak for the angle since that number was never touched upon or even approached for the rest of the year. Austin was programmed with Kurt Angle for the next big run at the top, leaving the newly named Alliance floundering away in the mid-card like the cosmic joke they were.

Months earlier, when the sale had first gone through, Jim Ross had condescendingly told Internet fans that he was around for the UWF fiasco in 1987 and the same thing absolutely wouldn't happen here, presumably because someone in wrestling had actually learned a lesson from the past. I had that one put onto a sampler and mounted on my bathroom wall, just in case I needed something to make me shit myself laughing.

A word on the UWF fiasco, if I may.

What I'm referring to here is an eerily similar situation that transpired in 1987, when there were three superpowers of wrestling: the WWF, Jim Crockett's dying NWA, and Bill Watts's surging UWF. All things being equal, Watts would have parlayed his national TV distribution deal into big houses and lots of money across the U.S. by promoting the younger and up-and-coming new stars of wrestling in addition to hardworking veterans. However, a spiteful Vince

McMahon began picking off Watts's talent base one by one, until a sudden collapse of the Oklahoma economy (Watts's UWF was based there) and an ugly divorce left him losing thousands of dollars per week and in need of a sucker to buy his operation. He offered it to Vince McMahon for a song, but Vince (who actually does have a brain) laughed it off.

So Watts brought Vince's "offer" to Jim Crockett, used it to leverage a good deal for himself, and got out of the business entirely, leaving Crockett with his entire remaining talent base and television deal. The TV shows were quickly cancelled in favor of NWA programming, and the stars were rapidly absorbed into Crockett's own talent base . . . and jobbed out. Why? Crockett's fragile ego couldn't handle the concept that another promotion might have offered a challenge to his "boys," even though he set up the matches and controlled all the outcomes. So everyone in the UWF was portrayed as a jobber, the invasion angle fizzled, and the only one to survive was a young and very green kid named Sting, who was over enough to escape on his own merits.

The same sort of thing happened with the 2001 version of the invasion, as Vince's ego wouldn't let "dubbya see dubbya" get anything over on him, the bad boy of sportz entertainment. His thinking was, "If those WCW losers can make us money in an invasion angle, then our WWF superstars can make us even more!" I have no parallel to draw with Vince's daughter, Stephanie, being made into the figurehead leader despite her adverse effect on ratings and the audience's eardrums, except maybe to note that Dusty Rhodes also booked himself into a similar position of power during the UWF fiasco, and he also has enormous breasts.

But one parallel I can safely draw is that of Sting and the young stud who managed to survive the *InVasion* fiasco unscathed, Rob Van Dam. RVD was brought in to shore up the talent roster in case of a promotional split, although the WWF had no real interest in him or they would have signed him months before. Rob's problems have always been twofold:

1) A dependence on flashy highspots over coherent interviews.
2) Pot. And making no secret about it.

Apparently feeling that he could straighten out both areas of deficiency if given a shot, the WWF programmed him with the most likely candidate for someone who could keep up with his frenetically paced matches: Jeff Hardy. And they stole the show at *InVasion* as a result. Here's my review:

Hardcore Title Match:
Jeff Hardy v. Rob Van Dam

Flippy floppy to start, and RVD stops to pose, allowing Jeff a shot from behind. Dropkick gets two. Weird rollup gets two. RVD gets a standing Moonsault for two. Rolling senton splash gets two. Rob goes up and gets tossed to the railing by Jeff, however. Jeff baseball slides him, but Rob counters the railrunner and they crash into the crowd.

Back to ringside, Rob uses the legdrop onto the railing, but Jeff powerbombs him off the apron. Jeff grabs his usual seventy-foot ladder and heads up, but Rob pushes him up and splats him onto the floor. They brawl up the ramp, but Rob fires off a Van Daminator and sends Jeff flying. The twisting legdrop gets two.

Back in, Rob dropkicks a chair into Jeff's face, but the Moonsault hits knee. Hardy DDTs him for two, and a nasty German suplex gets two. Jawbreaker and Jeff goes up, but the swanton misses and Rob makes a miraculous recovery to finish with the * * * * * Frog Splash and win the hardcore title at 12:32. Good spotfest, but Rob seemed too concerned with getting the RVD character over and not enough with getting the angle over. * * * 1/4

Hey, I wasn't a big fan right away, I'll admit it. In fact, I was downright sick of the guy in ECW. But he worked hard in the early stages of his WWF career, and turned the laid-back interview into an artform, and now he's a pretty cool guy. And I can appreciate anyone who's even more self-absorbed than I am. I know how much work it is.

SCENE ELEVEN
What?

Speaking of self-absorbed, shooting was finishing on *The Scorpion King* about this time and The Rock was ready to make his big return and presumably jack up the ratings again after the WWF had completely blown the *InVasion* angle. Keep in mind that this was less than a month after shooting a show that was supposed to drastically alter the direction of the company for the rest of the year. Everyone expected Rock to return and make threats against Steve Austin (the guy who had run him out of the WWF months earlier), but instead the writers decided to buck that boring trend of making sense and instead had him challenged by a jealous Booker T right away.

WWF Rule of Political Correctness #193A: Two wrestlers of the same race will inevitably either team up or feud within two months of debuting. Rock started insulting Booker's intelligence (which, in one of those "shoot comments that aren't supposed to be shoot comments" moments, was proven true by Booker's appearance on *The Weakest Link* game show) and before you could say "racial stereotyping," a match was set for *Summerslam*, sucka.

But on the bigger scale, Rock's big return after months of being away from the WWF was supposed to magically pump their ratings back up to 2000 levels, presumably because Rock has 4 million good friends who watch the show just for him, I guess, but that didn't happen. The ratings were pretty good again for a couple of weeks, but once it was established that

1) Rock was going to the WWF side of things.
2) He was just going to be involved in an Insta-Feud™ with Booker T rather than anything meaningful, like settling the score with Austin.

the fans turned off their sets and did something else. The WWF was back to the beginning, with ratings sliding again, having blown both the *InVasion* angle and The Rock's return.

The WWF brain trust has since decided that this ratings downfall did not in fact happen, and that we Internet fans just don't understand about the importance of having the right people on top of the promotion. See what I mean about changing history?

Summerslam was a pretty darn good show for the most part. Angle had completed the transition from completely dorky sidekick into all-American Ass-Kicker, and was ready to challenge Steve Austin for the WWF title again, and probably win this time. Probably. Here's my review:

WWF Title Match:
Steve Austin v. Kurt Angle

Fight on the floor to start, and Austin whales on him. Into the ring, Angle takes him down and they pound on each other like schoolkids fighting over a girl. Angle stomps a mudhole, but makes a crucial tactical error by not walking it dry, and Austin gets his own shots in. Angle clothesline and bodyblock get

two, however. He puts his head down and gets caught, and Austin works on the knee. Stepover toehold is countered with the anklelock, but Austin makes the ropes.

Outside, Austin hits a clothesline and they head in, where Austin dumps Angle again to soften up the ankle. Back in, a triple suplex gets two, but Angle comes back and gets seven German suplexes. HEY! That's gimmick infringement! Angle Slam is blocked, and Austin sends him to the turnbuckle. Austin puts him on top, but Angle blocks a superplex. Austin keeps wearing him down and gets it on the second try. Good psychology there. KICK WHAM STUNNER out of nowhere . . . gets two. Again, and Angle goes flying out of the ring on the rebound. Austin viciously posts him, drawing blood as promised on RAW. Another two postings are added for good luck, then one for the road and one to grow on.

Angle, as you might guess, looks like Tommy Dreamer after taking a tour of the cheese grater factory. Austin slugs him down for two, then tosses him back out and back to that post again. Angle finally sends Austin into the crowd, but Austin suplexes him onto the concrete. As Austin climbs back in, however, Angle catches the anklelock, then drags him into the ring by the foot and keeps it on until Austin makes the ropes. Austin bails as Angle bleeds to death.

Belly-to-belly on the floor turns the tide for Angle, and a backdrop suplex there helps. Back in, Angle hits the Anglesault for two. Austin grabs a Million Dollar Dream (!!), but Angle shows awesome psychology by using the Bret Hart Counter from Survivor Series '96 for two, which Austin then counters by rolling out of it and maintaining the sleeperhold. I bow to the Buddha nature of these guys and am not worthy to recap their matches.

Angle dumps him to break, but Austin sneaks back in, KICK WHAM STUNNER . . . gets two. The crowd and my young cousins nearly have a collective heart attack. Angle crawls up, blocks another Stunner, and gets the Angle Slam for the double KO. Angle crawls over for two. Anklelock, but Austin is in the ropes, and *just in case, he decks the ref. DDT from Angle, but a second ref counts two. Austin takes that ref out. Third ref in, third ref out. Angle Slam, no ref. Nick Patrick comes in, disqualifies Austin for grievous mistreatment of WWF officials, and the crowd is PISSED at 23:11. Man, they totally booked themselves into a corner with this match—they couldn't put Austin over because it would destroy Kurt Angle, but they couldn't put Angle over because they need Austin strong for the unification match against Rock. And that's why DQs were invented. If it had had a finish, it would be Match of the Year, but it didn't, so it ain't. ****½*

Well, better luck next time for Kurt. Rock beat Booker without any such shenanigans, claiming the WCW world title for himself, while the rest of the under-card featured the usual, endless "Alliance v. WWF" matches that never seemed to settle anything and never seemed to result in the Alliance getting any sort of strong wins over their WWF counterparts. *Summerslam's* buy rate was just slightly over "bomb" in terms of the usual numbers for the show, and people started panicking again. And when the WWF panics, Shane and Stephanie get even more TV time because standard McMahon logic says that low TV ratings must mean people haven't seen enough McMahons out there yet, so throw a few more out!

But even more annoying than Stephanie's "look at me!" mentality was Steve Austin's newest catchphrase. The result of a bored Austin playing games with Christian's voice-mail messaging, Austin developed a bizarre new interview style for himself with which he would conduct entire conversations between himself and whatever imaginary voices were in his head. His interviews started sounding like this. "What?" I said his interviews started sounding like this. Armed with his newest character quirk, Austin prepared to defend the WWF title against Kurt Angle, again, at *Unforgiven* in September.

However, on September 11, the World Trade

S teve Austin has since apologized for starting the "What?" nonsense.

Center was attacked and from the WWF's standpoint it couldn't have come at a worse time because they were building for their big show. So while all the other sports and entertainment franchises were shutting down for the week to mourn, the WWF did a live *Smackdown* two days after the tragedy in which they spent the better part of the show congratulating themselves for "helping America get on with their lives," as though a pro-wrestling show was integral to the national morale or something. Most sickeningly of all, Stephanie McMahon, queen of tact, did a short promo near the middle of the show in which she said she knew that America would fight back against the terrorists, "just like" when her daddy fought back against the federal government in 1994. Needless to say, the WWF PR department quickly made sure this little bon mot was cut from all further international and recapped airings of the show. Or maybe she really did want to compare the federal government to Al Qaeda, who knows what goes on in her mind sometimes.

SCENE TWELVE
However You Spell It, They Suck

And speaking of "What was going through their minds?" a good word from the Undertaker brought the team of Bryan Adams and Brian Clarke, aka Kronik, into the WWF in September 2001. Truly a head-scratcher of epic proportions, Kronik's signing came about only because no one in the WWF had watched any WCW programming near the end of the line, and thus were spared the pain of watching Adams and Clarke stink up the ring with every match. But as far as Vince was concerned, he knew Adams from his days as Crush and Clarke from his days as Adam Bomb, so they couldn't be *that* bad, could they? At *Unforgiven*, we all found out together, as they met Undertaker and Kane in only their second match in the promotion, and I just have to share it with you:

WCW Tag-Title Match:
Undertaker and Kane v. Kronik

Big brawl to start, with some punches even making contact! Adams takes a big boot and legdrop for two, brother. Elbow gets two for UT. Kane comes in with an elbow of his own for two. Adams comes back with a backbreaker and Clarke works on Kane with some big kicks. Somebody better tell him to stop showing effort or he might lose his job. They get two. Kane gets a neckbreaker, but misses a charge. He figures, "What the hell, it's only Kronik," and decides to ignore this potential point for selling, however, choosing instead to do the only logical alternative: nothing.

UT comes in and works the arm, as kind of an inside joke for those of us expecting an actual match or something. Well, that's my theory, anyway. ROPE-WALK OF DOOM follows. Kronik gets him in the corner and works him over with stuff one could laughingly refer to as "offense" if one was in a particularly generous mood and/or under the influence of some sort of alcoholic beverage. You know, I used to think that Ultimate Warrior would always hold the all-time record for blowing up in the first minute of the match, but Brian Adams appears to have broken that record by channeling all his conditioning programs into his hair. He might be dead by 0:30, but his hairstyle is ready to party even forty minutes into the match! I wonder if he and HHH exchanged styling tips backstage.

Adams gets a dropkick for two, but Taker no-sells (I'm as shocked as you) and slugs away. Nothing I can pick out makes contact. Adams no-sells Taker's no-selling and they both hit the floor, perhaps due to some obscure law of physics in the "unstoppable force v. immovable force" area. I'll have to ask Stephen Hawking the next time I see him.

They brawl out onto the floor, no one sells anything. This is turning into a bizarre sort of battle of wills, I think. Either way, we all lose. Back in, Kronik gets a double-shoulderblock on Taker and Adams hits the chinlock. Well, of course, this wouldn't be complete without someone taking a break from the non-stop action to rest, and God knows if I were betting beforehand I'd go with Undertaker and Adams being the ones involved. So, yeah, that lasts awhile. Clarke comes in, but Taker DDTs him, making his own comeback before tagging Kane. I'd call it the hot tag, but that would require Taker to actually show some emotion or vulnerability. I suppose if you count spitting his chewing tobacco in a particularly menacing fashion and wearing an evil-looking bandana, you could argue for Undertaker showing some personality depth, but I wouldn't count them.

Anyway, Kane comes in and JR decides to remind us that Kane is indeed a hoss, in case we had forgotten and needed the reassurance of knowing that. You'd have to think that unless being a hoss entitles you to a 15 percent discount at Home Depot or something, it's not really a useful designation to give someone. "Sure, he's one of the slowest human beings alive and hasn't done anything more involved than a powerslam since 1999, but he's damn sure a HOSS, BY GAWD."

Kane cleans house on both Kroniks with a double-clothesline, and then just in case that house wasn't clean already, UT comes in and cleans his yard with the same. That's one clean house. He gets ready to finish Clarke, but Stevie Richards comes in and gets killed. Kane gets the flying clothesline on Adams, and UT finally gets the elusive chokeslam on Clarke to finish at 10:21.

I'd say that's a pretty good sign that Kronik is about to pull a Buff Bagwell and exeunt, stage left. The sad thing is that Undertaker is probably gonna walk around backstage telling everyone how all these WCW guys can't work and are dragging him down. The only thing that disturbs me more than Undertaker systematically destroying the careers of every WCW guy to come through the promotion is the realization *that we're a mere three months or so away from sitting through UT and Kane v. The Outsiders at Royal Rumble, assuming there is a higher power and he is a sick and twisted individual with nothing but hatred for me. Oh, and one would have thought UT and Kane would sell for guys their size, and one would have been wrong. I've had migraine headaches that left me with a better sense of well-being than this match. DUD. In the interest of leaving on an up-note, however, I would like to reinforce that Brian Adams has very well-maintained hair.*

And indeed, shortly afterward Kronik was fired and Undertaker went around backstage making sure everyone knew exactly where the fault in that match lay. But remember: It only takes one to drag a good match down to a bad match, but it takes two (or in this case, four) to have the Worst Match of the Year winner for 2001 (which this was), for several reasons.

O**ther contenders for "Worst Match of the Year" in 2001: Booker T v. Buff Bagwell from the Tacoma *RAW*, and DDP getting squashed by Undertaker's wife on *RAW*.**

Kurt Angle finally won the WWF title from Steve Austin in another great match, and people began to wonder if they could have anything other than great matches, but the WWF's plan to use 9/11 to turn Angle into a mega-patriotic babyface backfired when people suddenly realized that it wasn't 1985 anymore and fans wouldn't cheer him. The same strategy had also backfired on the WWF in 1991 with the Hogan-Slaughter "Desert Storm" feud, but to a much greater degree than this did. Here, they decided to hedge their bets and simply changed the title back when William Regal turned to the Alliance and cost Angle the title, which went back to Austin a couple of weeks after *Unforgiven*.

That show's buy rate was guarded more closely than Fort Knox before finally coming in at a lackluster number. The Alliance, for their part, was just dying by the show because the entire thing was revolving around Stephanie instead of anything meaningful, and when Alliance guys *did* get promo time, they had to spend it kissing up to Steve Austin. Even Booker T was killed by The Rock at *Unforgiven* in a handicap match with Booker and Shane McMahon against Rock that was won handily by the Great One. It was becoming the biggest joke in wrestling, only it wasn't "funny ha ha," you know?

SCENE THIRTEEN
Jericho Shatters the Glass Ceiling!
Just Kidding

Speaking of people being jokes, Chris Jericho was getting tired of being treated like one. After blowing another big match against RVD at *Unforgiven*, he was verbally dressed-down by Shane and Stephanie until he was mad enough to challenge RVD and Shane to a tag match, with The Rock as his partner. However, once again Jericho blew it, hitting Rock with a chair by mistake to cost his side the big win. Rock confronted Jericho, blows were exchanged, and suddenly we had a hot feud for the WCW title. And of course, it wouldn't be a hot feud without Stephanie having to shoehorn herself into things to siphon off the heat, in this case making veiled threats of using Alliance enforcer Rhyno to mess up Jericho should he continue insulting her.

Rock and Jericho began an awesome war of words with Rock accusing Jericho of being a whiner who couldn't win the big one, while Jericho accused Rock of being an obnoxious jerk who was taking him too lightly. Would the eventual match rule as much as the buildup? Would Stephanie get involved yet again? The answer to both questions was a resounding "Yup." Here's my review:

Rock and Jericho are pretty much best friends in real life, which is why Rock was the only one in the promotion with the balls to put Jericho over in a meaningful way, unlike, say, HHH, who turned his feud with Jericho into a feud with Stephanie and then blamed Jericho for the resulting ratings disaster.

WCW World Title Match:
The Rock v. Chris Jericho

Lockup battle to start, and Rock works the arm. Jericho armdrags him, and works Rock's arm in turn. Jericho slugs him down and chokes him out. Jericho unloads CANADIAN VIOLENCE, but Rock counters with the Rock Bottom, which Jericho counters in turn with the Walls. Awesome. Rock bails to the apron and gets dropkicked to the floor. Back in, Jericho gets a flying elbow for two. More CANADIAN VIOLENCE, but Rock tries his own and gets hit with a leg lariat for two. Pair of backbreakers get two, but Rock reverses the pinfall for two. Nice touch.

Jericho forearms him down, but gets hit with a Rock forearm in turn. He comes back quickly with a hotshot and the crowd starts chanting "Rocky Sucks" like old times. Jericho goes up, but gets crotched. Superplex and double-KO, and the crowd actually counts along with the ten-count. But then it's St. Louis, so they're already trained. Rock slugs away and gets a Samoan drop for two. Kip-up and Rock lays the smackdown, drawing a very noticeable heel reaction. Jericho comes back and walks into a lariat for two. Suplex gets two. Rock dumps Jericho, and he gets two back in the ring. He goes to a heelish chinlock to put sympathy heat on Jericho, and indeed Jericho escapes, but misses a dropkick. Rock catapults him and lariats him. They head up, and Jericho gets a missile dropkick. Double KO again, Rock is staggered. Slugfest is won by Jericho, and he overpowers Rock and gets a neckbreaker and rana for two. Someone call HHH, Jericho's wrestling like a cruiserweight again.

Jericho hits a Rock Bottom! Lionsault gets two.

Bulldog sets up the Canadian Elbow, which misses. Rock gets an ugly dragon-screw into the Sharpshooter, and the crowd freaks until Jericho makes the ropes. Jericho bails and Rock preps the Spanish table and Rock Bottoms Jericho through it. Rock breaks the count like a heel and smacks Jericho around, and after Jericho crawls back in, Rock sets up for the Rock Bottom . . . and the crowd BOOS. Jericho blocks, but walks into a spinebuster. People's Elbow is caught and REVERSED into the Walls of Jericho! This match is so awesome. I'm thinking it might be the finish, but Steph McJugs bounces out and distracts Jericho for the millionth time.

Rock DDTs him and goes after Steph with a Rock Bottom that looked like he was fighting the combined forces of gravity and inertia trying to get the McMammaries in the air, but Jericho grabs the chair left by Stephanie, hits a forward legsweep with it, and wins the WCW title at 23:47! Finally he wins the big one! Awesome match, a total MOTYC if not for the screwy finish. ****½ My faith in Jericho is restored and Rock shoots him a heelish glare, only to hand him the chair as if to say, "You won this time, but you needed this chair to do it." I smell rematch. I'm there, dudes.

Indeed, there was a rematch two weeks after *No Mercy* in which Rock regained the title in another great match, this time on free TV. But this, and a zillion other title changes a week, were making most observers question the insane number of titles and title changes booked on a weekly basis. In fact, one notable *Smackdown* taping saw Christian winning the European title from Bradshaw, with the match being so important that it was edited off the show for time! Even Mick Foley, who was growing increasingly unhappy with the direction of the company, did a live interview in which he made this very point. Foley actually quit the WWF, on good terms, soon after in order to pursue his writing career.

But Rock was the champion again and Vince McMahon, like everyone else in the Western hemisphere, was sick of all this Alliance crap and all the titles, so the main event of *Survivor Series* was made into a "winner take all" ten-man elimination tag match, with Team WWF (Rock, Jericho, Undertaker, Kane, and Big Show) taking on Team Alliance (Austin, Angle, Booker T, Rob Van Dam, and Shane McMahon), with the winning "company" getting everything and all the losers getting fired. I know, I know, Angle is on Team Alliance after just being a huge babyface a month earlier—that's part of the problem they were having with the booking. The under-card would feature all unification matches, with the goal being to get down to one set of titles once and for all. And thank God for that goal, because it was getting ridiculously hard to keep track of who the WCW tag-team champions and/or the WWF tag-team champions were at any given time.

At the show, the WWF won the match (I know, I'm shocked, too), thus killing the Alliance and firing everyone involved. Oh, well, except of course for those members who already had titles because a prematch stipulation said that they would keep their jobs. And Test (who joined early in the angle), who won an "immunity battle royale" and thus couldn't be fired. And William Regal, who kissed Vince McMahon's ass on *RAW* the next night, literally, in order to win his job back. And the various members who reappeared in the weeks ahead through loopholes or begging. In fact, come to think of it, the match didn't really accomplish much, did it? Which is kind of the point of this year—a whole lot of time and effort wasted on something that was doomed to failure from the moment it was started.

The year ended with a pair of bright spots: the WWF finally caved in and signed Ric Flair to a contract, bringing him in to act as the co-owner of the WWF and as Vince's foil. The idea being that he had bought the stock off of Shane and Stephanie back in July, enabling them to purchase the Alliance. Flair injected some much needed life into a stale role and gave Vince someone truly worthy to play megalomaniac off of.

Flair's debut also turned Steve Austin back into his old babyface self because Flair endorsed Austin while Vince endorsed the still-hated Kurt Angle, putting Austin back in the position he's always been suited for. And with the WCW and WWF world titles still separated, a unification tournament was held at the last PPV of 2001, *Vengeance*, where Chris Jericho defeated The Rock to win the former WCW title, then defeated Steve Austin to unify the belts into the undisputed world title. As the year ended, fans were left with some hope that the glass ceiling had been shattered, for good.

Ha ha, just wanted to see if you were still paying attention there.

[Fade Out]

Afterword (One Last Thing . . .)

As 2002 began, our story came full circle back to where it had begun: Hulk Hogan. Desperate for a boost in ratings, Vince McMahon completed negotiations with Hogan, Kevin Nash, and Scott Hall to begin the year.

HHH returned from his leg injury in January, and instantly bombed in the ratings. Two months later, he still didn't look 100 percent (although he looked 40 percent bigger), and I have to wonder if he'll ever be at that level again.

Jericho appeared to be having a shot to run with the titles since he hadn't lost them yet, but there was always tomorrow or the next show.

The title changes have been toned down significantly as there were no changes of note between *Survivor Series* and *Royal Rumble*, and that's a good sign.

Ratings continued to stagnate, and so did the product. With each passing day, Vince appeared to be losing touch with his audience and resorted to bringing guys from 1996 back into the fold in order to restimulate the hot business he once had.

So what's the lesson here? How and why exactly did the WWF go from beating WCW to being WCW in the space of three years?

Well, ratings and fan apathy are a fickle bitch mistress when you come right down to it, but there are other reasons, too.

1) Lack of competition. The "war" was effectively over with at the beginning of 1999 when WCW's big comeback angle was to have Hulk Hogan pin Kevin Nash with one finger to win the WCW world title *Nitro*. It was all downhill from there, and *Nitro* never even won another quarter hour in the ratings again. WCW went through bookers like normal people change underwear (even turning the proverbial dirty undies inside out a few times in the form of Russo and Bischoff) and was never able to gets its shit together enough to mount another serious threat against the WWF machine. As a result, the WWF's ratings dropped steadily because Vince McMahon thrives above all else on getting his ass kicked, no matter what he may claim. The one other sure way to get Vince's product in full gear is to start beating him at his own game, which is what WCW (and earlier in the '80s, the Dusty-

169

booked NWA) managed to do long enough to start a sizable lead before coughing it up in the end. Without any serious competition (and no one counts the fledgling XWF and WWA groups picking at the corpse of WCW to be "serious"), there's simply no motivation for Vince to keep trying to win anymore.

2) Inmates running the asylum. Again, like WCW. Ever since WCW's problems started in 1998, the WWF's big crowing point has always been the harmonious locker room and how Vince is the guy in charge, but in early 2000, with his increasing focus on the XFL and the sudden boost in new faces, people started feeling threatened and things changed. Undertaker went from locker-room leader to locker-room bully, telling anyone who would listen how the new guys didn't know how to work. HHH started playing political games even more ruthlessly than his old friend Shawn Michaels had, maneuvering himself into a relationship with the boss's daughter and ensuring that he never, ever looked bad. Career mid-carders like Bradshaw suddenly felt it was their duty to dictate locker-room etiquette to people who were in a position to be pushed above them, and if the ignorant newcomer didn't comply, well, sucks to be him. Hazing rituals became commonplace and started becoming public, with very negative reactions from the fans resulting. For example, referee Billy Silverman was forced to buy drinks for everyone on the plane after violating the "unwritten rule" about only main-event guys upgrading their coach tickets to first class. He quit after weeks of such abuse over a minor thing. Seemingly the only guys on top who would do jobs without griping about it

were Steve Austin and Rock, and they're exactly the guys who shouldn't have been doing jobs that often. Morale became a mess, mid-carders started feeling they had no chance to advance up the card, and fans caught on to that feeling, too.

3) Weak story lines. Can't emphasize this one enough. You can trace the beginning of the downfall of the WWF's run at the top of the cable world almost to the day that Stephanie McMahon took over as head writer. What resulted was a series of watered-down, soap-opera story lines, or angles started and then dropped two weeks later, or people getting pushed one week and jobbed the next, or people acting completely outside their established characters for the sake of a gag or turn, or a million other little goofs that started getting noticeable after months and months of them. Sometimes all of the above happened at the same time! Adding to the pain even more was Stephanie's insistence on booking herself to be one of the top stars of the promotion, even when she's not an athlete by any stretch of the imagination and has only wrestled in one PPV match in her life. Bookers like Kevin Nash and Dusty Rhodes could get away with stuff like that in the past for a short time, if only because they're actually wrestlers, but a twenty-four-year-old girl putting herself on TV for forty minutes a show simply stretches the bounds of credibility to the breaking point.

4) Overexposure. With RAW, Smackdown, and Heat providing five hours of original content every week, plus a PPV every month, plus three hours of recap shows every week, it simply got to the point that there was too much WWF programming for the average Joe to digest without

switching over to something else for a change.

5) Main-event style. When Steve Austin revolutionized the WWF main-event scene in 1998 by creating the most successful formula match they've ever used, it also brought with it the inherent problem of making the athlete fit the match rather than the other way around. Guys like Chris Benoit were forced to drastically alter their styles in order to fit in with the punch-kick mentality, and although Benoit is an in-ring genius and adjusted fine, it took someone like Chris Jericho months to make his more high-flying tactics credible as "main-event offense." There is no longer a difference between the various main eventers—the variations in moveset are merely cosmetic, with everyone doing the same basic set of moves (the spinebuster is a particularly favored setup move) with punching to set them up, and the requisite ref bump before the big pinfall finish. Shane McMahon's involvement in main events got so clichéd that fans actually became trained to not pop for any near-falls toward the end because they knew that at some point Shane would pull the referee out of the ring at the two-count to stop him from getting to three. By the end of 2001, the main events were so homogenized that someone like Rob Van Dam was nearly ostracized from the main event completely because his style was both completely different and much more over than anyone else's was. It required, in my opinion, too much effort for the bookers to adjust the style of the match to play someone else's strengths, so they simply found someone who could instead adjust to the cookie-cutter matches. Which is not to say that these matches weren't fabulous as a

rule, because they were, but champagne every night gets boring, even really good champagne. Sometimes you need a shot of whiskey to cleanse your palette.

6) Lack of elevation. This was related to the last point, since guys were regularly deemed "not ready" for the main event due to a style difference, those guys were simply left to rot in the mid-card with nowhere else to go. Edge had been stuck in a rut since his singles push began—he began at the intercontinental title, and he's still there. People come into the WWF, immediately get shoehorned into either under-card, mid-card or main-event slots, and are unable to move anywhere but laterally from there. Raven is a terrific example. He was brought in to freshen up the hardcore division, did so, and then couldn't get any higher up the totem pole because the writers no longer knew what to do with him. An even better example is that of The Hurricane, Shane Helms. Brought in as a cruiserweight jobber in the WCW invasion, his obsession with Green Lantern led to the writers giving him a joke gimmick of "deluded superhero," and he would make a grand entrance and pretend to fly around the ring with his cape on. However, the writers were so enamored with their little in-joke that they ended up spending huge amounts of TV time on a guy who never won! Finally, instead of actually pushing him to justify the time spent, they simply jobbed him down to the under-card for good, no matter how over the gimmick had become.

7) Lack of long-term direction. Who's going to be world champion three months from now? Who knows? One week we get *RAW* filled with clean finishes and no McMahons, the next it's Vince-Vince-Vince

and everyone running in for the DQ all night. Things are done last minute so fans have no long-term incentive for tuning in—they know that if they skip two or three weeks and come back later, all the story lines will have changed anyway. Or even worse, they'll still be at exactly the same place they were three weeks ago, like with the never ending Austin-Angle feud of mid-2001 or the ridiculous *InVasion* angle. Lots of stuff going on, but nothing really happening, ya know?

In the end, it all comes back to the writing, I think. The originality and gung ho mentality of 1997–99 has been missing ever since the WWF became a public company, and it doesn't look to be coming back anytime soon. The WWF has long needed a shakeup of the backstage personnel, and instead all we've seen is faceless executives coming and going, most of whom make more than the average wrestler does! I assure you that hiring a new executive vice president of Internet sales and marketing isn't going to turn the product around, but getting rid of Daddy's Little Girl as head writer and hiring some actual wrestling fans to write the product might. By the time you read this, the WWF should have split into two separate promotions in order to freshen up the matchups a bit, but then they've been saying that since the WCW buyout. Logic would say that unless they double the writing staff and let both sides operate independently, it'll just be the same, stale product, times two. But, hey, if I knew the real solution, I'd find a sucker, er, I mean backer, and start my own promotion.

In the end, it's much more fun doing what I'm best at—taking potshots from the cheap seats—and like I always say, go with what you know.

Appendixes

Pay-Per-View Revenue History

Buyrates are the ratings for Pay-Per-View events, calculated by dividing the number of people who actually ordered the show ("buys") by the number of people who are *capable* of ordering the show ("The PPV Universe"). In this case, there are roughly 30,000,000 homes (give or take 5,000,000) in the PPV Universe, and, thus, you get the buyrate for a show by dividing the number of buys by 30,000,000. The "magic number" for a show to make money these days is 1 percent (called a 1.0 buyrate), which means that 1 percent of the people who could order a show did so, which amounts to about 300,000 people buying your PPV. (300,000 divided by 30,000,000 = 0.01, or 1 percent). The highest grossing PPV ever was 2001's *Wrestlemania X-7*, which did roughly 1,000,000 buys, or a 3.0 percent buyrate.

	Show	Buy Rate	Advertised Main Event
3/31/85	Wrestlemania	1.1	Hulk Hogan & Mr. T v. Roddy Piper & Paul Orndorff
11/7/85	The Wrestling Classic	2.53	Hulk Hogan v. Roddy Piper
4/5/86	Wrestlemania	7.01	Hulk Hogan v. King Kong Bundy
3/29/87	Wrestlemania	8	Hulk Hogan v. Andre the Giant
11/26/87	Survivor Series	7.01	Hulk Hogan's Team v. Andre's Team
1/24/88	Royal Rumble	8.2	Royal Rumble Match
3/27/88	Wrestlemania	6.52	World title tournament
8/29/88	SummerSlam	4.5	Hulk Hogan & Randy Savage v. Ted Dibiase & Andre the Giant
11/24/88	Survivor Series	2.82	Hulk Hogan's Team v. Ted Dibiase's Team
1/15/89	Royal Rumble	1.51	Royal Rumble Match
4/2/89	Wrestlemania	6.01	Hulk Hogan v. Randy Savage

Pay-Per-View Revenue History, *continued.*

	Show	Buy Rate	Advertised Main Event
8/28/89	SummerSlam	4.81	Hulk Hogan & Brutus Beefcake v. Randy Savage & Zeus
11/23/89	Survivor Series	3.34	Hulk Hogan's Team v. Zeus' Team
12/12/89	No Holds Barred	1.6	Hulk Hogan & Brutus Beefcake v. Randy Savage & Zeus
1/21/90	Royal Rumble	1.9	Royal Rumble Match
4/4/90	Wrestlemania	3.8	Hulk Hogan v. Ultimate Warrior
8/27/90	SummerSlam	3.9	Hulk Hogan v. Earthquake/Ultimate Warrior v. Rick Rude (double main event)
11/22/90	Survivor Series	3	Hulk Hogan's Team v. Earthquake's Team
1/19/91	Royal Rumble	3.04	Royal Rumble Match/Ultimate Warrior v. Sgt. Slaughter
3/23/91	Wrestlemania	2.8	Hulk Hogan v. Sgt. Slaughter
8/26/91	SummerSlam	2.7	Hulk Hogan & Ultimate Warrior v. Sgt. Slaughter & Col. Mustafa
11/28/91	Survivor Series	2.21	Hulk Hogan v. Undertaker
12/3/91	Tuesday in Texas	1.02	Hulk Hogan v. Undertaker
1/19/92	Royal Rumble	1.8	Royal Rumble Match
4/5/92	Wrestlemania	2.33	Hulk Hogan v. Sid Justice/Ric Flair v. Randy Savage (double main event)
8/29/92	SummerSlam	1.63	Ultimate Warrior v. Randy Savage
11/25/92	Survivor Series	1.4	Randy Savage & Mr. Perfect v. Ric Flair & Razor Ramon
1/24/93	Royal Rumble	1.24	Royal Rumble Match
4/4/93	Wrestlemania	2	Bret Hart v. Yokozuna
6/11/93	King of the Ring	1.12	Hulk Hogan v. Yokozuna
8/30/93	SummerSlam	1.32	Yokozuna v. Lex Luger
11/24/93	Survivor Series	0.82	Yokozuna's Team v. Lex Luger's Team
1/22/94	Royal Rumble	0.92	Undertaker v. Yokozuna
3/20/94	Wrestlemania	1.68	Bret Hart v. Owen Hart/Lex Luger v. Yokozuna (double main event)
6/19/94	King of the Ring	0.73	Bret Hart v. Diesel
8/29/94	SummerSlam	1.25	Undertaker v. Undertaker
11/23/94	Survivor Series	0.9	Undertaker v. Yokozuna
1/22/95	Royal Rumble	1	Bret Hart v. Diesel
4/2/95	Wrestlemania	1.4	Shawn Michaels v. Diesel/Lawrence Taylor v. Bam Bam Bigelow (double main event)
5/14/95	In Your House	0.83	Diesel v. Sid
6/19/95	King of the Ring	0.65	Diesel & Bam Bam Bigelow v. Tatanka & Sid
7/23/95	In Your House	0.7	Diesel v. Sid
8/27/95	SummerSlam	0.9	Diesel v. Mabel

	Show	Buy Rate	Advertised Main Event
9/24/95	In Your House	0.7	Diesel & Shawn Michaels v. Owen Hart & Yokozuna
10/22/95	In Your House	0.4	Diesel v. British Bulldog
11/23/95	Survivor Series	0.57	Diesel v. Bret Hart
12/17/95	In Your House	0.33	Bret Hart v. British Bulldog
1/21/96	Royal Rumble	1.1	Bret Hart v. Undertaker
2/18/96	In Your House	0.74	Bret Hart v. Diesel
3/31/96	Wrestlemania	1.2	Bret Hart v. Shawn Michaels
4/28/96	Good Friends, Better Enemies	0.65	Shawn Michaels v. Diesel
5/26/96	Beware of Dog	0.45	Shawn Michaels v. British Bulldog
6/23/96	King of the Ring	0.65	Shawn Michaels v. British Bulldog
7/21/96	International Incident	0.37	Shawn Michaels & Sid & Ahmed Johnson v. Owen Hart & British Bulldog & Vader
8/18/96	SummerSlam	0.58	Shawn Michaels v. Vader
9/22/96	Mind Games	0.48	Shawn Michaels v. Mankind
10/20/96	Buried Alive	0.4	Undertaker v. Mankind
11/17/96	Survivor Series	0.58	Shawn Michaels v. Sid
12/15/96	It's Time	0.35	Sid v. Bret Hart
1/21/97	Royal Rumble	0.72	Shawn Michaels v. Sid
2/16/97	The Final Four	0.5	Bret Hart v. Steve Austin v. Vader v. Undertaker
3/23/97	Wrestlemania	0.77	Undertaker v. Sid/Bret Hart v. Steve Austin (double main event)
4/20/97	Taker's Revenge	0.5	Undertaker v. Mankind
5/11/97	A Cold Day in Hell	0.57	Undertaker v. Steve Austin
6/8/97	King of the Ring	0.5	Steve Austin v. Shawn Michaels
7/6/97	Canadian Stampede	0.59	The Hart Foundation v. Steve Austin's Team
8/3/97	SummerSlam	0.8	Bret Hart v. Undertaker
9/7/97	Ground Zero	0.45	Undertaker v. Shawn Michaels
10/8/97	Badd Blood	0.6	Undertaker v. Shawn Michaels
11/9/97	Survivor Series	0.89	Bret Hart v. Shawn Michaels
12/7/97	D-Generation X	0.4	Shawn Michaels v. Ken Shamrock
1/18/98	Royal Rumble	0.94	Shawn Michaels v. Undertaker
2/15/98	No Way Out of Texas	0.52	D-Generation X v. Steve Austin's Team
3/29/98	Wrestlemania	2.34	Shawn Michaels v. Steve Austin
4/26/98	Unforgiven	0.85	Steve Austin v. Dude Love
5/31/98	Over the Edge	0.58	Steve Austin v. Dude Love
6/28/98	King of the Ring	1.13	Steve Austin v. Kane
7/26/98	Fully Loaded	0.9	Steve Austin & Undertaker v. Kane & Mankind
8/30/98	SummerSlam	1.63	Steve Austin v. Undertaker
9/27/98	Breakdown	0.86	Steve Austin v. Kane v. Undertaker
10/18/98	Judgement Day	0.89	Undertaker v. Kane
11/9/98	Survivor Series	0.89	World title tournament

Pay-Per-View Revenue History, *continued.*

	Show	Buy Rate	Advertised Main Event
12/13/98	Rock Bottom	0.78	The Rock v. Mankind
1/24/99	Royal Rumble	1.91	The Rock v. Mankind
2/14/99	St. Valentine's Day Massacre	1.21	The Rock v. Mankind/Steve Austin v. Vince McMahon (double main event)
3/28/99	Wrestlemania	2.32	The Rock v. Steve Austin
4/25/99	Backlash	1.06	The Rock v. Steve Austin
5/23/99	Over the Edge	1.12	Steve Austin v. Undertaker
6/27/99	King of the Ring	1.14	Steve Austin v. Vince & Shane McMahon
7/25/99	Fully Loaded	0.94	Steve Austin v. Undertaker
8/22/99	SummerSlam	1.71	Steve Austin v. Mankind v. HHH
9/26/99	Unforgiven	1.02	HHH v. British Bulldog v. The Rock v. Big Show v. Mankind v. Kane
10/17/99	No Mercy	0.88	HHH v. Steve Austin
11/9/99	Survivor Series	1.14	HHH v. Rock v. Steve Austin
12/12/99	Armageddon	1.1	HHH v. Vince McMahon
1/23/00	Royal Rumble	1.58	HHH v. Cactus Jack
2/27/00	No Way Out	1.2	HHH v. Cactus Jack
4/2/00	Wrestlemania	2.08	HHH v. Mick Foley v. Big Show v. The Rock
4/30/00	Backlash	1.62	HHH v. The Rock
5/21/00	Judgement Day	1.05	HHH v. The Rock
6/25/00	King of the Ring	1.19	HHH & Vince & Shane McMahon v. The Rock & Undertaker & Kane
7/23/00	Fully Loaded	1.04	HHH v. Chris Jericho/The Rock v. Chris Benoit (double main event)
8/27/00	SummerSlam	1.4	HHH v. The Rock v. Kurt Angle
9/24/00	Unforgiven	1.5	HHH v. Kurt Angle
10/22/00	No Mercy	1.31	The Rock v. Kurt Angle
11/19/00	Survivor Series	1	HHH v. Steve Austin
12/10/00	Armegeddon	1.15	HHH v. Steve Austin v. The Rock v. Kurt Angle v. Rikishi v. Undertaker
1/21/01	Royal Rumble	1.35	HHH v. Kurt Angle
2/25/01	No Way Out	1.31	HHH v. Steve Austin/The Rock v. Kurt Angle (double main event)
4/1/01	Wrestlemania	2.18	Steve Austin v. The Rock
4/29/01	Backlash	0.9	Steve Austin & HHH v. Undertaker & Kane
5/20/01	Judgement Day	0.76	Steve Austin v. Undertaker
6/24/01	King of the Ring	0.96	Steve Austin v. Chris Benoit v. Chris Jericho
7/22/01	InVasion	1.63	Team WWF v. Team WCW/ECW
8/19/01	SummerSlam	1.32	Steve Austin v. Kurt Angle
9/23/01	Unforgiven	0.82	Steve Austin v. Kurt Angle
10/21/01	No Mercy	0.8	Steve Austin v. Kurt Angle v. Rob Van Dam

Composite TV Ratings for Wrestling Events, 1997–1999

Composite		Composite		Composite	
1/6/97	2.14	1/5/98	3.52	1/4/99	5.74
1/13/97	2.31	1/12/98	3.82	1/11/99	5.53
1/20/97	2.23	1/19/98	4.07	1/18/99	5.6
1/27/97	2.2	1/26/98	3.53	1/25/99	5.53
2/3/97	2.63	2/2/98	3.55	2/1/99	5.81
2/13/97	2.71	2/9/98	3.22	2/13/99	4.3
2/17/97	2.13	2/23/98	3.22	2/15/99	5.94
2/24/97	2.5	3/2/98	3.9	2/22/99	5.6
3/3/97	2.44	3/9/98	3.63	3/1/99	6.4
3/10/97	2.34	3/17/98	4.41	3/8/99	6.44
3/17/97	2.34	3/23/98	3.62	3/15/99	5.84
3/24/97	2.53	3/30/98	3.83	3/22/99	6.43
3/31/97	2.71	4/6/98	4.43	3/29/99	6.54
4/7/97	2.23	4/13/98	4.63	4/5/99	5.83
4/14/97	2.22	4/20/98	4.42	4/12/99	6.33
4/21/97	2.74	4/27/98	5.71	4/19/99	6.1
4/28/97	3.42	5/4/98	5.53	4/26/99	6
5/5/97	3.41	5/11/98	4.81	5/3/99	6.43
5/12/97	3.23	5/18/98	5.41	5/10/99	8.13
5/19/97	3.63	5/25/98	4.22	5/17/99	6.4
5/26/97	2.74	6/1/98	4.39	5/24/99	7.2
6/2/97	2.51	6/8/98	4.33	5/31/99	6.33
6/9/97	2.24	6/15/98	4.33	6/7/99	6.6
6/16/97	2.44	6/22/98	4.34	6/14/99	6.64
6/23/97	2.43	6/29/98	5.44	6/21/99	6.03
6/30/97	2.5	7/6/98	4.03	6/28/99	6.83
7/7/97	2.64	7/13/98	4.65	7/5/99	6.03
7/14/97	2.63	7/20/98	5.02	7/12/99	6
7/21/97	4.04	7/27/98	4.92	7/19/99	6.31
7/28/97	2.92	8/3/98	4.93	7/26/99	7.13
8/4/97	2.8	8/10/98	4.55	8/2/99	5.9
8/11/97	2.93	8/17/98	4.23	8/9/99	6.4
8/18/97	3.2	8/24/98	4.72	8/16/99	6.62
8/29/97	1.63	9/5/98	2.61	8/23/99	5.7
9/5/97	2.13	9/14/98	4.03	8/30/99	4.24
9/8/97	2.22	9/21/98	4.03	9/6/99	4.43
9/15/97	2.6	9/28/98	4.65	9/13/99	6.02
9/22/97	2.4	10/5/98	4.55	9/20/99	6.1
9/29/97	2.8	10/12/98	4.84	9/27/99	6.81

Composite TV Ratings for Wrestling Events, 1997–1999, *continued.*

Composite		Composite		Composite	
10/6/97	3.1	10/19/98	5.04	10/4/99	5.93
10/13/97	2.82	10/26/98	4.53	10/11/99	6.14
10/20/97	3	11/2/98	4.84	10/18/99	5.42
10/27/97	2.83	11/9/98	5.03	10/25/99	5.6
11/3/97	2.61	11/16/98	5.54	11/1/99	5.94
11/10/97	3.42	11/23/98	4.91	11/8/99	5.41
11/17/97	3.14	11/30/98	5.03	11/15/99	6.31
11/24/97	3.12	12/7/98	5.14	11/22/99	5.54
12/1/97	3.02	12/14/98	5.23	11/29/99	6.53
12/8/97	2.73	12/21/98	4.73	12/6/99	6.02
12/15/97	3	12/28/98	4.92	12/13/99	6.12
12/22/97	3.12			12/20/99	5.82
12/29/97	3.62			12/27/99	5.9

Composite TV Ratings for Wrestling Events, 2000

Composite		Composite	
1/3/00	6.42	1/1/01	4.51
1/10/00	6.63	1/8/01	4.83
1/17/00	5.94	1/15/01	5.24
1/24/00	6.8	1/22/01	5.5
1/31/00	6.64	1/29/01	5.43
2/7/00	6.52	2/5/01	5.01
2/14/00	4.34	2/12/01	4.83
2/21/00	5.94	2/19/01	4.91
2/28/00	6.5	2/26/01	5.12
3/6/00	6.43	3/5/01	4.54
3/13/00	6.3	3/12/01	4.93
3/20/00	6.2	3/19/01	4.62
3/27/00	6.63	3/26/01	4.71
4/3/00	6.4	4/2/01	5.72
4/10/00	6.22	4/9/01	5.42
4/17/00	6.74	4/16/01	5.12
4/24/00	7.13	4/23/01	5.11
5/1/00	7.42	4/30/01	4.93
5/8/00	6.23	5/7/01	4.64
5/15/00	6.14	5/14/01	4.52
5/22/00	7.12	5/21/01	4.22
5/29/00	6.43	5/28/01	4.24

Composite		Composite	
6/5/00	5.92	6/4/01	4.34
6/12/00	6.83	6/11/01	4.1
6/19/00	5.8	6/18/01	4.21
6/26/00	6.4	6/25/01	4.65
7/3/00	5.3	7/2/01	4.62
7/10/00	6	7/9/01	4.73
7/17/00	6.2	7/16/01	5.03
7/24/00	6.9	7/23/01	5.35
7/31/00	6.4	7/30/01	5.68
8/7/00	6.3	8/6/01	5.4
8/14/00	5.9	8/13/01	5.16
8/21/00	6.2	8/20/01	5.16
8/28/00	4.93	8/27/01	4.85
9/4/00	4.21	9/3/01	4.62
9/11/00	5.81	9/10/01	4.62
9/18/00	5.81	9/17/01	4.8
9/25/00	5.54	9/24/01	4.47
10/2/00	5.43	10/1/01	4.43
10/9/00	5.32	10/8/01	4.47
10/16/00	4.83	10/15/01	4.11
10/23/00	5.52	10/22/01	3.92
10/30/00	4.92	10/29/01	4.1
11/6/00	5.14	11/5/01	3.95
11/13/00	5.03	11/12/01	4.12
11/21/00	5.02	11/19/01	4.81
11/27/00	4.92	11/26/01	4.41
12/4/00	5.02	12/3/01	4.19
12/11/00	5.84	12/10/01	4.67
12/18/00	4.91	12/17/01	3.99
12/25/00	3.84	12/24/01	3.2
		12/31/01	2.4

WWF Tag-Team Title History

Champion	Date Won	Location
Luke Graham & Tarzan Tyler	06/71	New Orleans, LA
Karl Gotch & Rene Goulet	12/06/71	New York, NY
Baron Mikel Scicluna & King Curtis Iaukea	02/01/72	Philadelphia, PA

(All title histories courtesy www.puroresu.com)

WWF Tag-Team Title History, *continued.*

Champion	Date Won	Location
Sonny King & Chief Jay Strongbow	05/22/72	New York, NY
Toru Tanaka & Mr. Fuji	06/27/72	Philadelphia, PA
Tony Garea & Haystacks Calhoun	05/30/73	Hamburg, PA
Toru Tanaka & Mr. Fuji [2]	09/11/73	Philadelphia, PA
Tony Garea & Dean Ho	11/14/73	Hamburg, PA
Jimmy Valiant & Johnny Valiant	05/08/74	Hamburg, PA
Dominic Denucci & Victor Rivera	05/13/75	Philadelphia, PA
Dominic Denucci & Pat Barrett	06/75	
Blackjack Lanza & Blackjack Mulligan	08/26/75	Philadelphia, PA
Tony Parisi & Louis Cerdan	11/18/75	Philadelphia, PA
Executioners (Killer Kowalski & John Studd)	05/11/76	Philadelphia, PA
Chief Jay Strongbow & Billy White Wolf	12/07/76	Philadelphia, PA
Toru Tanaka & Mr. Fuji [3]	09/27/77	Philadelphia, PA
Defeat Tony Garea & Larry Zbyszko.		
Dominic Denucci & Dino Bravo	03/14/78	Philadelphia, PA
Yukon Lumberjacks (Pierre & Eric)	06/26/78	New York, NY
Tony Garea & Larry Zbyszko	11/21/78	Allentown, PA
Johnny Valiant & Jerry Valiant	03/06/79	Allentown, PA
Ivan Putski & Tito Santana	10/22/79	New York, NY
Samoans (Afa & Sika)	04/12/80	Philadelphia, PA
Bob Backlund & Pedro Morales	08/09/80	New York, NY
Samoans [2]	09/09/80	Allentown, PA
Tony Garea & Rick Martel	11/08/80	Philadelphia, PA
Moondogs (Rex & King)	03/17/81	Allentown, PA
Moondogs (Rex & Spot)	05/81	
Tony Garea & Rick Martel [2]	07/21/81	Allentown, PA
Mr. Fuji & Mr. Saito	10/13/81	Allentown, PA
Chief Jay Strongbow & Jules Strongbow	06/28/82	New York, NY
Mr. Fuji & Mr. Saito [2]	07/13/82	Allentown, PA
Chief Jay Strongbow & Jules Strongbow [2]	10/26/82	Allentown, PA
Samoans [3]	03/08/83	Allentown, PA
Rocky Johnson & Tony Atlas	11/15/83	Allentown, PA
North-South Connection (Adrian Adonis & Dick Murdoch)	04/17/84	Hamburg, PA
Mike Rotundo & Barry Windham	01/21/85	Hartford, CT
Iron Sheik & Nikolai Volkoff	03/31/85	New York, NY
US Mail Express (Mike Rotuno & Barry Windham) [2]	06/17/85	Poughkeepsie, NY
Dream Team (Greg Valentine & Brutus Beefcake)	08/24/85	Philadelphia, PA

Champion	Date Won	Location
British Bulldogs (Dynamite Kid & Davey Boy Smith)	04/07/86	Chicago, IL
Hart Foundation (Bret Hart & Jim Neidhart)	01/26/87	Tampa, FL
Strike Force (Rick Martel & Tito Santana)	10/27/87	Syracuse, NY
Demolition (Ax & Smash)	03/27/88	Atlantic City, NJ
Brainbusters (Arn Anderson & Tully Blanchard	07/18/89	Worcester, MA
Demolition [2]	10/02/89	Wheeling, WV
Colossal Connection (Andre the Giant & Haku)	12/13/89	Huntsville, AL
Demolition [3]	04/01/90	Toronto, ON
Hart Foundation [2]	08/27/90	Philadelphia, PA
Nasty Boys (Brian Knobs & Jerry Sags)	03/24/91	Los Angeles, CA
Legion of Doom (Hawk & Animal)	08/26/91	New York, NY
Money Inc. (Ted DiBiase & Irwin R. Schyster)	02/07/92	Denver, CO
Natural Disasters (Earthquake & Typhoon)	07/20/92	Worcester, MA
Money Inc. [2]	10/13/92	Regina, SK
Rick Steiner & Scott Steiner	06/14/93	Columbus, OH
Money Inc. [3]	06/16/93	Rockford, IL
Rick Steiner & Scott Steiner [2]	06/19/93	St. Louis, MO
Quebecers (Jacques & Pierre)	09/13/93	New York, NY
Marty Janetty & 1-2-3 Kid	01/10/94	Richmond, VA
Quebecers [2]	01/17/94	New York, NY
Men On a Mission (Mabel & Mo)	03/29/94	London, ENGLAND
Quebecers [3]	03/31/94	Sheffield, ENGLAND
Headshrinkers (Fatu & Samu)	04/26/94	Burlington, VT
Shawn Michaels & Diesel	08/28/94	Indianapolis, IN
1-2-3 Kid & Bob Holly	01/22/95	Tampa, FL
Smoking Gunns (Bart Gunn & Billy Gunn)	01/23/95	Palmetto, FL
Owen Hart & Yokozuna	04/02/95	Hartford, CT
Shawn Michaels & Diesel [2] #	09/24/95	Saginaw, MI
Owen Hart & Yokozuna [2] #	09/25/95	
Smoking Gunns [2]	09/25/95	Grand Rapids, MI
Bodydonnas (Skip & Zip)	03/31/96	Anaheim, CA
The Godwinns (Henry & Phineas)	05/19/96	New York, NY
Smoking Gunns [3]	05/26/96	Florence, SC
Davey Boy Smith & Owen Hart	09/22/96	Philadelphia, PA
Shawn Michaels & Steve Austin	05/26/97	Evansville, IN
Steve Austin & Dude Love (Mankind/Cactus Jack)	07/14/97	San Antonio, TX
The Headbangers (Mosh & Thrasher)	09/07/97	Louisville, KY
The Godwinns [2]	10/05/97	St. Louis, MO

WWF Tag-Team Title History, *continued.*

Champion	Date Won	Location
Legion of Doom [2]	10/07/97	Topeka, KS
The New Age Outlaws (Billy Gunn & Jesse James)	11/24/97	Fayetteville, NC
Terry Funk & Cactus Jack	03/29/98	Boston, MA
The New Age Outlaws [2]	03/30/98	Albany, NY
Kane & Mankind	07/13/98	East Rutherford, NJ
Steve Austin & The Undertaker	07/26/98	Fresno, CA
Kane & Mankind [2]	08/10/98	Omaha, NE
The New Age Outlaws [3]	08/30/98	New York, NY
Ken Shamrock & The Big Boss Man	12/14/98	Tacoma, WA
Jeff Jarrett & Owen Hart	01/25/99	Phoenix, AZ
Kane & X-Pac	03/30/99	Uniondale, NY
The Acolytes (Faarooq & Bradshaw)	05/25/99	Moline, IL
The Hardy Boyz (Jeff Hardy & Matt Hardy)	06/29/99	Fayetteville, NC
The Acolytes [2]	07/25/99	Buffalo, NY
Kane & X-Pac [2]	08/09/99	Chicago, IL
The Undertaker & Big Show (Paul Wight)	08/22/99	Minneapolis, MN
The Rock (Rocky Maivia) & Mankind	08/30/99	Boston, MA
The Undertaker & Big Show [2]	09/07/99	Albany, NY
The Rock & Mankind [2]	09/20/99	Houston, TX
The New Age Outlaws [4]	09/21/99	Dallas, TX
The Rock & Mankind [3]	10/12/99	Birmingham, AL
Hardcore Holly & Crash Holly	10/18/99	Columbus, OH
Mankind & Al Snow	11/02/99	Philadelphia, PA
The New Age Outlaws [5]	11/08/99	State College, PA
The Dudley Boyz (Buh-Buh Ray & D-Von)	02/27/00	Hartford, CT
Edge & Christian	04/02/00	Anaheim, CA
Too Cool (Grand Master Sexay & Scotty Too Hotty)	05/29/00	Vancouver, BC
Edge & Christian [2]	06/25/00	Boston, MA
The Hardy Boyz [2]	09/24/00	Philadelphia, PA
Los Conquistadores [3]	10/22/00	Albany, NY
The Hardy Boyz [3]	10/23/00	Hartford, CT
Right To Censor (Goodfather & Bull Buchanan)	11/06/00	Houston, TX
Edge & Christian [4]	12/10/00	Birmingham, AL
The Rock & Undertaker	12/18/00	Greenville, SC
Edge & Christian [5]	12/19/00	Charlotte, NC
The Dudley Boyz [2]	01/21/01	New Orleans, LA
The Hardy Boyz [4]	03/05/01	Washington, DC
Edge & Christian [6]	03/19/01	Albany, NY

Champion	Date Won	Location
The Dudley Boyz [3]	03/19/01	Albany, NY
Edge & Christian [7]	04/01/01	Houston, TX
The Undertaker & Kane	04/17/01	Nashville, TN
Steve Austin & Hunter Hurst Helmsley	04/29/01	Chicago, IL
Chris Benoit & Chris Jericho	05/21/01	San Jose, CA
The Dudley Boyz [4]	06/19/01	Orlando, FL
The Acolytes [3]	07/09/01	Atlanta, GA
Diamond Dallas Page & Kanyon	08/07/01	Los Angeles, CA
The Undertaker & Kane [2]	08/19/01	San Jose, CA
The Dudley Boyz [5]	09/17/01	Nashville, TN
Chris Jericho & The Rock	10/22/01	Kansas City, MO
Booker T & Test	10/30/01	Cincinnatti, OH
The Hardy Boyz [5]	11/12/01	Boston, MA
The Dudley Boyz [6] Unify WCW World Tag Team Title.	11/18/01	Greensboro, NC
Tazz & Spike Dudley	01/07/02	New York, NY
Billy Gunn & Chuck Palumbo	02/19/02	Rockford, IL

WWF World Title History

Champion	Date Won	Location
Buddy Rogers	04/63	
Bruno Sammartino	05/17/63	New York, NY
Ivan Koloff	01/18/71	New York, NY
Pedro Morales	02/08/71	New York, NY
Stan Stasiak	12/01/73	Philadelphia, PA
Bruno Sammartino [2]	12/10/73	New York, NY
Superstar Billy Graham	04/30/77	Baltimore, MD
Bob Backlund	02/20/78	New York, NY
Antonio Inoki	11/30/79	Tokushima, JAPAN
Bob Backlund [2]	12/12/79	New York, NY
Bob Backlund [3]	11/23/81	New York, NY
Iron Sheik	12/26/83	New York, NY
Hulk Hogan	01/23/84	New York, NY
Andre the Giant	02/05/88	Indianapolis, IN
Randy Savage	03/27/88	Atlantic City, NJ
Hulk Hogan [2]	04/02/89	Atlantic City, NJ

(all title histories courtesy www.puroresu.com)

WWF World Title History, *continued.*

Champion	Date Won	Location
Ultimate Warrior	04/01/90	Totonto, ON
Sgt. Slaughter	01/19/91	Miami, FL
Hulk Hogan [3]	03/24/91	Los Angeles, CA
Undertaker	11/27/91	Detroit, MI
Hulk Hogan [4]	12/03/91	San Antonio, TX
Ric Flair	01/19/92	Albany, NY
Randy Savage [2]	04/05/92	Indianapolis, IN
Ric Flair [2]	09/01/92	Hershey, PA
Bret Hart	10/12/92	Saskatoon, SK
Yokozuna	04/04/93	Las Vegas, NV
Hulk Hogan [5]	04/04/93	Las Vegas, NV
Yokozuna [2]	06/13/93	Dayton, OH
Bret Hart [2]	03/20/94	New York, NY
Bob Backlund [4]	11/23/94	San Antonio, TX
Diesel	11/26/94	New York, NY
Bret Hart [3]	11/19/95	Landover, MD
Shawn Michaels	03/31/96	Anaheim, CA
Sycho Sid	11/17/96	New York, NY
Shawn Michaels [2]	01/19/97	San Antonio, TX
Bret Hart [4]	02/16/97	Chattanooga, TN
Sycho Sid [2]	02/17/97	Nashville, TN
Undertaker [2]	03/23/97	Rosemont, IL
Bret Hart [5]	08/03/97	East Rutherford, NJ
Shawn Michaels [3]	11/09/97	Montreal, PQ
Steve Austin	03/29/98	Boston, MA
Kane (Glen Jacobs)	06/28/98	Pittsburgh, PA
Steve Austin [2]	06/29/98	Cleveland, OH
Rocky Maivia	11/15/98	St. Louis, MO
Mankind	12/29/98	Worcester, MA
Rocky Maivia [2]	01/24/99	Anaheim, CA
Mankind [2]	01/26/99	Tucson, AZ
Rocky Maivia [3]	02/15/99	Birmingham, AL
Steve Austin [3]	03/28/99	Philadelphia, PA
Undertaker [3]	05/23/99	Kansas City, MO
Steve Austin [4]	06/28/99	Charlotte, NC
Mankind [3]	08/22/99	Minneapolis, MN
Hunter Hearst Helmsley	08/23/99	Ames, IA
Vince McMahon	09/14/99	Las Vegas, NV
Hunter Hearst Helmsley [2]	09/26/99	Charlotte, NC
The Big Show (Paul Wight)	11/14/99	Detroit, MI

Champion	Date Won	Location
Hunter Hearst Helmsley [3]	01/03/00	Miami, FL
"The Rock" Rocky Maivia [4]	04/30/00	Washington, DC
Hunter Hearst Helmsley [4]	05/21/00	Louisville, KY
The Rock [5]	06/25/00	Boston, MA
Kurt Angle	10/22/00	Albany, NY
The Rock [6]	02/25/01	Las Vegas, NV
Steve Austin [5]	04/01/01	Houston, TX
Kurt Angle [2]	09/23/01	Pittsburgh, PA
Steve Austin [6]	10/08/01	Indianapolis, IN
Chris Jericho	12/09/01	San Diego, CA

Index

Adams, Bryan, 164–66
Anderson, Arn, 73–74
Anderson, Ole, 8–9
Andre the Giant v. Hulk Hogan, 11, 12
Angle, defined, xiii
Angle, Kurt, 3, 117, 130–31, 154
    v. Chris Benoit, 145, 154
    v. HHH, 133–34, 136, 141–42
    v. Rikishi, 127
    v. The Rock, 135–36, 141–43
    v. Shane-O-Mac, 155–56
    v. Steve Austin, 163–64, 166
    v. The Undertaker, 128
Arezzi, John, 50, 85
Austin, "Stone Cold" Steve, xiv, 2, 33–38, 41–48,
    69, 79, 90–91, 132–33, 160–61, 171
    3:16 interview, 33, 35
    Canadian Stampede, 43–45
    Mike Tyson and, 64–65
    Royal Rumble, 87–89, 142
    v. Bret Hart, 34, 35–36, 40–43
    v. Brian Pillman, 33–34
    v. Canadian Violence, 151–52
    v. Chyna, 102
    v. HHH, 101–2, 108, 135–36, 137, 142, 143
    v. Kurt Angle, 163–64, 166
    v. Mankind, 81
    v. Mick Foley (Dude Love), 69, 70–71, 72,
        134–35
    v. Owen Hart, 46, 61
    v. The Rock, 92, 109, 140–41, 146–47, 149
    v. Rocky Mavia, 61
    v. The Undertaker, 72–73, 77–78, 82–83, 96,

    151; v. Bret Hart v. Vader, 37–38; v. Kane,
        80, 149–50
    v. Shawn Michaels, 66–68
    v. Vince and Shane McMahon, 100–101
Awesome, Mike, 159–60

Backlund, Bob, 7–8, 16, 23, 97
    v. Bret Hart, 23–24, 31
    v. Diesel, 25
Bagwell, Marcus "Buff," 144, 156
    v. Booker T, 157, 158
Bearer, Paul, 51–52
Benoit, Chris, 3, 117, 127, 171
    v. Chris Jericho, 142
    v. HHH, 135
    v. Kevin Sullivan, 113, 114
    v. Kurt Angle, 145, 154
    v. The Rock, 129–30; v. Undertaker v. Kane, 133
Big Bossman (Ray Traylor)
    v. Al Snow, 103–4
    v. Big Show, 109, 110
    v. The Undertaker, 94–95
    Big Show, 118
    v. Big Bossman, 109, 110
    v. HHH, 113–14
    v. The Rock: v. HHH v. Mankind v. Bulldog v.
        Kane, 105–6; v. Shane McMahon, 117–18
Billionaire Ted's Rasslin' Warroom, 28–29
Bischoff, Eric, 2, 16, 28, 33, 68–69, 98, 100,
    126, 139, 140
Blackman, Steve, 76
Blade, defined, xiii
Blind charge, defined, xiv

Blue Blazer (Owen Hart), 95–98
Bollea (Boulder), Terry. *See* Hulk Hogan
Booker T (Booker Huffman), 3, 156, 160
    v. Buff Bagwell, 157, 158
    v. The Rock, 162–63, 164, 166
Bourne, Matt, 20
British Bulldog, 124
    Canadian Stampede, 43–47
    v. The Rock v. Mankind v. Big Show v. Kane v.
        HHH, 105–6
    v. Shawn Michaels, 48–49
Buffer, Michael, 75
Busch, Bill, 113

Cactus Jack. *See* Foley, Mick
Cain. *See* Kane
Callaway, Mark. *See* Undertaker, The
Canadian Stampede, 43–45, 56
Canadian violence, defined, xiv
Canadian Violence Connection, 151–52
Candido, Chris, 26–27
Cantebury, Mark, 76
Cassidy, Leif, 4, 103
Chainsaw Charlie (Terry Funk), 64, 65–66, 71–72
Christian (Jay Reso), 4
    and Edge, 4, 149; *v.* Conquistadors, 136–37;
        v. Hardy Boyz, 108, 120, 123, 131–32,
        136; *v.* Too Cool, 124
Christopher, Brian, 123–24
Chyna (Joanie Laurer), 68, 86, 91, 99, 102, 107,
    117, 148
Clarke, Brian "Kronik," 164–66
Cole, Michael, 49
Conquistadors, 136–37
Copeland, Adam. *See* Edge
Cornette, Jim, xv–xvi, 4
Crockett, Davey, 10
Crockett, Jim, 9, 161

Dark Patriot, 47
D-Generation X, 49–50, 61, 66
    Mike Tyson and, 65
    MSG Incident, 50
    v. Nation of Domination, 73–74
    v. The Radicalz, 117
    v. Shawn Michaels v. The Undertaker, 52–54
Diamond Dallas Page Falkenberg, 153–54
Dibiase, Ted, 33
Diesel (Kevin Nash), 1–2, 16, 24–29, 170
    v. Bob Backlund, 25
    v. Bret Hart, 31, 32
    v. Shawn Michaels, 26; *v.* Razor Ramon and
        1-2-3 Kid, 24–25
Disco Inferno, 54

Doink the Clown, 20, 79
Dooley, Norm, xv–xvi
Double KO, defined, xiv
Dude Love. *See* Foley, Mick
Dudley Boyz, 118–20, 123, 131–32
Dumpsters, 65–66

Edge (Adam Copeland), 3, 4, 69, 122
    and Christian, 4, 149; *v.* Conquistadors,
        136–37; *v.* Hardy Bozys, 108, 120, 123,
        131–32, 136; *v.* Too Cool, 124

Fake Diesel (Glen Jacobs), 51, 52, 94
Falkenberg, "Diamond Dallas" Page, 153–54
Farooq, 69
Ferrera, Ed, 106
Flair, Ric, 9, 13, 15, 168
Foley, Mick (Cactus Jack; Dude Love), 2, 79–80,
    98, 118, 128, 131, 132
    Have a Nice Day, 45–46, 147–48
    v. Chainsaw Charlie, 64, 65–66
    v. HHH, 47–48, 114–17
    v. The Rock, 89–90, 104–5
    v. Steve Austin, 69, 70–71, 72, 134–35
    v. The Undertaker, 71–73
Funk, Terry (Chainsaw Charlie), 64, 65–66,
    71–72

Georgia Championship Wrestling, 8–9
Gig, defined, xiii
Gill (Gillberg), Duane, 122
Glossary of terms, xiii–xv
Gobbledygooker, 65
Godfather, The, 96
Goldberg, 122, 144
Goldust (Dustin Rhodes), 51, 91, 92, 144
    Canadian Stampede, 43–45
    Royal Rumble, 88
    v. Owen Hart, 121
Graham, Billy, 7
Greater Power, 98–100
Greene, Kevin, 26
Guerrero, Eddy, 117, 122
Gunn, "Bad Ass" Billy, 54–55, 88, 91, 92, 99,
    123
Gunn, Bart, 76–77

Hakushi, 31
Hall, Scott (Razor Ramon), 24–25, 26, 29, 33, 169
Hardy, Jeff, 3, 119, 150–51
    v. Rob Van Dam, 162
Hardy Boyz, 3, 119, 148, 150–51
    v. Edge and Christian, 108, 120, 123, 131–32,
        136

Hart, Bret, 1, 16, 17, 30–31, 32, 34, 35–36, 41–45, 55–58, 75
    Canadian Stampede, 43–45
    v. Bob Backlund, 23–24, 31
    v. Diesel, 31, 32
    v. Hulk Hogan, 16
    v. Owen Hart, 21–22, 97
    v. Shawn Michaels, 42–43, 58–60
    v. Sid, 39–40
    v. Steve Austin, 34, 35–36, 40–43; v. Vader
        v. Undertaker, 37–38
Hart, Owen, ix, 41–46
    as Blue Blazer, 95–98
    Canadian Stampede, 43–45
    Royal Rumble, 88
    v. Bret Hart, 21–22, 97
    v. HHH, 68, 121
    v. Ken Shamrock, 76
    v. Steve Austin, 46, 61
Hart, Stu, 8
Hart Foundation, 42, 43–45, 56, 97
Have a Nice Day (Foley), 45–46, 147–48
Heath, Dave, 69
Hebner, Earl, 59–60, 121
Heel beatdown, defined, xiv
Hennig, Curt, 73, 97
Henry, Mark, 29, 74, 75
Heyman, Paul, 140, 151, 160
HHH (Hunter Hearst Helmsley), x, 2, 33, 47, 49–50, 75–77, 91, 94, 108, 148–51, 170
    Curtis Hughes and, 36
    MSG Incident, 50
    Royal Rumble, 88
    Stephanie and, 110, 120–21, 127–28, 130, 132
    v. Big Show, 113–14
    v. Cactus Jack, 114–17
    v. Canadian Violence, 151–52
    v. Chris Jericho, 120–21, 127–28, 129, 150
    v. Kurt Angle, 130, 133–34, 136, 141–42
    v. Owen Hart, 68
    v. The Rock, 73–75, 77, 109–10, 122–23, 124–26; v. Bulldog v. Mankind v. Big Show v. Kane, 105–6
    v. Rocky Maivia, 38–39
    v. Steve Austin, 101–2, 108, 135–36, 137, 142, 143
    v. The Undertaker and Kane, 149–50
    v. Vince McMahon, 111
Hickenbottom, Michael. *See* Michaels, Shawn
Holly, Bob, 30
Honky Tonk Man, 54–55
Huffman, Booker. *See* Booker T
Hughes, Curtis, 36

Hulk Hogan (Terry Bollea), 1, 7, 9–10, 16, 28–30, 32–33, 149, 169
    filmography, 11, 13
    v. Andre the Giant, 11, 12
    v. Bret Hart, 16

Insta-Feuds, 144–45
Irvine, Chris. *See* Jericho, Chris

Jacobs, Glen (Isaac Yankem), 2, 31, 51–52. *See also* Kane
Jammes, "Road Dogg" Jesse, 54–55, 92, 99
Jannetty, Marty, 24
Jarrett, Jeff, 18, 55, 96, 97, 107–8
Jarrett, Jerry, 18
Jericho, Chris (Chris Irvine), 3, 169, 171
    and Kane v. Lance Storm and Mike Awesome, 159–60
    v. Chris Benoit, 142
    v. Chyna, 117
    v. HHH, 120–21, 127–28, 129, 150
    v. Kane, 136–37
    v. The Rock, 166–67
Johnson, Ahmed, 28, 38
Johnson, Dwayne. *See* Rock, The
Juice, defined, xiii
Junkyard Dog, 7, 10

Kane (Glen Jacobs), 51–52, 76, 91
    and Chris Jericho v. Lance Storm and Mike Awesome, 159–60
    and Undertaker, 63–64, 66, 77–78, 127, 149; v. Kronik, 165–66; v. Steve Austin and HHH, 149–50; v. The Rock v. Chris Benoit, 133
    v. Chris Benoit, 136–37
    v. HHH, 91, 127
    v. Mankind, 72–73; v. HHH v. Bulldog v. Rock v. Big Show, 105–6
Keibler, Stacy, 86, 131
Kick Wham Stunner, defined, xiv
King Lear (1993–96), 15–34
Knight, Dennis, 86
Koloff, Ivan, v. Pedro Morales, 6–7
Kronik (Brian Clarke), 164–66
Kwang, 30

Laurer, Joanie (Chyna), 68, 86, 91, 99, 102, 107, 117, 148
Lawler, Jerry "The King," 2, 17, 30, 31, 78
Lazarus (1997), 35–62
Lee, Brian. *See* Underfaker
Legion of Doom, 55
    Canadian Stampede, 43–45

LeRoux, Lash, 89–90
Levesque, Paul. *See* HHH
Leyfield, John "Bradshaw," 76
Lichacelli, Ray, 20
Love, Dude. *See* Foley, Mick
Luger, Lex (Larry Pfohl), 2, 16–18, 21–22, 28
Lying in wrestling, ix, x–xi

Mabel, 26, 27, 88
McMahon, Linda, 99, 118, 138, 145–46
McMahon, Shane, 4, 77, 78, 80, 95–96, 144,
    145–46, 152, 154, 157, 159, 160–62, 171
   v. Kurt Angle, 155–56
   v. The Rock, 166; *v.* Big Show, 117–18
   v. Steve Austin, 100–101
   v. Test, 102–3
   v. X-Pac, 93–94
McMahon, Stephanie, 4, 102, 114, 130–31, 136,
    143–44, 151, 160–62, 168
   Hunter and, 110, 120–21, 127–28, 130, 132
McMahon, Vince, Jr., x, 1, 169–72
   1963–1993, 7–13
   1993–1996 (King Lear), 16–20, 26–30, 32–33
   1997 (Lazarus), 35–40, 42, 46, 47, 48, 50, 51,
    55–62
   1998 (Austin *v.* McMahon), 63–83
   1999 (Russofiction), 85, 98–99, 105
   2000 (McMahon—Helmsley Era), 117–18, 132,
    137–38
   2001, 140, 143–49, 153, 156–58, 161,
    167–68
McMahon, Vince, Sr., 5–6, 7, 8
McMichael, Debra, 77
MacMichael, Steve, 26
Maivia, Rocky, 39, 42
   v. Steve Austin, 61–62
Malenko, Dean, 122
Mankind, 30, 80, 81
   v. Kane, 72–73; *v.* The Rock *v.* HHH *v.* Bulldog *v.*
    Big Show, 105–6
   v. The Rock, 81–82, 89–90; *v.* Ken Shamrock,
    78
   v. Steve Austin, 81
   v. The Undertaker, 51–52, 71–73
Marshall, Debra, 26
Martin, Andrew (Test), 3–4, 102–3, 111
Maven, 140
Mean Street Posse, 102–3, 124
Mero, Marc, 76, 86
Mero, Rena, 86–87
Micelli, Debbi "Medusa," 28
Michaels, Shawn, 1, 16, 24–29, 35–39, 49–51,
    56–60, 90, 124–25

and Diesel *v.* Razor Ramon and 1-2-3 Kid, 24–25
Montreal Incident, 58–60
Syracuse Incident, 27
   v. Bret Hart, 42–43, 58–60
   v. British Bulldog, 48–49
   v. Diesel, 26
   v. Ken Shamrock, 61
   v. Sid, 26, 27, 36, 37
   v. Steve Austin, 66–68
   v. The Undertaker, 45, 47, 52–54, 63–64
Ministry of Darkness, 91, 98, 100
Mondt, Toots, 5
Montoya, Aldo, 38–39
Morales, Pedro *v.* Ivan Koloff, 6–7
Morley, Sean, 69
Morton, Ricky, xiv–xv

Nash, Kevin. *See* Diesel
Nation of Domination, 69
   v. D-Generation X, 73–74
Neidhart, Jim, 97
   Canadian Stampede, 43–45
New Age Outlaws, 77, 99
Nidia, 140
Nitro, 28–29, 35, 36–37, 48, 69, 77–78

". . . OF DOOM," defined, xv
O'Haire, Sean, 158, 159
1-2-3- Kid (Sean Waltman), 24–25, 29, 68–69
Outlaws, the, 54–55, 65–68, 92

Palumbo, Chuck, 123
Patriot (Del Wilkes), 46–47
Patterson, Pat, 6, 18, 22
Pay-per-view revenue history, 173–76
Pfohl, Larry (Lex Luger), 2, 16–18, 21–22, 28
Pillman, Brian, 33–34, 51
   Canadian Stampede, 42, 43–45
Piper, Rodney (Roddy), 7, 10
Playing Ricky Morton, defined, xiv–xv
Plugg, "Sparky" Thurman, 30
Plunder, defined, xv
Potato, defined, xv
Pritchard, Bruce, 59–60
Pritchard, Tom, 26

Radicalz, The, 122
   v. D-Generation-X, 117
Ramon, Razor (Scott Hall), 24–25, 26, 29, 33, 169
Ratings for wrestling events, 177–79
Rating the matches, xv–xvi
RAW, 35, 37–41, 47, 48, 61, 65–66, 75, 92–93
Reso, Jay. *See* Christian

Rhodes, Dustin, xv, 144, 170. *See also* Goldust
Richter, Wendi, 86
Rikishi (Solofa Fatu), 3, 124, 127, 135–36, 137
Rios, Essa, 122
Rizzo, Alex "Big Dick Dudley," 119
Road Dogg (Jesse Jammes), 54–55, 92, 99
Roberts, Jake "The Snake," 29, 104
Rock, The (Dwayne Johnson), 2–3, 69, 75–76, 78–79, 87, 114, 127, 166–68
    v. Booker T, 162–63, 164, 166
    v. Cactus Jack, 104–5
    v. Chris Benoit, 129–30; *v.* Undertaker *v.* Kane, 133
    v. Chris Jericho, 166–67
    v. HHH, 73–75, 77, 109–10, 122–23, 124–26; *v.* Bulldog *v.* Mankind *v.* Big Show *v.* Kane, 105–6
    v. Ken Shamrock, 67–68; *v.* Mankind, 78
    v. Kurt Angle, 135–36, 141–43
    v. Mankind, 81–82, 89–90; *v.* Ken Shamrock, 78
    v. Mick Foley, 89–90, 92, 104–5
    v. Shane McMahon, 166; *v.* Big Show, 117–18
    v. Steve Austin, 92, 109, 140–41, 146–47, 149
Rogers, Buddy, 5, 6
Ross, Jim, xv, 47, 77, 93–94, 147, 161
Royal Rumble, 86–89
RTC (Right To Censor), 126–27
Rude, Rick, 13, 47–49
Runnels, Terri, 7, 51
Russo, Vince, 1, 50, 65, 73, 75, 81, 85–111, 95–96, 113, 139

Sammartino, Bruno, 6, 7
Sarven, Al (Leif Cassidy), 4, 103. *See also* Snow, Al
Savage, Randy, 7, 13, 18, 28
Severn, Dan, 76, 87–88
Shamrock, Ken, 4, 40, 79–80
    Canadian Stampede, 43–45
    Royal Rumble, 88
    v. Owen Hart, 76
    v. The Rock, 67–68; *v.* Mankind, 78
    v. Shawn Michaels, 61
    v. Val Venis, 91–92
Shamrock, Ryan, 91–92
Shoot, defined, xiii
Smith, Davey Boy, 41–42
Snow, Al, 4
    v. Big Bossman, 103–4
Snuka, Jimmy "Superfly," 10, 48, 65
Spotfests, 145
Springer, Jerry, 85, 86, 127

Stasiak, Stan "The Man," 7
Steiner, Scott, 3, 144, 145
Stiff, defined, xiii
Stomping a mudhole, defined, xv
Stone Cold Steve Austin. *See* Austin, "Stone Cold" Steve
Stone Cold Stunner, xiv
Storm, Lance, 159–60
Stratus, Trish, 130–31, 143–44, 145–46
Stuntman bump, defined, xv
Sullivan, Kevin *v.* Chris Benoit, 113, 114
Sytch, Tamara "Sunny," 26, 42

Tag-team title history, WWF, 179–83
Taylor, Scott "Too Hot," 123–24
Taylor, Terry, 107
Tazz, xiii, 117
Test (Andrew Martin), 3–4, 102–3, 111
Thesz, Lou, 5
Too Cool, 123–24
Too Hot (Scott Taylor), 123–24
Too Much, 123–24
Traylor, Ray. *See* Big Bossman
Turner, Ted, 8, 9, 28–29, 63
TV ratings for wrestling events, 177–79
Tyson, Mike, 64–65

Underfaker *v.* The Undertaker, 2, 22, 23
Undertaker, Sara, 153
Undertaker, The (Mark Callaway), 2, 49, 86, 100, 153
    and Kane, 63–64, 66, 77–78, 127, 149; *v.* Kronik, 164–66; *v.* Steve Austin and HHH, 149–50; *v.* The Rock *v.* Chris Benoit, 133
    v. Big Bossman, 94–95
    v. Kurt Angle, 128
    v. Mankind, 51–52, 71–73
    v. Shawn Michaels, 45, 52–54, 63–64
    v. Steve Austin, 72–73, 77–78, 82–83, 96, 151, 159; *v.* Bret Hart *v.* Vader, 37–38; *v.* HHH, 149–50
    v. The Underfaker, 22, 23
    v. Yokozuna, 18–20
UPYOURS, 96

Vader, 37–38
Van Dam, Rob, 161–62, 171
    v. Jeff Hardy, 162
Vega, Savio, 27
Vegas, Vinnie, 24. *See also* Diesel
Venis, Val, 51, 97, 122, 124
    v. Ken Shamrock, 91–92
Ventura, Jesse, 102

Vicious, Sid, 26, 27, 39
    v. Shawn Michaels, 26, 27, 36

Wacholz, Kevin "Nailz," 22
Waltman, Sean (1-2-3- Kid), 24–25, 29, 68–69.
    See also X-Pac
Watts, Bill, 9, 161
Webb, Alicia, 91–92
Wilkes, Del "Patriot," 46–47
Williams, Steve, 2. *See also* Austin, "Stone Cold"
    Steve
  as Dr. Death, 76–77, 94
Wilson, Torrie, 157–58
Working stiff, defined, xiii
Workrate, defined, xiii–xiv
World title history, WWF, 183–85

XFL, 140, 147–48, 157, 170
X-Pac, 68–69, 74, 121–22
    Royal Rumble, 88
    v. Road Dogg, 99
    v. Shane McMahon, 93–94

Yokozuna, 16–20, 64, 104
    v. Lex Luger, 17
    v. The Undertaker, 18–20
Yurple the Clown, 79, 105

Zahorian, George, 18, 22